My Buddy, King of the Hill

Frank X. Pagano, Sr.

Hardcover ISBN 978-1-105-68525-5
Paperback ISBN 978-1-105-68527-9

TO

My wife Judy Nell
Whose assistance has helped me put my
memories down on paper
and whose encouragement has led to its final
completion.

A Special Thank You
to
PEB
(Pierre Bellocq)
My dear friend, for generously granting permission to publish
some of his world famous caricatures in this book.

Howard "Buddy" Jacobson

Acknowledgment

To my long time friend Pasquale Tuosto and his lovely wife
Vicky.
Thanks for all of your help and support in the making of this
book.
Without your encouragement this might still be on my to do
list.
You have made the process of writing this book much more
fun than it should have been.

Introduction

Everyone alive today, past a certain age, can tell you where they were on November 22, 1963. I can. If you haven't been around that long ask someone, someone with graying temples, someone whose eyes have dark circles and skin is not as firm as it once was, or someone whose paunch hangs, with disregard, over a tarnished buckle. Or ask those of us with those added signs of age. It was a day that we needn't refer to Jim Bishop's masterful work on the assassination of John F. Kennedy. For those of us who lived it, it sounds so odd. For those of us who lived through the President's death, we need no film or book. We only need memory.

That is our collective memory. It was that way when Mr. Lincoln was murdered and unfortunately, it will someday be that way again. Days like that happen only once or twice in a lifetime, but there are days, from our personal memory, that have as much impact on us and our lives as the death of a President. Days that come and go in our lives and network of family and friends. Days and people whose passings do not shake the world as the passing of a President, and yet, to us, they're as important as any head of state.

What the President was to his field...politics, my Buddy was to his...horse racing. He was Howard "Buddy" Jacobson and he too was a president—President of the Horseman's Benevolent and Protective Association. He was a union leader, where unions were anathema. He was a, "troublemaker, a Jew against the WASP and he was one of, if not the greatest, racehorse trainers of all time." Those are the recollections of his contemporaries. What Caesar Chavez did for the grape pickers in California, Buddy Jacobson did for the grooms at the racetrack, except the grooms were making less money. No grape picker worked for such storied money on those farms, but there was plenty of it on the farms of the racing world.

What set Buddy apart was a thing called excellence. You can look in the record book and tell me names of great horses: Vanderbilt's Native Dancer, Calumet Farms' Citation, King Ranch's Assault, or DuPont's Kelso. And you might tell me of great union leaders like Reuther, Lewis, or Meaney and fail to mention Chavez.

You might also forget Buddy Jacobson never had a great racehorse. The magic of his hands made nags, who should have been retired or sold to a riding school, into winners. In this process, he made a lot of little people winners. He also made a lot of people losers. He caused a section of backstretch to be named for a kid from Oklahoma—"Ussery's Alley," and it was the middle of Aqueduct Race Track. When Bobby Ussery rode for Buddy Jacobson, the crowd of 40,000 fans knew when the gate opened and Bobby pulled the horse away from the rail— down the alley—the race was over.

It was also the beginning of the end of large crowds at the racetracks. It was the downhill flight when state Governments decided there was just too much money around and tapped into it. Making themselves partners in a business that had been successfully run 120 years before there was a Nation or a Constitution. The "old money" was fading from racing like a weak winded thoroughbred. And politicians made themselves partners in the racing business better than Don Corleone could ever have dreamed. Always with the lame excuse, "they were going to put the bookmakers out of business." Never suspecting they were creating generations of degenerates and building illegal gambling empires. As the State's business got bigger and bigger the crowds got smaller and smaller.

When the old money controlled the game there was a certain amount of leisure connected to it. When the state made themselves partners, it was the antithesis of a civil service mentality. There were more racing days, marketing schemes like so much perfume or coffee, more wagering gimmicks and as a result, there was a decline in the quality of the product. Not to be forgotten…more people went to bookmakers because they could get credit and better prices on the payoffs. These were the very institutions that state governments across the country were claiming to be putting out of business, and they were flourishing. But I'm getting ahead of myself. The sociology of racing is for another time, but the passion for racing is about Buddy and a thousand more who would kill to be like him or even just to be near him.

This is the story of a man convicted but so were many others. The question for you to decide is, was he guilty? Was he just another loser behind concrete and barbed wire or a winner that wound up there because he knew too much?

A winner or a loser? It depends on who's telling the story. There was one other thing Buddy was known for...murder. Again, it depends on who is telling the story. The whole story has never been told. It's a plot Oliver Stone could do wonders with—that the fates came together to deny Buddy that certainty of light that attends every celebrity accusation or crime today. Indeed, since the time of Buddy's trial, the media has raised the mixture of crime and celebrity to an art form. The eerie thing, there was media but yet no media coverage for Buddy's trial. Would Saco and Vanzetti be a cause celeb without the media? Would there be new industries of trial lawyers and legal *experts* were it not for the murder of two people connected to a celebrity? Reflect on the absence of newspapers when O.J. was charged and arrested and you will understand the trail of my Buddy.

Buddy Jacobson, was charged with murder, at the same time the city of New York went dark with the 1978 newspaper strike. There was beauty, money, intrigue, and the lingering question was always, why? There wasn't a newspaper in town and television hadn't been raised to tabloid formats yet! There wasn't DNA or a parade of experts. It was just another murder in New York.

The mellowing effect of time, which brings a wisdom of its own, leaves some, if not most, wishing we could do something over again. Some mistake, a left turn when we should have gone right. That's one of the conditions of life. What happens though when it is society collectively wishing it could do things differently—undo or erase some act of its past?

Kids at play call it a *do over*. And, if it's not a do over the event leaves some doubts—doubts that become if, only, and what if.

Should we have dropped the atomic bomb on Japan or electrocuted the Rosenberg's? The larger the question, the more philosophical we get. Should Buddy Jacobson have been convicted of murder? Was it payback or was it justice?

What is payback and what is justice? One could reasonably argue payback is another name for justice when doled out by society. Then it becomes a question of evenness and application at law. Law is, however, not a good barometer when we discuss justice. The Dred Scott decision was the law of the land, but it had nothing to do with justice. On the other hand, Buddy Jacobson would have walked away from the charge of murder were he tried for it today, as probably would have, the people mentioned earlier, Saco and Vanzetti. One last thing, there is an envy connected to excellence. It is human nature. When that envy is mixed with some of the strongest opinions known to man and when a pinch of money is added we have all the elements for murder and mayhem.

The day, like a thousand days before it, was ending or so I thought, with my drive on the Southern State Parkway. The traffic, like the day, was bumper to bumper, and I cursed the memory of Robert Moses for not having the foresight to anticipate the great eastward movement of the masses. As I said, it was ritual of a thousand days before it. Always at the same spots, toll booth plazas or bridges designed to keep city people away from Jones Beach.

I had left Belmont Park, where I labored daily at a job I loved, seven days a week. There is no slavery known to mankind more demanding than slavery to self. A slavery of ritualism, a slavery of adoration and love; if you have a job or profession that you miss or can't take a day away from, no explanation is possible. With rare exception, even on my days off, there was a need to go to work. That is the way it is with all horse trainers. I wasn't always a horse trainer. Like most, it came to me later in life. Some, like Buddy Jacobson, grew up around and in it.

That's the way it's been every day of my life since I met Buddy. It was a career started like a scene from *The Sting*. It was quite by accident, but as I reflect on it now, it's understandable–the unfriendly way people have when motives are suspect, particularly where money is involved. The more rarified the air the more suspect and cautious one becomes. It has less to do with snobbery as much as it has to do with security, something less sophisticated than insider trading but amounting to the same thing. At a racetrack there are thousands of people that want to meet and get friendly with a trainer as talented as Buddy Jacobson. For me, it started out with a simple accident and grew to a wonderful, albeit complex, friendship...a friendship that forever changed my life.

Chapter I

Breaking News

When the lanes on the parkway went from four to three and the traffic backed up, as it did every day, I cursed old Bob Moses again, like the guy driving behind me cursed me. Pointless, aimless frustration that makes up such a large part of our existence. I remember the exact spot I was when the radio was interrupted for a news flash. But unlike the news flashes that happen every hour on the hour in places like metropolitan New York, this flash was different.

"New York City Police have just announced the discovery of a body inside a burning crate on the shoulder of the Henry Hudson Parkway. As we reported from Chopper Two, there was a tie-up on the Northbound Henry Hudson. Firemen arrived to extinguish the blaze and discovered the body of a white male, approximately six feet tall. According to police at the scene, the victim had been left mutilated with multiple stab wounds about the body and appeared to have been shot several times."

It was a story that was shocking, but not too shocking, because in the city, stories like these are a daily occurrence. When I heard the location, I thought it was just another drug buy gone bad. Someone had ventured into a neighborhood he didn't know—and he paid for it with his life.

The damn traffic was almost at a complete standstill, and I was about to change lanes when the announcer came on with more news.

"We've just been informed by the police that noted horse trainer Buddy Jacobson is being held for questioning."

I stopped mid-lane. My head was ringing, and my vision narrowed. I couldn't believe what I had just heard. Horns were blaring, but I didn't care. I rolled down the window to flag a car over. I had to know this was real, that someone—anyone—had heard what I had just heard…but they kept driving around me. They ignored me as I had almost ignored some faceless stranger in a crate. I needed confirmation. I had to know this was real, so, as my hands trembled at the knob, I scanned the radio, straining my ears to catch any news in the sea of white noise. Nothing.

The horns and curses grew louder. The drivers trapped in their faceless snakes of steel, like me, were only trying to get home, so I hit my signal and tried to make my way to the shoulder.

I continued to turn and twist the dials, but my head was throbbing and sweat was starting to gather in the folds of my shirt. I was too nervous, I was…and then I heard it—"Anonymous sources in the police department have confirmed Howard Buddy Jacobson was arrested. The noted horseman and playboy millionaire is a suspect in the slaying of a man found murdered in a blazing crate on the Henry Hudson Parkway. Stay tuned for further details."

Again, my disbelief and shock took over the muscles of my hands and fingers as I turned the dial again, pushing further into a wall of static. In rage and disbelief, I put the car in drive and cut across three lanes of traffic, desperately trying to make it just four more exits and then home. My mind and my foot were in a tight race, and my lips, stuck on autopilot, were steadily repeating, "Buddy, Buddy what happened? It just can't be."

As soon as I made it home I flung open the door and headed straight for the phone. I had to call someone…but who? I figured the police headquarters was the best place to start. I dialed the number and was greeted by a voice pattern familiar to me since childhood.

"Police headquarters, Sgt. Bluerru speaking."

That's the way, it seems, police are trained to answer telephones, not just in New York but worldwide.

"I'm trying to find out about the arrest of Buddy Jacobson."

The faceless voice asked me with cold practiced regimen. "Who's Buddy, whatever his name is?"

"Jacobson...Jacobson. He was arrested today in connection with the body found in a crate on the side of the road."

"What precinct was it?"

I lost it. "What the hell do you think I'm calling you for?" The voice just droned on, oblivious to anything but his scripted monologue.

"Look Mister, I can't tell you what number to call if you don't tell me what number you want...got it?"

As slowly and calmly as I could, I repeated the name. "Jacobson, Buddy Jacobson. He was arrested in connection with a slaying on the Henry Hudson Parkway."

The policeman cupped his hand over the phone, and I could hear the muddled voices as he passed my question along. A few seconds later, with a different tone and clarity of voice, he gave me the number for the precinct that made the arrest. I made the call and readied myself to start over with a new apathetic voice as flat and listless as the one before.

I managed to find out I had to call the detective squad. The phone rang busy. I hung up and tried again but with the same nagging tone as before. I couldn't just sit still and wait. I was, by now, in a state of frustration that was bringing on a panic attack. If you're from New York, you know what I mean.

I decided to forego any attempt to reach the police and instead, called Irwin Klein. Win Klein, as he was known to friends, was a polished criminal attorney and had known Buddy and I for a long time through his ownership of race horses.

"Win, did you hear about Buddy?" I blurted into the phone.

"Who is...oh, Frank...yeah, I was just on the phone with..."

He never finished. I don't remember who he said he was talking to. "The radio said he was being held by the cops and I tried to find out where. Forget it."

"What can we do to find out?"

"I can find out where he is alright, but I don't know if he wants me for his attorney."

"Tell him I retained you, but do what you can and do it now."

"Okay Frank, I'll call you back as soon as I got something."

When I hung up the telephone, for the first time, I realized I was soaking wet, but now, after speaking to Win, I sat back with the thought that at least the load was being shared now. Win Klein would get some pieces to the puzzle. I turned dinner aside for the moment, kicked my shoes off, and just started to muse on my friendship with Buddy. Do you remember I said it could have been a setup out of *The Sting*? Try this on for size.

It wasn't anything but a sheer accident. I'd always had an appreciation for the horses. At the time, I didn't recognize it. It wasn't only the horses I loved, it was the action that went with them. My livelihood was ownership of discotheques in New York—a business I enjoyed. It gave me a lot of free time during the day. Whenever I could, I'd be at the race track: Aqueduct, Belmont, or Saratoga, it made no difference. There were a lot of beautiful girls running around the disco business, but the only girls I was interested in had four legs.

I knew of Buddy Jacobson but had never met him. For me to approach him as a devotee would be like Rupert Pumpkin in a scene from the *King of Comedy*. Everybody wanted to know Buddy and by the fates, I got to know him. He was an aloof individual, as many successful people must train themselves to be, and he was successful. He was a student of thoroughbred horses that exceeded the expectations of his teachers and mentors. He didn't trust many people and confided in fewer.

I closed my eyes and relived the scene again—that first up-close and personal meeting with Buddy Jacobson. It was in the early 60s, at the end of September, and the Belmont Meet was over and the Aqueduct Meet was beginning. To those that have never been to a racetrack on the New York circuit, suffice it to say, Belmont is like a day in the country and Aqueduct is like coming back to an apartment house. There was a certain efficiency at Aqueduct, but it could be as cold as the wind whipping across Jamaica Bay. Belmont, on the other hand, is the jewel of New York racing.

It was on such a day, windy and damp, too windy and too damp for September, but this was normal for Aqueduct. A crowd of about 20,000 was on hand which, for that time, was average for a weekday. I was making my way down one of the many humongous stairways to the paddock. Except for the last race, when everyone is trying to get out of the track at the same time, the stairways are usually deserted. The paddock is also called the walking ring. Here, most of the gamblers—and that's what they are though the marketing says to call them patrons—take up positions trying to catch a wave or high sign of a trainer or maybe a groom or jockey. The patrons are not allowed in this saddling area, except by invitation of an owner or trainer. I too was on my way to the paddock but much too cocky to think that I needed anything other than my own look at the horses to see which one would cross the finish line first.

A guy about my age went whizzing past me on the staircase, taking the steps two at a time. He was using the steel banister to steady himself and make the tight turns as one might do riding a horse or at the Indy 500. Coming up the stairs was another guy, neatly dressed from the waist up: white shirt, tie, jacket, the whole bit, but he wore a pair of plain gray slacks. Two people, objects, meeting at the same point in time collided. The guy coming down had a container of coffee in one hand and gave the guy coming up a bath. An accident to be sure but true to the tenets of all horse players and gamblers, they both were right according to the way they saw it. The down guy, a little larger and seemingly more rambunctious started to curse out the up guy.

"You dumb son of a bitch, you got me covered with coffee."

The up guy started shaking his clothes to remove as much coffee as possible without saying a word, thus not offering an apology the down guy felt he was entitled to. Justice demanded I stick my nose in.

"Hey," I told the down guy, "you're out of order. What do you mean spilling your coffee?"

"Who asked you?"

"Hey, you bumped into this guy minding his own business."

"Maybe that's what you should do...mind your own business."

"I happened to see it. What are you yelling at him for?" I stared and glared at him.

He looked at the up guy who finally spoke. "No problem, no problem. Forget it. Thanks."

The down guy said, "Well, maybe it was an accident and walked away."

I said, "Are you okay?"

He was continuing to clean his coat. "Yeah, but I've got to saddle a horse in here, but that was nice of you."

"No problem," I said. "I saw what happened and that was kind of nasty of him to try and pretend it was your fault.

"Do you get to the races often?"

"Yeah, I'm here once in a while."

"Would you like to see the races from a box seat?"

"Sure, why not?" I said.

"Go up there and tell the usher Buddy said to put you in 6E. That's my box. I'm Buddy Jacobson."

"I know," I said. "I've seen you around before."

"Now look," he cautioned me. "I don't give out any tips or anything like that, but I would like to have you sit there, if you want."

"No problem, not necessary at all, but if you insist...and by the way, about the tips, that's good because I don't take any tips."

Buddy went down to saddle the horse and then later joined me in the box.

"What do you do for a living?" It was at this point, I realized, he hadn't even asked me my name. So I introduced myself and true to his word, he didn't give me any information...that day. I spent the rest of the day with him, and he invited me back. From that point on we became fast friends. The chemistry, for whatever reason, worked. That was the start of it, a simple accident that changed my life.

Chapter II

Buddy in Florida

The next time I met Howard "Buddy" Jacobson it was at Aqueduct Race Track. We then had dinner a few times, usually at Johnny's Steak House, one of his favorites, off Queens Boulevard, near Buddy's apartment at the Silver Tower. We spoke about horses, and I was interested in getting into the business. Before we finalized anything I was called out of town and got involved with my disco business. The racing season in New York came to a winter close, and Buddy moved to Florida with his horses.

It was a cold day in January that I decided to take some time off and make a trip to Miami. My second day there I went to the races. I was standing by the rail at Hialeah Race track watching the horses get ready for the third race when I realized Buddy had a horse in this race, and he was putting the saddle on the horse. Since I had not seen him for a few months I did not call to him, but as the horse was walking to the track, he saw me on the rail.

"Frank, Frank," he called out and waved to me to come to the gate and meet him.

I was surprised and happy to get his greeting. We shook hands and he said, "Come on. Follow me." We went to the box area and took our seats.

"So, how ya been?"

"Good," I said. "But busy with the disco."

No one else came to the box and in about two minutes the announcer said, "They're off!"

He gave a look toward the track and we watched with very little emotion as his horse won by three lengths.

"He won! He won!" I shouted.

"Yeah," he said without changing his expression. "Not a bad horse. So, how about dinner tonight?"

"Fine," I said. "Bud, he was four to one, but I didn't bet. I like to bet when I come to the track."

"Okay, don't worry there's plenty more winning. Got to go, see you about Eight p.m. at King Arthur's Court, Miami Spring Villas."

He waved, and he was gone—no picture with the winning horse… out to the parking lot, and off he went.

I made my way down to the walking ring, no sense to leave on such a beautiful day, and I liked a horse in the fifth race and this time I'd bet. After all, why would you come to the race track and not bet? As I walked along I kept repeating, "Four to one. Four to one." And this information from one of the leading horsemen in the country. Visions of dollars danced in my head.

Everyone wants to be around a person who can help you make a quick profit. Stock brokers can give you tips, but you need a lot of money and time to wait for a return. A horse trainer, who is good, knows when his horse is doing well in training. It might take him a few months to get ready, but when he tells you it's for now or maybe tomorrow, there can be instant success. Of course this depends upon the source of the information. I had spent all of my life going to the track and restaurants and seeing how the trainers were treated by those who would do almost anything to get in the position that I now found myself. Was I there? Maybe. The fifth race was over and my horse won. At two to one, it was not a great profit, but it was better than losing. On this beautiful, sunny Florida day the sixth race was running, and I turned and headed for the exit—Miami Springs Villa, now where was that?

I got my car and drove toward the beach. I was staying in a four-star hotel on the beach…expensive and glitzy. It took me about thirty-five minutes to get there. I went directly to the front desk and asked about Miami Springs Villas. I was told it was in the south, near the airport, an easy ride of about forty minutes. I jumped on the elevator and headed for my room. Now I'm not the type that attracts lots of women, and as a matter of fact, I have to work at meeting new people, but today the only other person on the elevator was a young, barely eighteen-year-old red headed, petite beauty. She was having trouble with her bathing suit cover-up which slipped off her shoulder as she was swinging a large beach bag. My floor was seven, and as we were facing each other, she giggled. I offered her a hand and she remarked how the sun was so hot today she was anxious to get to her room and apply sun cream. I smiled, and as we reached my floor, I wondered if I was supposed to follow up on her comment and offer to help her apply the sun cream to protect her lovely body. As the door opened I decided the best word is the word left unsaid, and considering her age, I feel it was a good decision. Besides, I needed to change and make the drive to Miami Springs still not knowing exactly how to get there.

It was easier than I thought to find the Miami Springs Villas Hotel. It was located on the south side of the road, in clear sight of the Miami Airport. Across the road on the north side was what appeared to be a beautiful oasis. There were a number of private villas almost like mini-townhouses. They surrounded a lovely lake where ducks and some swans made it look like a paradise. Off to one side was the restaurant named King Arthur's Court. The dining room was big enough to seat 300. It looked like King Arthur's Court with a large round table with room for about thirty. There were two pianos, numerous smaller tables, all of which were painted in bright colors. The walls were covered with great flasks and swords, chest armor and medieval weapons. When you entered you were back in merry old England. The bar was circular and always crowded, but even with all this atmosphere the best feature was the food. The menu offered fine British beef, Maine Lobsters, and large jumbo shrimp.

On the right side of the restaurant was a large swimming pool. As I entered the restaurant, Buddy was at the bar. "Frank," he called and waved. He was sitting next to a very pretty, young lady who he introduced as Amy.

"I invited her to have dinner, hope you don't mind"

"A pleasure," I said while wondering how we could talk business with her around.

"By the way, I have a girlfriend who can join us if you like."

"Thanks, maybe another time," I said.

"Come on, let's eat," said Buddy.

Our table was in a quiet corner of the dining room. Buddy and I both drank coke and Amy a glass of red wine. Buddy had shrimp cocktail and a sirloin steak. I had crab cakes and prime rib. Amy just had shrimp and a salad. She was afraid to eat too much, as she was graduating next week. Buddy explained that Amy was living here on the grounds, and she was attending Eastern Airline's flight attendant school. Classes started every three months and 125 new recruits would be arriving next week.

"They live and train right on the grounds," Buddy said. "And if you're up early and by the pool they practice sinking those rubber rafts into the pool."

We finished dinner and Buddy turned to Amy, "Babe, why don't you wait in the room while Frank and I talk?"

"Oh sure," she said as he handed her a room key. In a flash she was up and gone. She was about 5' 8" with dirty blonde hair and a playmate body, just on the slim side. I didn't appreciate how attractive she was while she was sitting.

"Great gal, a little older than I like, twenty two. I think from Ohio, loves disco and next week, she will be gone. That is the best thing about the girls here, they are always moving on after they graduate from the flight attendant school. Now, let's make a date to talk business when we get back to New York."

Chapter III

Main Count

"Now Frank, still interested in the horse game?"

"Yes, I am".

"Good, I have a horse for you when we get back to New York. It is $5,000 and ready to run. I have another owner, Jerry Maccheroni, who is a restaurant guy. I think maybe the two of you should get together and it will make it easy on you."

"Buddy, whatever you say. I'm ready."

With that he rose quickly and said he would see me in NY. Again a quick exit. I wondered about the check. I hadn't seen him pay it. Maybe it was my treat. I was not sure, so I called the waiter. He said everything was taken care of and that Mr. Jacobson had an account and I was his guest.

"OK, then…," I said good night to all and as I walked into a wonderful Miami night with millions of stars in the sky I thought this must be what paradise is like—beauty, luxury, abundance of youth, and someone to help you earn all you would need to keep it going. Was I dreaming? If so, I certainly did not want to wake up.

I left paradise and the sunshine behind and returned to New York. A short time later, on a rainy Monday morning, the phone rang. I was feeling just about as cheerful as the day.

"Frank, it's Buddy."

"Oh, hi."

"Can you come to the barn about 2:00 today?"

"Sure."

"Good, see you there." Click. Conversation Over.

I arrived at Buddy's barn at the Aqueduct Race Track a little early. I had met Jerry Maccheroni and had dinner with him the week before. We got along fine and were both anxious to own our first race horse. I had no problem having a partner since the expense would be cut in half. The reality was that what I wanted was to be near the action and to bet on some winners.

Jerry saw me and came to greet me. "Frank, we have a problem."

"What?"

"The horse we are buying is lame."

"What?"

"Come on, I'll show you."

He pointed to stall number thirteen, and I looked in and saw a large brown horse wearing a winter blanket, standing near his feed tub.

"My God, Jerry, he looks fine," I said. With that the horse took a step and his large head seemed too big for his body. As he began to walk it was amazing, but he was indeed, very lame.

I turned and looked at Jerry. Now normally when horses take bad steps, an owner might just not be knowledgeable enough to tell the difference, but in this case there was no error.

"Look Jerry, I'm sure Buddy knows what he is doing. Maybe the horse is a little off or needs some exercise? Let me speak to him."

I went down to Buddy's office where he had arrived and was sitting behind his desk reading the newspaper.

"Buddy," I said in an excited tone, "the new horse, is he lame?"

He slowly raised his head from the paper and looking me right in the eyes said, "Naturally."

Just one word. He switched the whole mess on me. How could I even think to question him? After the shock, I wondered myself. He then explained to me that the horse was Main Count, a five-year-old winner who was trained by John Lipari, who was down on his luck. So Buddy bought him, and that's why we got him so cheap. When I run him he will be sound. My job was to convince Jerry to trust Buddy. I did that, telling him I was giving Buddy my check for half today. He did the same. I began a long up and down journey and saw a different side of Buddy. Over time, I was to see many more. The ride had begun.

Three weeks later on a cloudy, wet, gloomy New York day another call came in.

"Hi, Frank."

"Hello, Bud," I responded.

"We run tomorrow…Aqueduct…third race."

"Great. How is he doing?"

"Good. See you there, bye."

This is not what I expected. I was beginning to see that life on the track was not like the movies where the poor kid hooks-up with a prominent horse trainer, forms a great friendship, and they get rich together and go on to enjoy all the things poor kids are told really matter in life. Fade out. The end. But then that's the movies. It was maybe a little early in our relationship, but I had hoped for some insight, some word about the race, the condition of the horse, or the bet. Buddy didn't know much about me. We had dinner a few times but the discussions were always in general or about my disco business which was doing well. He knew we were both kids from Brooklyn. I was an only child. He had a sister. His father was an Adam Hat salesman who had an eye for the ladies and left his family. I don't think Buddy ever forgave him. Buddy's mother was a Jacobs. She was the sister of Hirsch Jacobs, a prominent horse trainer. Later on he told me, how after his father left they would spend Sundays with his uncle and upon leaving, Uncle Hirsch would give his mother $100. This was a great deal of money at the time.

My dad went through good and bad times, and I lived in the Red Hook section and spent my youth with great friends. I always loved horses and would say, "Someday I'll own a horse." The reply I usually got was, "Pagano, you got holes in your sneakers. How you going to have horses?"

Growing up I wanted to get a job and help out, but my parents said, no. School is too important. I earned a scholarship to a Catholic high school and upon graduation went to college for a year, then I did a three-year stint in the United States Coast Guard. Two of those years were spent aboard a cutter in the North Atlantic. I married and had kids. When I left the service, I entered St. John's University and in six and a half years of night school I received my BA. I worked in the NYC office of the mayor and then in the department of human resources, as a case worker—a job I loved but pay I hated. When the chance came to go into a disco operation, I jumped at it and turned to a new love of money and the lifestyle it would buy. I often wondered which part of me did Buddy think he knew?

Rain, rain and more rain. Why did it wait for today? Jerry and I met for lunch at the track. Buddy was a no show. We discussed the horse and how much we should bet.

"Does he like a wet track?" Jerry asked. On his form in the paper there were no races on a wet track. All we could do was speculate. A half hour before the race we went to the paddock to see the race and the trainer.

After saying hi, Buddy was busy putting the saddle on the horse. The rain continued as the jockey came into the stall where Buddy was working on the horse.

"The track is slush," he said. He was one of the leading riders at that time.

"I had the blacksmith change his shoes. He should handle it okay. I want you on the lead or as close as you can be."

"Okay," said the rider.

"Riders up," was the call from the paddock judge.

As the horses walked out I realized my colors, my own colors were going to the races...not bad for a kid from Brooklyn with holes in his sneakers.

Jerry was in a panic. "Ask him can the horse win? Should we bet?"

"Okay, relax," I said.

"Buddy, what do you think?"

"Frank, every horse I run, I run to win. The mud is against us and the going will be hard on his leg, but he is as good right now as he will ever be. How about dinner, 7:30, Johnny's Steak House?"

"Okay, Bud. Good Luck."

I told Jerry, he went to the hundred dollar window. The odds were 5/2, a good price. I made my bet.

"They're off!" The announcer cried. Main Count was third, two lengths off the lead, a good position to be in. The rain continued and you could see the mud flying from the horse's hoofs. The crowd was sparse, but we were all shouting for our selections. As they made the turn for home my orange and black colors became prominent. The horse was in the center of the track and closing fast on the two front runners who had raced as a team. The horse closest to the rail began to slow and was quickly losing ground, leaving the gray horse on the lead. The jockey hit Main Count once, twice, as he seemed to slide on the track, but by now his head was up to the gray's saddle number. One more surge.

Lights flashed as they passed the finish line. Did he get there? The tote board lit up, "Photo" for the win. The moment of truth was here. He tried so hard. Jerry came to the box where I was watching the race.

"What do you think? Did he get it?"

"Hard to see from here," I said. "But he sure was trying."

"Do you think we should go down for a picture?" he said.

"No, let's wait".

We were number three, and the gray was number seven. Then it was on the board and official—number seven win, number three, second place. I was still on a high but down a notch. Win or lose, this was definitely the game for me.

It was 7:17 that night when I arrived at Johnny's Steak House, the restaurant near the Silver Towers Apartments where I knew Buddy lived with his wife, Joan, and his two sons, David and Douglas. The restaurant was quiet tonight, and Johnny was not in the kitchen but having a drink at the bar with Buddy.

"Hi, all," I said. Buddy smiled and said something to Johnny who turned to greet me as if I was an old friend.

"Nice to see you again. Wet night, huh?" he said as he shook my hand.

I wondered how big his kitchen was because at about six feet tall and 240 pounds, he made for a commanding presence.

"Johnny, since we have been coming here I just cannot decide which steak I love best."

"Ahh," he laughed. "They're all good—prime, you know. All of our meat is prime. I better get inside. Thanks for the drink, Buddy. Catch you later."

"How about you Frank, a drink?"

"I'll have a coke with lots of ice. What are you having?"

"The same."

"Funny," I said, "I was born in an apartment over my grandfather's bar, my mom and dad have wine with their meals, I make a living in gin joints, and I don't drink. I never do drugs or drink because I want to control my actions and my body... not some phony drug."

"I don't drink very much myself and spend my life in a gambling business and very rarely gamble. Oh, I did when I was young but today, every time I send a horse to the track I put my reputation on the line and that's enough for me."

"Let's go to the table."

Buddy told me his theory about weight. He was only 5' 8", slim and most of the time very serious, with dark piercing eyes and nice features, lots of dark slightly wavy hair. "I order anything I want, but always drink a large glass of water before dinner then I eat half of whatever I order. It sure works great for me."

"Now Frank, I guess you were wondering why I wanted you to buy the horse? Well, I'll tell you. I've only known you a short time, but I enjoy our time together. I trust you and most of all you are smart, but you never brag about it."

"Well, thanks. That's nice."

"Frank, I know you like this business. Well, I like the disco business. Now you have a license and can be at the track more. I'll teach you my business and you teach me yours. That's it. What do you say?"

I don't drink, and I never used drugs. Was this a hallucination or a dream? But, I was here and one of my heroes was asking me to teach him. I babbled a few sounds and said, "I think it's okay...good luck...great. Yeah, yeah, let's do it!"

We clicked coke glasses, and my new life was under way.

After we ran Main Count and I became eligible to claim, Buddy said his knee was hot, so we should run him at Suffolk Downs Track in Boston for a $2500 claiming race. "Somebody will surely claim him and we can recoup some of the money," he said.

Jerry and I agreed, and we sent him out. The day before the race Jerry called and asked if I wanted to go and watch the race. He had his own plane, and we could fly up and back in a few hours. I said fine and spoke to Buddy about it.

"It's a waste of time. I spoke to the vet, and he will tap the knee before the race. He can't win," he said.

"Well, I'll go to keep Jerry company."

The next morning I met Jerry at a small private airport in Flushing, Queens. His plane was a four passenger single engine job. It was very fast and had all kinds of equipment, so you could fly in fog or bad weather. He figured the coarse to Logan Airport and wrote the numbers he needed on a long sheet of paper. As you arrived at a landmark a bell would go off, and he would feed the next numbers into the computer. The trip was bumpy but easy. As we arrived we were told to land on runway L-13. As we made our approach a voice screamed over the radio, "Abort landing! Abort landing! Mayday!" Jerry pulled hard on the wheel and pulled up. I just sat and watched as a large commercial jet roared below us.

He began to sweat, and I asked, "What happened?"

"I was going into the wrong landing strip," he said.

I was still very calm and didn't think very much of it. I just didn't realize how close to disaster we had come. Jerry landed the plane and was still very upset. "I guess I'll be hearing from the FAA."

"The American Automobile Club?" I asked.

"No, the people who issue my pilot's license."

"Only kidding, Jerry. Just relax and I'll rent a car and we can drive to the track."

We arrived just in time for the first race, and the horses were nearing the starting gate.

"Want to bet?" he said.

"I don't think so. I don't know any of these horses."

The race ran and number eight won. The rider was the leading rider at the track, John Giovanni. When we checked the program he was due to ride our horse.

"I think we will lose the horse. He has a good New York form and the leading rider. Trainers up here don't think Buddy would put the leading rider on a bad horse. Let's get down to the paddock."

The tote board flashed the first flash and our horse was two to one, the favorite in the betting.

"What do you think of that?" he said.

"Well, if I didn't know he had a broken knee I'd run and bet."

"Do you think he can win?"

"Jerry we came to lose him and try to get back some of our money. No, he can't win."

The horse came into the ring, and was jumping around like a two year old.

"He looks great," Jerry said.

I kind of agreed but when he was put in the stall to put the saddle on I looked at his knee. There was a small but visible drop of blood. I had never seen this on a horse about to race. It was obvious he had just been injected. I reached down and checked his knee and removed the blood. Just then the jockey, John Giovanni, arrived.

"Hi guys," he said. As we all shook hands, I introduced him to Jerry.

"Boy," he said, "I like him today. I got a $50 double with him and the winner I rode in the first race." He reached into the top of his boot and showed us the ticket. "Looks like easy money to me."

As he mounted the horse we wished him good luck.

"See you in the winner's circle," John said.

I saw a few trainers I knew watching him go to the track. I knew he had to be claimed.

"Frank, that kid is a top jockey and he loves the horse. Maybe he can win."

"Jerry, you saw the blood. Buddy says he is finished. You can't bet."

"But maybe he can last with these cheap horses. We should bet a little."

I can't believe that he was getting to me. I knew the horse was lucky to make it to the gate. Could it be possible he would make some kind of great effort, overcome all, and win? Maybe.

As we walked to the window Jerry said, "He is the favorite at five to two. I've got to bet."

"Okay, but just a few dollars," I said as I approached the $10 window. I wanted to bet $10 for luck, after all I was too smart to get suckered in. "Number four, ten times." I would bet $100, just in case. Jerry was coming over from the $50 window.

"I hope you didn't bet too much."

"Just $800," he said.

The horse was now down to 2 to 1.

"They're off! Main Count for the lead."

Jerry screamed. I held my breath.

"Main Count in front," was the second call.

"Main Count dropping back," was the third call.

It was over. The jock pulled him up and the ambulance took him off the track. There were six claims in for him so we got back a few bucks. The ride home was long, and we hardly spoke. I felt so stupid. I still believed in fairytale endings. I guess I was a true horse player—betting with my heart instead of my brain.

Poor Jerry had almost crashed and could have been killed. He was going to hear from the FAA. His horse lost, he lost more than half his investment, and on top of all that he lost his $800 bet. No wonder he was so quiet. But Jerry was a good sport and never complained and stayed with the business and later Buddy ran quite a few winners for him.

Chapter IV

Days at Barn Learning and Nights at Disco

The following days were spent learning from Buddy. "Just follow me around and watch. Ask questions when you want," Buddy said, and that was it for the first few weeks. At night I would have dinner with Buddy, and he dominated the conversation and talked mainly about horses, discos, and girls.

"Most owners lose money with only about 3 percent showing a profit each year, and about 10 percent of the trainers get rich while 40 percent make a living, the rest have part time jobs or wives that work. It's a very hard game, this he said over and over.

"I'll teach you the condition book, that's the key to winning races…this is a book put out by the racing secretary every two weeks. It lists races to be held each day for the next two weeks. It's very important to place your horses in the best race with the least competition. A good trainer or a good jockey agent knows the horses on the ground and is able to judge what races to run them in. Your job is to take advantage of this knowledge and pick the right spot for your horse. Knowing when your horse is due to run will help you train him and bring him to his best form on that race day."

Buddy told me, I get the book as soon as it comes, the same day, then I work for one or two hours placing the names of my horses next to the race I will run in, after that I put the book away and try not to change it. This was very important to Buddy and for the next few years I watched him follow this procedure. He was always a man that liked to think things through, to always be the smartest guy with the newest information, and a stickler for having his rules followed and not questioned. There was so much to learn, feeding proper hay, what vitamins to give, how to take a temperature, what to feel for in the legs, be able to see the difference in the horse from day to day. He never said much but what he said was on the money—learning the business takes years.

Chapter V

The Apartment

"I hate August," Buddy said as we drove towards his new apartment in Queens.

"Don't you like the heat?" I asked.

"No, no, it's Saratoga time. I have a farm there so I try to avoid seeing a lot of people, but you can't escape the race track."

"I think it sounds great."

"You would!" he said as we arrived at the apartment building he had just moved into. "I've got a few boxes in the trunk. Give me a hand."

"Right." He had a large bag of groceries and a box with pots and pans. We left the Caddy with the top down.

"Doesn't look like rain today, let's go."

The entrance was crowded and two young girls with tennis racquets and dressed in shorts were saying hi to these other girls in flight attendant uniforms leaving the building. As we passed I said, "Bye girls. Have a good flight."

They smiled and said, "Bye."

"Can you get that door please?" Buddy said.

"Sure," the taller girl replied as she held up the heavy glass door.

"Thanks."

"Looks like someone is cooking up a storm," the little blonde said.

"15-C girls, at 7 p.m., and you and your pals are invited. It's a moving-in party and come as you are. Hope you like pasta. Hold the elevator, Frank. Don't forget girls, 15-C…"

I held the door as he stepped in, the girls were still at the front door laughing and waving goodbye.

"Do you think they will come?" I asked.

"Yeah, but not to worry, I've got some gofers...young guys who live in the building. When they get home from work they come to the apartment, and I send them to ring bells and invite all the stews in the building for dinner...works like a charm."

We reached the apartment which was located at the end of the hall. As he opened the door he said, "This building is more than 75 percent airlines. Almost all of them are women—alone, young and poor, and all of them are looking for adventure, love, and rich husbands. Get that stuff in the kitchen, Frank."

We entered into a very large living room, the outside wall was to the left and the three windows faced the side of the building. The kitchen was right behind the living room and open on both ends. Behind this was the bedroom. In there a mattress was on the floor and a small dresser on one wall. There were a couple of mirrors leaning against the wall and a pile of clothes in the corner—a typical bachelor pad with the bare necessities.

As we unpacked the sacks he began to talk. "You know it's hard now that I moved out. Joan is so bitter." Joan had been Buddy's sweetheart since his school days. She was Irish, Catholic, very pretty, slim, and bright. She was a good wife and a great help in the early days, doing the books, talking to owners, keeping house and caring for the two boys. She had lots of talent but her only interest was her family and she was now devastated by his womanizing.

"She just doesn't understand. I don't know what happened.

I was never a player as a young guy. I had Joan and the kids and I just wanted success with the horses. Then one day I flew to Boston for a race, had a conversation with the stewardess and realized I wasn't as bad as I thought. I guess I wanted to make up for the times I wasted in my youth. Who knows! Leave the pasta on the stove it's for tonight. Why don't you stay for dinner and watch the operation?"

"Thanks, but its Friday and I hope a good night at the disco..."

"Come on, why don't you stay for dinner? You'll get a kick out of it."

"Yeah, well maybe."

Buddy got up to meet some people at the door, and as I sat on a large, black pillow in the corner of the room I thought about the last two months and having to be up and out by 6:00 a.m. every morning and then out late most nights. The glamorous lifestyle of the rich and famous was exhausting, and I was only getting started.

I spent each day observing the routine and watching Buddy at work. I realized there were two persons in Buddy Jacobson's body. At the track he was never late, arriving at 6 a.m. and getting right to work. In the evening hours, clocks had no value and only food and the laughter of beautiful young women were important and his escape from the pressures of life and business were not discussed. For Buddy failure was not an option, and he was constantly placing himself under pressure to win.

The barn at Aqueduct was owned and operated by the New York Racing Association. The NYRA was a private group who had a state license to operate three tracks in New York: Belmont, in Nassau County, Aqueduct in Queens, and Saratoga in Saratoga County. The NYRA controlled every aspect of racing, and they would allocate space at these tracks to owners and trainers to keep their horses and train them for the races. There was no charge for the stalls. These stalls were in great demand because without them a person would be limited to the number of horses he could race. Buddy had his stalls at Aqueduct where there were about 1,000 stalls. At Belmont, there were about 2,200 stalls.

Buddy's barn had been assigned to him for the last ten years and there were no other trainers in his barn. He got to this point because of his past successes. He was the leading trainer in races won for the past ten seasons. In 1965, he broke the NYRA record for races won by winning 200 races in one year. This at a time when the racing season was a short eight and a half months long. There was no winter racing and the New

York tracks closed from November to March. Today the New York tracks run the full twelve months.

With so many accomplishments it was no wonder he commanded great respect at the track. Buddy wanted me to learn, so I tried. I saw he was all business. Most of the men called him Mr. Jacobson. There was very little chatter and there were no radios playing. The horses were in numbered stalls and Buddy knew each and every one of the thirty he had, but he would refer to them by number only. For example, he would say, "Number six and number twelve go together. Number fourteen walks today. Put number sixteen on the pony track" Since he was primarily in the claiming business, he did not want people to know who the horses were. People could not see or study the conditions of the horses if they did not know their names. Secondly, by using numbers, he was distancing himself from any attachment since they were, in reality, inventory.

Most of the time, he would just let me wander and do my own thing, help muck a stall, walk a horse, or hold one as the vet would draw blood or inject a joint. But one day he took me aside and said, "Frank, if you watch, you will see that every day when the horse takes his first step out of the stall, I check his front legs for heat or any changes. And I have my assistant, Joe Porter, take the temperature of each horse. I always do those two things." And in a minute he was gone. I never forgot, and I tried to follow his instructions. I also noticed over the years that whenever he was interviewed there were many things that he did with a horse that he never talked about— including taking the temperature and checking the front legs. Buddy, like so many of the good trainers, had his own theory about the feeding of the horses. The biggest difference in his theory was that he would feed pellets which were specially made to his specification by his feed company. Buddy was the only trainer that I ever knew that subscribed to the United States Department of Agriculture literature which he received each month. The publication was free and it would detail any new medications that were currently being introduced to be used in the development of livestock. This publication helped him develop the specification he wanted in his pellets.

"Hey Frank, want to help make the sauce? I know you like to cook."

"Sure Buddy. Why not?" As I moved to the kitchen I noticed the living room was rather dark and that someone had lit some candles. The shelf in the corner held the largest reel to reel tape player I had ever seen. The music was varied but there were a number of French and Spanish songs. I wondered how many here could understand.

With no chairs in the room, it was a good idea to hang on to the large pillows unless you wanted to stand. I looked over the counter that separated the two rooms and saw Buddy with a tall blond standing at the bar, which was the only piece of furniture in the room. It was an old table about six feet long and covered with a red and white checked cloth. There were a few bottles of wine, white and red, a large bucket of ice, a lot of plastic glasses and the last section had some vodka, rum, and American whiskey.

"Hi," I said to the young fellow at the stove. "I'm Frank."

"Hi, I'm Andy. Are you a friend of Dennis'?"

"Who?"

"Okay, I thought Dennis sent you."

"No, Buddy did. He said I might be some help."

"Well great," Andy said as he began to stir the tomato sauce.

"I'm just going to add the meat," and he proceeded to place some chopped beef into a large pot of boiling tomato sauce.

"Did you cook that from scratch?" I asked.

"No, it's Presto. Canned is much easier."

"Yeah, well it smells good."

"Buddy said to peel plenty of onions and garlic," Andy said with a large smile.

I noticed he was average height, with light hair and complexion with a tooth missing and was still suffering from acne.

"You live in the building, Andy?"

"Me? No, no, I live with my mom and dad. I'm just looking for a job. I graduated a few months ago..."

"Hi, here is Dennis." Dennis, I found out, was Buddy's number one gofer. He was about twenty years old with a rather odd nose and an ordinary face. He was about as tall as Buddy but very thin.

"Boy, wait till you see the hotties I picked up tonight."

Andy introduced us, and I immediately didn't like him. Buddy came into the kitchen.

"How's it going guys?"

"Buddy, these new girls I got are so hot. The dark haired one had her skirt up to her ass in the Caddy. Oh yeah, I bought some bread and stuff, about $10."

Buddy handed him $10. "Where did you park the car?"

"On the avenue, near the cleaner. It's good until 8 a.m."

"Come on. I'll set you up with the little one."

I watched as Buddy and Dennis walked into the living room.

The music seemed to get louder and the lights lower. The apartment door was open and more people started to appear. The girls outnumbered the men, two to one.

The pasta was ready, and Andy mixed it up and began to put it on small plastic plates. "Come and get it," he yelled. And they did. It looked to me like many had come because they were hungry and food was being served at a good price.

Dennis made drinks for Buddy and the little dark haired girl. She looked too young to be a stew, but all her five foot frame was well put together and she acted rather high for someone having her first drink. I watched Dennis as he kept pushing her towards Buddy but always placing his hands all over her. Buddy was drinking a coke and laughing as I saw him disappear into the bedroom with Little Miss Sunshine.

Dennis closed the door and placed a sign on the handle that read, "Men at Work," as he returned to the party. I decided it was late enough for me, and I said good night to Andy and left.

The next few months were hard work. I was in the barn every morning and at the disco at night.

"Frank," Buddy said one morning. "You're doing a good job and I can tell you like it. Spend some more time in the office. I'd like you to learn how to do the payroll. It's once a week, maybe an hour, okay?"

"Sure, Bud. I do it at the disco. It's not bad."

Buddy was coming to the disco more often too. He loved to sit and watch the kids dance. "You should have more strobe lights," he said. "And I would put a projector on all the time, maybe Old Charlie Chaplin films and a better DJ. That's important."

"Well, all that costs money, and I have partners in this joint."

"Yeah, that's too bad. I like this place, and maybe I could buy it."

"I don't think it's for you. These fellows are new to the business and want to give it a chance, but you never know."

"Well, if anything comes up let me know. See you in the morning." And he finished his coke and left.

The next few days we worked hard in the barn. Buddy had a new plan. "Now that you have your owner's licenses I want to claim some horses for myself but put them in your name. I can't put them in my name because the owners would want to know why I didn't buy the horses for them. I'll run a horse in your name and you will be eligible to claim. I'll put up the money and give you 10% of any profits. What do you think?"

I was in shock. Claiming meant an owner who had a horse running at the current race meet could buy a horse out of special races called claiming races. The price was set for the race by the racing secretary who worked for the racetrack. When the horses were entered in the races, other owners could claim or buy them by placing a sealed bid in the amount of the claiming price fifteen minutes before the race. The sealed bid was stamped with a time machine at the track and placed in a box at the track's racing office. After the race, the box was opened in public at the office and the bids were opened. If you were a qualified owner, had enough money in your racetrack account and the bid was stamped at least fifteen minutes prior to the start of the race and you were the only bid for that horse, you were the new owner. If there was more than one slip submitted for the horse, the racing secretary would number the slips and place numbered round balls into a small jar and shake and draw one of the *pills* as they were called. Of course there would be as many *pills* as there were slips. This process was called "shake for a horse." If I did what Buddy said, I would be on thin ice at the track, but I would also become a fixture in a business I loved.

"Great, whatever you say."

Just like that it was done. He began right away, the next week he claimed three horses. People were beginning to buzz about who this new owner was. In no time at all I was in the middle of a storm.

Jockeys are stars at the track and they have agents who work at securing mounts for them. A good agent will see trainers early in the morning, every day at the race track. The agent will then go to the races to watch the horses and meet with the owners and become friendly and helpful with the hope that the owner might help him influence the trainer. Then in the evening the agent will make phone calls and try to secure mounts. It is a job that requires a great amount of persistence. As I became known at the track I met so many of the agents who wanted to get close to Buddy.

I liked the action and the attention. I went to the races everyday and reported to Buddy what I thought about the horses I saw, he would then tell me what was right and what was not. I began to see how he judged horses.

It was at Belmont on a warm afternoon that I was standing by the rail near the walking ring watching the horses for the next race when someone said, "Nice day for a race?" I turned and saw a very young man of about twenty-five or so. He was tall, about six feet, and had dark black wavy hair. He was very handsome, dressed in a black shirt, pants and black leather jacket.

"Sure is," I responded.

"I'm Vince De Gregory, agent for Angel Cordero,"

"Nice to meet you. He is a jockey right?"

"I know you're kidding, he is a great jockey and will be one of the best soon."

"I saw him ride, and he did look good."

"I know you claimed a horse a few days ago named No Snakes.

Well Angel would like to ride him for you."

"I leave that to the trainer," I said with a smile.

"But I heard you and Buddy are close friends and Buddy is so hard to get to see, maybe you could tell him? Angel knows this horse, and he can do a good job for you. He knows the horse only has one eye and needs a strong rider. Please keep us in mind."

I thanked him, and this was the first time I had heard the horse only had one eye. I liked Vince and over the years we became good friends. He was a very good agent, but I told him he would have been great in the movies—big, strong, and handsome.

I told Buddy about the conversation, and he said he would like to try the rider because the horse did need someone who could handle a one-eyed horse…someone strong and this new kid, Angel, looked okay.

It was two weeks later on a stormy day with lots of rain that Buddy found a race for No Snakes. "He likes the mud, so I think he can win today." He grunted as I kept after him for some encouragement about our chances today.

That afternoon I arrived early to watch the races. The track was a sea of mud, horses were sliding and there were lots of scratches. We were entered in the last race and the rain never stopped; I was having a drink at the soda stand when a person I did not know approached me.

"Bad day for a race, but your horse should love this track. I'm Frank Fiore."

"Hi, I hope you are right."

"I own the two horse in the race, and I think he is second choice in the betting, but he can't stand up in the mud."

"Well, I'm sorry to hear that for you but happy for me." We both laughed.

"I've seen you around and meant to say hi. I have been an owner for about twenty years."

"Nice to know you. I've only been in the game for a short time but it's lots of fun. By the way I know a trainer with the same name."

"No relation, I know him but never did any business with him, but we claim from each other."

"Well thanks a lot for the information. I was afraid of your horse and I do like my horse, now even more. See you around."

Nice guy I thought but now I can bet more than I intended.

As we left the paddock the rain was still falling and then a strong wind followed. I spoke to our jockey and he said the horse looked great and then, "See you in the winners circle." That sounded good to me.

Buddy had a special cup over the eye socket and a run out bit to help keep the horse on a straight course. He told Angel he was sure he knew the horse and to ride him towards the lead but to adjust as the race ran.

It was good to get inside out of the weather. I saw our horse was two to one and the next horse was five to two, that was the two horse of Frank Fiore. I took extra money out to bet, I knew our horse was doing well and that the jockey liked him and the owner of the next best horse said his horse could not do well in mud. Boy did I feel good.

I went to the $100 window and made my bet. I looked at the betting board and there were only two minutes to post. When I arrived at the box area it was less than one minute to post time. The betting board was now showing my horse at five to two the same as the two horse. The poor public didn't know the two didn't like the mud, too bad.

"They're off."

A good start right in front of the stands. The race was once around and we were second with the two horse in the lead. Into the first turn, No Snakes settled for second place about three lengths behind the leader who was traveling at an even pace. The rest of the field followed behind at a slower pace down the backside. The leader was now five lengths in front and racing off the rail. We were about six lengths in front of the third horse around the turn and the leader showed no sign of stopping and looked very strong. I glanced over and about four rows to my left I saw Frank Fiore waving and encouraging his horse. In an instant I realized he was *cold watering* me, a term used when trying to fool your competition. I said a silent prayer for Cordero to dig in and try. At the top of the stretch the leader was now in front by three lengths but going wide and now in the middle of the racetrack. Our rider began to work on his horse. His strong hands pushed and a crack or two with the stick and we were now only one length off the leader but running wide on the outside. Why doesn't he go inside the other horse, I said to myself. Darkness came over the finish line and lights began to blink, with one last dash our horse prevailed.

"He won!" I shouted to Buddy who only gave a slight smile.

"Go get your picture taken," he said, and I did.

I passed Frank Fiore and saw him in a serious conversation with his trainer. There was no joy in their box.

After the race I thanked Angel and asked him why he did not go inside of the other horse, "Was the track bad on the inside?" I asked.

"No Frank, the rider on the other horse knows my horse has no eye on the right so if I go inside he will not see the other horse, so I stayed outside."

"Great work and thanks."

I went to the window to cash my tickets and found my pal Sidney there.

"I know you made a good bet, so did I, but I was not sure after I saw that guy Fiore who owns the two horse bet $2000 on his horse. I just knew you and Buddy would do it."

I had learned a lot today, and I got a better idea of why Buddy kept to himself and had few, if any, friends on the track.

Chapter VI

Linda

I had to go out of town, and I returned late on a Friday. On Monday I called Buddy.

"Great, you're back lets have dinner, seven p.m. By the way, I'm bringing a friend. See you at Johnny's."

I hoped it was not going to be one of his gofers. As I arrived at Johnny's, the rain had stopped and the streets were quiet as a Monday night usually is. Buddy was at the bar. He seemed different, smiling and all polished—new shirt and hair combed. There was a young girl sitting next to him who I had never seen before.

"This is Linda," he said as she extended her hand.

"Buddy told me a lot about you," she said.

I shook her hand and noticed she had a firm grip for such a soft hand. "Well don't you believe what he says, I do like girls." She laughed and we all seemed at ease.

"Linda is our new secretary," he said. "She has been here three days and likes the barn and the horses."

"That's great," I said. "How do you like the hours?"

"Well, I was working for the airlines and traveling a lot with so many different shifts, it's great to have steady hours."

"Have a drink," Buddy said.

"Sure, a coke, please."

"Wow, another guy like Buddy. I thought everyone in New York drank," she said.

"Buddy, your table is ready. I made some special appetizers for you guys. Hi Frank, how are you doing?"

"Good Johnny," I said.

"Excuse me, I'll meet you at the table," she said as she went toward the ladies' room.

We went to the corner table that Johnny had prepared.

"Well, what do you think?" Buddy asked.

"Aside from the fact she is pretty, has a great figure, and appears sweeter and smarter than anyone I've seen you with, what can I say."

"We met on a flight I took from Maryland. She had a layover and I asked her to dinner. We went to the barn and she just loves horses. I took her to a hotel and we have been together ever since."

"What about the apartment?"

"I couldn't let her see that joint, with all the broads and guys. I got us a new apartment in Forest Hills today and signed the lease on it—a one bedroom, nice neighborhood. I told her I am getting a divorce. Here she comes."

Johnny made some special dishes and we had a great dinner and laughed a lot.

"I'm from a small town in Pennsylvania. I'm twenty and I've never been married. I'm telling you this because Buddy seems to like you. He said that you are helping him at the barn with a lot of things he wants me to do. I hope we can be friends. I like Buddy a lot."

"I tell you Linda, I like you and thanks for putting it on the line. I like Buddy and the horse business. I want to be around, but I'm happy for him, and I will give you all the help I can with the books and payroll. I never really liked that stuff but who can say no to Buddy!"

Her eyes seemed to sparkle. They were a dark blue and set off against her very white skin which looked as soft and smooth as a baby's. She was about 5' 7" with a slim figure, small bust, and round hips. Her dirty blond hair was cut short and framed her face. It was easy to see why Buddy was attracted to her.

She gave a quick smile and said, "Great, that wasn't hard."

"Listen Frank, I told Linda we would go shopping after the barn tomorrow, but I want us to go to the disco tomorrow night, and I want to go looking for a place to buy."

"You mean a disco?"

"Right, I want to try and I'll put up whatever we need. By the way, I just signed papers to buy a farm in Old Westbury, Long Island. It's the closest piece of land near the city line where I can keep horses. I'm getting so many and there just are not any more stalls available at the track. Besides, horses are like people they need vacations too! We can ship them out for one or two week's rest and they will come back in great shape. Plus if they get hurt, I'll have a place to lay them up, and I can check on them."

"That sounds great, but with all that you still want a disco?"

"Sure, we need something to do with our nights."

Linda laughed, "Boy, I wonder what I'm getting into."

"You guys don't realize that New York state is one of the few states that is without a breeding program. I was contacted by some upstate representatives from the state legislature who want a program to help the farmers who are getting out of the dairy business. That land would be great for raising horses. We will be in on the ground floor with our farm."

"A friend of mine, Al Bierd, we call him 'The Bird' is in the real estate business, and he is working on the deal for me. We may have to go into the city this week to sign the papers…"

The waiter brought the check and Buddy paid.

"That's a lot Buddy, but it all sounds good. I'm going to the disco and then home. I'll stop by in the morning and give Linda a hand. Thanks for dinner, and it was nice meeting you, Linda. Goodnight."

I walked out and they lingered at the bar talking to Johnny. My first impression was this was a nice girl who really liked Buddy and he seemed different with her. Maybe this was a good thing. I hoped it was.

The next morning I got out to the barn at 7:30. Everyone was hard at work.

"Good morning, Linda. How's it going?"

"Fine, Frank, I have a few questions, but Buddy is always so busy I can't ask him anything."

I sat at the desk with her and we worked for about an hour. She was smart and had no trouble learning the routine.

"One question, Frank, why do we carry all of these books and ledgers with us?"

"He takes them with him every day—the payroll book, the checkbook, the ledgers for expenses and income. Some people leave them in the office. He carries them home when he finishes here. Don't ask me why."

Buddy called, "Frank, come on."

I left the office and saw him walking towards the track.

"What's up?" I asked, as we walked towards the rail.

It was a beautiful sunny day and most of the horses had been out on the track for their exercise. The sound of a few galloping horses and their naying sounded like music. No one without a license is allowed on the grounds, and it made me think of a military installation where I did my boot camp training—lonesome but secure.

"I told her to buy some furniture for the apartment. I'm going to the old place and pick up some clothes and things. I'm keeping the old apartment for now. I signed a two year lease. I'll let Dennis and one of his friends stay there, but I'll still have to help with the rent."

"You seem to like Linda."

"You bet. She is swell, but a little small town. She has only been to New York city two or three times, and I don't think she would understand about the apartment, so we have to be sure she does not meet any of the people."

"I think you are right, but what about Joan?"

"I guess I'll always love Joan. We have been together so long. When I moved out I figured I'd go back one day but something changed. Oh, I'll take care of her and the kids, but I know I'll never go back."

We watched as the horses galloped.

Chapter VII

Buddy's First Disco

"Let's meet tonight, we will grab a pizza or something, but I want to scout out some locations for a disco. Okay?"

"Sure, Bud, where do you want to meet?"

"How about seven p.m. at Mario's on Queens Blvd."

We started to walk back to the barn. "You know, I never spend more than one night with a girl but Linda is different right now. I'm not thinking of anyone else."

"I'll pick up my car and get going. See you tonight. Say goodbye to Linda."

At 7:15 I arrived at Mario's, an Italian restaurant not far from Buddy's new apartment. He was sitting in his car parked outside the restaurant.

"How about getting some sandwiches to take along while we scout out some locations."

"Fine with me. What will it be?"

"I'll have a zucchini on a roll and Linda wants a meatball hero."

"Okay, I'll pick them up. What about a drink?"

"Just two cokes". I got the food and we ate while Buddy drove.

We covered Queens Boulevard, stopped at a bowling alley, a large Chinese restaurant and three or four small bars.

"Nothing any good," he said. "We can call it a night. I know we will find something soon. We've just got to keep looking. I'll take you back to your car, and we can do it again tomorrow."

"Okay, but we can try Nassau County, around Rockville Center and such."

We reached the restaurant, I said good night and headed home.

All that week we drove around and checked plenty of locations. Buddy had gotten some addresses from a local real estate agent and Linda checked the paper's classified section under the heading bars and restaurants for rent or sale—no luck.

During the day we were racing and Buddy had four winners that week. On Sunday Linda decided to stay home and work on the apartment so Buddy and I went to search alone. We found ourselves in Great Neck, on Long Island at about 9:30 p.m.

"I guess we should head home," I said. The town was so quiet and cut down the middle by the Long Island Railroad.

"Let's just stop for a drink before we head back. Look there is a restaurant on the right." Buddy said as he pulled in and parked the car. The restaurant had a large window looking into the bar area and you could see the place looked empty. We went to the bar, and he ordered a white wine. I had the same. The bartender was an older fellow, at least fifty years old. He looked timid as he poured the drinks.

"Pretty big place," Buddy said. I turned and realized it was a very large room. The bar was separated from the dinning area by a three foot partition topped with artificial plants. The restaurant itself was about fifty feet by a hundred feet. There were a number of black leather booths on the far wall and maybe twenty wooden tables in the room. In the back there was a wooden plank about thirty feet long. We realized it enclosed a dirt floor which was used as a bowling area for an Italian game call Bocce. There was a lot more room than it appeared from the outside.

"Kind of quiet tonight," Buddy said.

"Yeah," said the bartender.

"You serve food?"

"I can make you a couple of ham sandwiches if you like."

"Yeah, let's have two."

He left the bar and went into the back where the kitchen was located.

"You hungry Buddy?" I asked.

"No, no, I just wanted to get rid of him. What do you think?"

he said very excitedly.

"About what?" I asked.

"The place. The place! I think it's perfect for a disco."

"Take it easy Buddy, it's big and might do, but the location is no good. Look at that large glass window in the front on the side. You're right next to a very nice apartment building. There is no way you could run a disco. The noise of the bands, the cars, the kids coming and going. No chance here, Buddy."

The bartender returned with the sandwiches. They looked good, so we asked for mustard and began to eat.

"So, business good?" Buddy asked the bartender.

"Are you kidding, this is probably my last night. The electric bill is due tomorrow. I'm on COD with the liquor authority, and from there it only gets worse. I've been here three years. The area changed and five new restaurants have opened. It's time for a change, but I'm not able to do anything now."

"Would you like to sell the place?" he asked.

"Why, you know anybody who wants to buy?"

"Wait a minute, Buddy! You don't know what the rent is, if there's a lease, how much he is owed and..."

"That's okay Frank, we can check that out later. What's your name?"

"Dave...Dave Russo."

"Do you own this place?"

"Me and the creditors!"

"Well, how much do you owe?"

"For starters, I need $3,000 for the electric company tomorrow.

I owe the Landlord $1,500 by Friday and I'd like to get $1,000 for some small expenses."

"So, what's the price of the place?" I asked.

"Look, if I could pay off what I owe and walk away with about $5,000 the place is yours."

"Well, as long as you owe less than $10,000 I'll take the deal." Buddy said excitedly.

Dave looked happy but a little reluctant. "Look guys, it sounds good but by the time we go to the lawyers, get all the papers together, I'll lose the place and the landlord will take it back."

"Dave, are you ready to get out now? Well, I'll take over now. I'll pay the electric bill tomorrow and the rest by the end of the week."

"Can you put anything down now?" he asked.

Buddy turned to me. "You have any cash?"

I had about $500 but I wasn't going to give it to this guy. "I've got $100 on me. You want it!"

"Give it to Dave," Buddy said.

I handed it to Dave and I could not believe he took it. He went to the cash register and took a pile of letters and bills out and brought them to the bar.

"Here's the electric bill. It has to be paid by noon. The others are some small items, add them up and we will keep count."

Buddy took the bills and I turned to Dave. "Let me have the keys."

Dave went back to the register and brought a ring of keys and placed them on the bar.

"I expect some deliveries tomorrow, so you better be here to receive them. Good Luck. I'll be in touch. By the way, if you like, I'll lock up and turn out the lights, and the drinks are on me, Boss." He smiled broadly and I don't know who took advantage in this deal.

We said good night and walked out. We got in the car and Buddy was more excited than if he had just won the Kentucky Derby.

"Bud, you have to think this over. The area is too upscale for a disco, maybe you should open a nice restaurant?"

"Oh, your name might attract a nice crowd."

"This is the place, and the price is nothing. I've got some guys that will take a piece, and you will get a share for all your help, no money."

"Thanks, that's mighty generous of you, but there are lots of things that have to be taken care of here. You have to get the liquor license and a cabaret license, if you have music and dancing. We have to be sure that the taxes are paid or you might be buying a headache. I know you are excited, but get in touch with a lawyer and the accountant before you spend any more money…"

"Don't worry. I just know this place, and I know it will go."

"Buddy, let's make sure this guy is the owner."

He looked at me and then laughed long and hard. "Never happen," he said.

The next day was Monday, and I went to my disco to check the receipts and order some supplies. I worked until about 2 p.m. and decided to drive over to Great Neck to see if Buddy was still interested. I arrived at about 3 p.m. and was shocked to see about six of the black booths on the sidewalk. There were people coming in and out and lots of activity. I went inside and it looked like mass confusion. Buddy was helping some men tear out another booth.

"Buddy, what are you doing?" I exclaimed. "You can't do this. That stuff is valuable, and you don't even own the place yet."

He smiled, "Now Frank, we paid the guy and today Linda went to pay the electric bill. I called Tom at the bank, and he gave us a new checking account so we can pay the bills. I put $10,000 in and so far we have spent about $4,500, so I'd say we own the place. I have some partners. I sold shares for $5,000 each and so far I have about six sold."

I checked the list of the new owners.

Bill Collins, one of the best and most respected black smiths on the track who just happen to do all of Buddy's blacksmith work. Bob Ussery, a star jockey who had won the Kentucky Derby, twice. Pete Axhelm, a reporter and writer of note. Frank Wright, a well known trainer. Cortwright Wheatherall III, of Philadelphia was one of his owners, a very rich society figure who loved horses and horse players.

Irwin Klein, a well known criminal attorney who was Bobby Ussery's lawyer when he got divorced and who loved racing. Al McPeet, a contractor friend of Buddy's who was good at construction. So far that made seven and four of them were here in work clothes, tearing down almost everything and starting to paint the walls black.

"We're waiting for the dumpster to come to get rid of all this stuff. I want to open Friday or Saturday night."

"With music?"

"Sure, a real disco, lots of work to do!"

"It's not possible. You need a cabaret license."

"Okay, I'll get one. Win Klein is coming over tonight and he can handle it."

Linda popped up from behind the bar. She was holding a large scrub brush and had been scrubbing the sink and shelves. "This place needs a good cleaning if he wants to open this week."

"Linda, he can't. He needs a license and it could be trouble if he doesn't have it."

"Don't worry," she said. "He can get it." Buddy walked over and barked some orders to the guys working on changing out some lighting.

"Here Frank, these are your keys. The large yellow one is for the front door."

I grabbed them and looked around at the chaos. "Buddy, let's walk outside. I want to speak to you."

The action never stopped. He brought three men from the track and McPeet had five of his workers helping.

"Buddy, I appreciate your offer, but right now I am busy in my disco, and I think you have more than enough partners here, so here are the keys. I'll help you all I can."

I handed him the keys, and he was quiet for a minute then he said, "Well Okay, but your share will always be there and you can come in anytime." I thanked him again and said so long and left the mad house.

It was late Wednesday when I returned. The sidewalk was clear and there was still plenty of work being done inside. Pete Axhelm was walking around with the stub of a cigar in his mouth and telling Bob Ussery how he was tall and could paint up high and Bobby could do the lower part of the wall. Frank Wright was holding a drink and looked like he had just stepped out of a gentleman's fashion magazine. His date was a beautiful honey blonde from South Carolina and she had a wonderful southern accent. They seemed to be supervising and admiring the work. Linda was working on some dark drapes for the large windows. Buddy was walking around with a hammer looking to nail something.

"It's starting to shape up," I said. "When will you open?"

"Friday."

"What about the cabaret license?"

"I made a great connection. You remember about two months ago a police captain was in a fight outside the Copacabana in the city? Well he and his pal were drunk, and his friend hit him and he fell and fractured his skull."

"So?"

"His friend is a lawyer, named Donahue, and he came to see me. He said we can open, and he has connections to guarantee no one will bother us this weekend. After that we can apply for the license."

"Buddy, I don't think he can do it."

"Well, he wants $7,500."

"No way. It's a con. If you get lucky, no one will come the first week, and he makes a score. If someone comes he will just say sorry or return the money. I wouldn't do it."

"Don't worry. I trust him and it's a go. Now, I could use a good bartender. Can you help me with that?"

Buddy was a genius at the racetrack but as naïve as a newborn baby in business. I knew I couldn't talk him out of this bad deal, so I let it drop.

"I have a good friend, he works for the city and used to work for me when I had my big disco upstate. I'll get him for you."

"By the way, I took out an ad on a rock & roll station. It starts tomorrow. Let me know what you think of it."

Buddy went through with his plan and while he was getting ready on Friday about 2 p.m. when the restaurant received a visitor—the mayor of Great Neck! He was a small man, balding, and in his 60s. He went into the restaurant and it was busy and noisy. He approached the bar. He knew Buddy was running the place and wanted to meet him.

"Excuse me, I'm Mayor Schultz. Is Mr. Jacobson here?"

Buddy looked at him and without a word pointed to a worker in the far end of the room. The mayor approached and said, "How do you do Mr. Jacobson, I am Mayor Schultz, and I'd like to welcome you to our village." The man he spoke to was Tony, newly arrived from Italy and unable to speak or understand English. He faced the mayor with a blank expression and began to ramble in Italian. The place went from silence to outrageous laughter. The mayor was completely humiliated. His face turned ashen, and he gave a quick look around to make an immediate exit. It was this funny moment which was to prove costly.

Surprisingly the weekend went well—no inspection, a good amount of customers for a first week. All the partners had plenty to drink and enjoyed the music and the attractive crowd. Buddy was overjoyed. "What a night and that bartender friend of yours was great. I gave him an extra $20. He seemed happy. I had Linda on the door collecting admission, and I gave that guy, Dave, $500 towards the payment of the place. I like this business"

"And you paid that guy, Donahue, $7,500?"

"But it was worth it. This place is a winner. I have more ads next week, Buddy's of Great Neck and a band, no DJ...new strobe lights and I think I'm going to show old Chaplin movies. I'll buy a projector and rent the films. Come over this weekend."

"I'll try, but I'm busy in Brooklyn. Business is getting better each week."

Buddy worked hard and his crew had the place in great shape. They had new posters of old movies, they hired two waiters and another bartender to help Jack.

It was 2:30 a.m. on Saturday and we were getting slow. I told my cousin Joe I was leaving and he should close. I drove to Great Neck and as I approached the restaurant there was a flurry of activity. The street was blocked off and I had to park two blocks away and walk. They were three town police cars and about four other official cars. I saw Buddy standing by a police car with his hands on the hood and a police officer searching him. Next to him was my friend, Jack. There were about fifty people milling around and I asked someone what happened.

"Some kind of raid. They served an underage kid," he said.

"The mayor was even here."

I spotted Linda and McPeet. "What's up?"

"Oh Frank, I'm so glad you're here," she said. "We didn't have a cabaret license and they also said we served a minor. But, we checked everyone at the door and they all had ID's."

"Where is everybody?"

"They all left when the police came."

I walked over to a sergeant and told him I was a friend of Buddy's and asked him what was happening. "He's going to be arrested, we will take him to court in Mineola. You can come and see him there." I walked closer and Buddy was now in the police car and saw me and just shook his head. Jack was in the back of another car. I told Linda I was going to Mineola to see about getting Buddy out. She said she would come along. McPeet said he would go home. I told him we would take care of it.

We drove to Mineola Court and spoke to a police officer on duty. He told us to call a lawyer and wait until Buddy was processed. I called Win Klein. "I'll be there in an hour, don't worry I'll call a bail bondsman. We will get him out in the morning." So, Linda and I found a nice wooden bench and tried to get some sleep. I fell off for a while but Linda was too nervous to sleep.

About 5:30 a.m. Win arrived. "All set," he said. "I spoke to everyone and I've arranged bail for Buddy and Jack the bartender...they should be out by 6:00 a.m."

Linda jumped up and grabbed his hand as if he was the Pope.

"Thank you, thank you," she repeated. Win was grinning and almost seemed embarrassed. I patted him on the back and we were celebrating as if we had just gotten an acquittal.

About thirty minutes later Buddy and Jack appeared. "Wow, great!" Linda gave Buddy a hug, and I shook hands with Jack who appeared in shock. He was, after all, a New York city social worker who had never been arrested or even received a ticket for a driving offense. Now to be handcuffed and processed—pictures, fingerprints. I guess he was in shock.

"Come on, let's get out of here."

"Yeah, let's go."

The sun was just beginning to rise, and we all began to smile as we got away from the courthouse. Buddy thanked Win and said we would be in touch. I brought the car around front and Buddy, Jack, and Linda got in.

"I'll go back to the restaurant, so you can pick up your cars."

"I never want to be in jail again," Buddy said.

"Me neither," said Jack.

"Go home and have a good sleep, and we will straighten this out this week."

"Yeah, sure. Maybe you can take Linda home and I'll go to the barn?"

"Sure Buddy."

"Sorry about all this, Jack. I just don't know what happened but don't worry, the lawyer will take care of it, and I'll pay all the expenses."

Jack turned to Buddy, "I just can't figure it out either. One minute I was mixing a drink, and the next I was marching out with my hands up. Glad my mother wasn't there." We all laughed, we needed a bit of humor.

Buddy took his car and headed for the barn. Jack told me he would call and speak to me later. I drove Linda home and assured her everything would be fine. Then I made my way home to get some rest.

The next day was Tuesday and Buddy called to tell me he was meeting Klein for lunch at Johnny's at 1:00 p.m. He wanted me to be there. Klein and Buddy were already talking when I arrived. "Hi, guys," I said.

"Sit down. Want a drink?" Buddy asked.

"Sure, a large coke."

Win smiled and extended his hand. I liked Win, he was a happy person and always very positive. "I think we can solve our problems very easily." he said.

"Boy, that's good news."

"I spoke to the assistant district attorney, and he would dismiss all the charges against Buddy, if we can give him a manager who will plead guilty."

"How can we do that, and who can we give him?"

"Jack," he said.

"Wait a minute. He is a city worker. I can't jeopardize his job."

"No way. He will get a suspended sentence and a fine, which we will pay and there is no way it could affect his job."

Win replied, "We should give him something if he would do it, say two or three thousand dollars."

"That's generous Buddy, but I would want him to be sure it wouldn't affect his job."

"That sounds fair, Frank. You work on it and Win can set it up."

"What about the restaurant, Buddy?"

"Win says that I can't go back. There is too much exposure. I'll give it back to Dave and we can look for another spot."

"I'm going to call Jack and let him know."

"Fine, let's eat."

As I left the restaurant I had mixed emotions. I wanted to help Buddy. I know a conviction would be bad for his racing license, but I could not hurt Jack. He trusted me and had worked in my first disco. He was the main bartender and handled all the cash and supervised six other bartenders. I trusted him and we were close.

Jack and I met the next day. He was anxious and hoping all this could just go away. Jack Zwiebann, was forty-four years old, he was a college graduate, a social worker for about fourteen years, single, Jewish boy who still lived with his mother and did not smoke or drink but loved to play the horses. He knew who Buddy was and he respected him like a baseball fan would respect Joe DiMaggio or Babe Ruth. So when I explained to him what Klein had proposed he reflected and wanted to help Buddy.

"I'll just have to make sure it will not affect my job," he said. "I have too many years in and I just can't take a chance. I know a guy in the personnel office and I'll speak to him, and if it's okay I'll take the heat, the $3,000 and a good tip every once in a while. I guess Buddy would appreciate it if I did this for him."

"I can tell you the money will be there but he is such an odd duck, I don't know about the appreciation. But thanks from me and whatever you decide is okay with me." We had lunch and I went to Brooklyn to my disco and called Buddy from there.

"I think it is going to be okay, but he is checking about his job. We settled on $3,000, is that okay?" I asked.

"Sure, sure, tell him I'll have $1,500 for him tomorrow and the rest after the case. Thanks, Frank."

"Anytime, Bud."

Jack said okay and that everything checked out. I made arrangements to get the money for him and he was happy with the deal. Win Klein arranged everything and Buddy was cleared of all charges. Jack paid a fine and the matter was settled. Dave got his place back. The rent was up-to-date, the electric was paid, there was about $2,000 worth of liquor which Buddy had purchased, and all the equipment he left behind. That was the plus. He also received $1,100 cash. Of course he had no black leather booths, a lot of black walls, and a few holes in the walls, so I guess it evened out. So much for Buddy's first disco.

Chapter VIII

NYC and the High Life

Buddy was looking for a place but had no luck. In the meantime, we started to go to into New York more often. He wanted Linda to see the city. They were getting along well, and he was like a kid on his first date. One of his favorite places was Maxwell's Plum on First Avenue and 64th Street on the upper East side. The place was huge and decorated with large Tiffany lamps, heavy wooden tables, and chairs. It was a flamboyant, sexy restaurant and singles bar. The waiters wore aprons and the staff were all young and attractive, and they employed a number of Englishmen and Buddy loved to hear their accents. His favorite dish was the onion soup and the steamed mussels. They were well known for their hamburgers and even served wild boar, but that was not to our liking. It was a good place to start the evening and Linda liked it a lot.

After dinner we would walk just a few yards down to Mr. Laffs, a great meeting place with delicious burgers and such. The owner and manager was Duncan. He was Canadian and a great friend of all the hockey players, and on any given night if the Rangers were playing the place was full of Ranger players. Duncan was a tall man with a ruddy complexion, handsome, and blond. He liked to bet horses and therefore loved Buddy. We would listen to music, have a drink, and socialize. Linda loved the scene and everyone loved Linda. It was here one night I got to meet Al Bierd, the "Bird," as Buddy called him. He had helped Buddy buy the farm in Old Westbury and on this night he met Linda. Al was about ten years older than Buddy and he had a piece of a race horse, but Buddy always said he was too cheap to buy his own horses. He was tall about six feet, very slim, and rather ordinary looking. He owned some buildings in the city and lived on the rental income. It was apparent from the start that he was taken with Linda. He had known Buddy for a long time but had never seen him with this kind of girl. He sat next to her and began to ask all about her. Buddy was talking to Rod Gilbert, a famous New York Ranger hockey player. Rod was about the same size as Buddy, a little small for a hockey player, but he was a star, fast, and very smart. Al was asking Linda if she came to the city often, "Not really," she replied.

"Well, if you like the theater, I have a great agent and can get you tickets to any show. Just let me know."

"Thank you, that's very nice but you know Buddy just doesn't like shows that much."

"If you do, I'll be glad to take you." Just then Duncan came over and said he would like Buddy to meet a few of the New York Giant's football players. Buddy said hi, and told them to call him when they wanted to come out to the track. The Bird continued to talk to Linda, and she tapped Buddy and said she was tired and wanted to go home. Buddy said goodnight, paid the check and we left.

Later she spoke to me about all the attention she was getting and felt uncomfortable, she was afraid Buddy would be upset. I told her Buddy would understand and not to worry, this was New York and there were lots of jerks who think with a little money they are special. Just be yourself was the best advice I could give and if someone came on too strong to tell me first. She gave me a smile but never needed any of my help.

Chapter IX

Second Disco The Chanticleer

The next morning I went to the track and while Buddy was watching some horses on the track I spoke to him about the disco.

"Buddy, I know you are trying to buy a disco but haven't had any luck. You once asked me about my disco, the Chanticleer. Well, I think we can buy the partners out."

"Great," he said. "How much and when?"

"They might take $10,000. There are four of them and they put up $2,000 each, but they all work for the city and they don't want any trouble which might affect their jobs. I think I can arrange it, but we will have to get you your own liquor license. That could take a few months."

"Do you think they would let me run the place, if I paid for it now?"

"I don't know, but without the license in your name you are at risk if the State Liquor Authority thinks there is undisclosed ownership. If they sell, you will have to be quiet about it until the license is approved. Is that okay with you?"

"Positively."

"Well then I'll work on it right away." I spoke to my partners and they agreed. They were happy to make a small profit so the deal was made and Buddy paid them.

"Wow, I love this place. We can put in a projector and change the lights. I know a great DJ. I'll call him."

"Slow, Buddy. Take it easy while we apply for the license. Remember you just work here for now."

"Sure, sure, I understand. Don't worry so much."

It was a Tuesday and his plan was to make his changes by Friday and have a new approach for the weekend. The restaurant was located on Fourth Avenue and 93rd Street in Brooklyn. It was the Fort Hamilton area, a very commercial street but close to an upscale neighborhood. The bar was well known for its Sunday night entertainment. It was transformed into an Irish Pub. When we bought the place we continued to run the Sunday night event. We had a great Irish tenor, Harry Walker, and our piano player was Joe Fay. The bar, which was one of the longest in Brooklyn at more than fifty feet, had two bartenders who had been working there for more than fifteen years. I had my dad help, as he was great with this older crowd and enjoyed the sing along. I only went in a few Sundays and left everything to him and my cousin, Joe Ciniglio. I told Buddy that this was a great night, the income was high, and I didn't want to change it. He reluctantly agreed. I left Buddy to make his changes.

On Friday, I drove towards the restaurant coming from Long Island in heavy traffic. I switched on the radio and there it was, "Buddy's under the bridge, the hottest place in Brooklyn. Come early, stay late!" A loud blasting commercial.

"Oh no, Buddy," I said. "Oh no, keep it quiet." As I drove the commercial was repeated. I was in quite a shock. I drove past the restaurant and saw a new addition. A huge banner, bright red with white letters, that said, "BUDDY's." It had to be twenty by twenty feet tied to the front of the building. I was angry and upset. Buddy was by the front door and barking orders to the help.

"Hi, Frank. How you like it?" he asked.

"Buddy, is this a low profile?"

"You've got to advertise, if you want to do business, besides could be anybody. Don't worry so much," and he disappeared into the restaurant.

My cousin, Joe, came out of the restaurant, "This bastard is crazy," he said. "I almost cracked him. He is abusing everybody. It's nuts."

I calmed Joe who was not happy with Buddy's attitude. Joe was five years older than me. He worked in my first disco and handled the money, the bouncers, and always watched my back. He worked as a longshoreman until he was hurt when the hi-lo he was driving went off the pier and sent him into the water. It was winter so he was wearing a heavy coat and boots yet managed to swim out. A miracle some said. I think it was his determination. He was only 5' 9" but looked like a smaller version of Rocky Marciano and with a fist like a hammer. We were very close.

"Take it easy. It's his first night. Give him some help."

"That son of a bitch thinks he's important. Who the fuck is he!"

"He's okay, give him a chance."

"Okay, but you better hang around. The fucking cops from the 86th were by and said they will be back."

Having a disco in New York was a funny business, you would get lots of visits from different sections of the police department, sometimes weekly or monthly. It was necessary to make payments to the local car, the sergeants, Brooklyn South, P.C. and so on. One night, while I was having a drink with one of the detectives at the bar, I said, "Harry, how many guys are on the pad? I just paid the borough."

"Look Frank," he smiled, "if I walked into your men's room right now we both know the soap will be missing, and I'll have to write you up. You don't need that."

We both laughed, as a matter of fact I liked Harry and was glad that the twenty dollars I gave him gave me a friend. I didn't want to do anything wrong but things happen in discos and it pays to have friends. I never told Buddy about this. I took care of it myself.

The night went well, a large crowd. Buddy greeted and chatted with lots of the girls who appeared rather young. There were a lot of first timers and that was good.

A few weeks passed and Linda was doing well at the track. In fact, Buddy had put some horses in her name and she won her first race. Afterwards we celebrated in P.J. Clarke's on 3rd Avenue in NYC. The place became famous and was used in many films, but at that time, it really was most connected to the 1945 movie, *The Lost Weekend*, which starred Ray Milland. He won the Academy Award for his role. A landmark restaurant was owned by Danny Lavezzo, Sr. a big horseplayer/owner and gambler. His trainer was Al Scotti, a great guy who almost never went to the city but would never miss a morning at the barn. I always enjoyed the place and the food was good and lots of horse people would be here. We went home early as we were racing the next day.

It was a good day, we won two of the races and Buddy said, "See you tonight."

It was a Friday night at the disco and we had a good crowd. Buddy had a guest, Al "the Bird." He was there to see what the business was all about and maybe invest with Buddy in a larger spot in Manhattan. They took a table in the rear and were enjoying a drink and appeared to be in deep conversation. I was in the kitchen, which was very large and used as our office since we did very little cooking.

Joe came in to look for me. "We've got a problem," he said.

"What?"

"Someone is smoking dope in the place. One of the guys from the neighborhood told me a kid is selling stuff here!"

"Do you know who he is?" I asked.

"I can find out."

"Let's go." We went through the swinging doors and into the dimly lit bar area. Joe went and spoke to the young boy who pointed to someone sitting on a chair facing the dance floor.

"That's him," said Joe. He had his back to us and was clapping his hands in time with the music. He appeared tall, with long hair, and we noticed he had a brown paper bag on the floor under his chair. As I approached, I reached under the chair and picked up the bag. He never saw what happened. I turned and walked into the kitchen, Joe at my side.

"What do you want to do?" Joe asked.

"Nothing, just put this away." I never opened the bag. We heard a commotion on the floor and went out to see this tall slim fellow arguing with a waiter and Buddy and Al were standing by trying to calm him down.

"What's up?" I asked.

"Some motherfucker stole my bag," he shouted, and he continued to franticly carry on.

"Take it easy. Come with me," I said. As I walked to the kitchen he continued to swear and make threats. In a quick motion I turned and reached up and grabbed a handful of his hair and pulled him down to the ground between the dishwasher and the garbage bins. My left hand reached out and grabbed a longneck whiskey bottle and with one motion I smashed it on the metal leg of the dishwasher and ended up with about three inches of jagged glass. I put my knee on his chest and placed the glass about two inches from his face. Joe grabbed his arm and we tried to restrain him. He continued to struggle and it became obvious he was under the influence of drugs. Buddy and Al were standing close by. I shouted for him to lie still. I never moved the bottle, but he shook his head up and the glass cut his cheek about one inch below his eye. Blood started to trickle down his cheek and in an instant he stopped struggling.

"Oh my God," I heard Buddy exclaim. Al became sick and lost his supper in the garbage pail. I heard the door slam as they ran from the room.

"Now, cocksucker you come near here again and I'll slice you up for dog food. Do you understand?" I shouted in a loud voice. "Do you, you fuck?"

"Yes, yes. I hear you," he replied.

I moved back and let him up. He was about six feet and 150 pounds maybe, it looked to me he was a user as well as a seller. The blood wad running down and he brushed it away with his hand.

"Get out, you prick and don't come back!"

"What about my bag?" he asked.

Joe had been quiet but now he reached out and grabbed his shirt and threw him across the room. "You fuck. You come in here and sell your shit? You're lucky I let you walk out!" he shouted, as he escorted him to the door.

I asked one of the men at the door, and he said Buddy and Al just ran past him and never said a word.

Joe came back into the restaurant after watching the dealer run off. "What happened to your pal?" he said, with a Cheshire cat grin.

"I guess they had an appointment."

"No balls! That one guy looked like a baby, and I always knew your pal was a wimp and sure enough they ran home to mama."

"They're not used to violence, no stomach for it. Who could imagine that years later this guy would be accused of murder of a real tough guy?

It was about half an hour later when the man at the door said someone was asking for the boss. I told him to bring the guy to the kitchen. Joe was by the door, and he came in with the fellow. He was about sixty, short and stout with lots of hair and a slight limp.

"I'm Vito Catrone. I live about three blocks away. My nephew just came home and said there was a problem."

"Your nephew was out of line. What's your problem?" I asked.

"I've lived in the neighborhood all my life. I know your landlord. The kid was doing stuff on his own and I'm sorry. He was wrong but he took some stuff from some negroes, and if he don't pay or give the stuff back it could be bad. So I came to ask you for a favor, give me his bag and I swear he will never come near here and I'll personally kick his ass."

I looked at Joe. He never changed his expression.

"You know he got a pretty good cut on his face," he added.

"He's lucky that's all he got," Joe answered.

I looked at Vito and he mentioned the landlord who was a well respected friend of mine.

"Vito, this is your lucky day. We never looked in the bag, so maybe it's his lunch or his shorts. Whatever it is, it don't belong here and it was just about to go down the drain. Joe see if you can find the bag."

Joe walked to the refrigerator and brought the paper bag to me.

"Give it to Vito," I said.

Vito grabbed the bag, "Thank you, thank you," he exclaimed.

"We don't steal and we don't allow low life in here, so keep your nephew out of here."

Joe took Vito by the arm and said, "Come on, I'll walk you out," and he did.

Joe returned to the kitchen. "I don't like that guy, maybe we should have flushed that shit."

"Well, he mentioned the landlord, and I just don't want any more aggravation tonight."

The next morning was Saturday, and I went to the barn. Linda was making some coffee so I had some with her. "Buddy was so late last night. I wish he would not stay to close up. He gets up so early."

"Yeah," I said. "I tried to chase him out, but you know Buddy. He likes to do everything himself and has to be in on everything. Why don't you come tonight?" I asked.

"He says it's too much for me and maybe he's right, but I guess I could come one or two nights."

"Hey Frank, come on and bring your coffee." It was Buddy going to watch some horses on the track. "Don't say anything to Linda about last night. I don't want her to worry. Is everything okay?"

"No problem, it's fine."

"Boy, I never thought that stuff could happen. Poor Al was sick, and I don't think he will ever go into the business."

"Say Buddy, Linda said you were very late getting home. You okay?"

"I stopped by the old apartment. Dennis called me early and said they were having a new group of stews and he had a new Norwegian girl for me. We had a ball."

"Kind of dangerous, don't you think? Linda is no fool. You better be careful."

"Don't worry about me. I'll see you about four this afternoon. I got a horse in the second race, and I'll come after that."

I arrived about 3:30 and began to work in the bar. We didn't open until 7:00 p.m. but there was plenty of work to do to get ready. At 4:15 Buddy arrived. He was anxious to install some new lights and had one of the cleanup men helping him. At about 4:45 I had visitors.

"Hi Frankie," someone called. I turned around to see the landlord's father, Dick Fusco. His son-in-law was listed as the owner of the property, but Dick was the only member of the family I ever saw. He was with a younger fellow that I had never seen before.

"Hi Dick, welcome…come on in and have a drink." We shook hands and went to a corner table. "Have some wine?"

"Good for me, but my friend, Sonny, likes cold beer." I got the drinks and sat at the table. Buddy was working and they didn't know him and I left it that way. Dick liked red wine and seemed to enjoy the one I chose for him. He was about sixty-five or so almost six feet and about 260 pounds—a big fellow with a ruddy complexion looking more Scandinavian than Italian. He used to tell stories about the old rum running days when he was known as Tricky Dick because of his fast boat and an ability to outrun the Coast Guard. His friend, Sonny, was just a bit shorter but maybe forty and built like an oak tree. His face showed signs of the fight game, and it was obvious his nose had been broken more than once. I wondered if they were here about the trouble last night.

"Everything okay, Dick?" I said.

"Sure, sure…I wanted my friend Sonny to see your place. He likes the disco business," Sonny never said a word. "I wanted to show him the bowling alley below." The restaurant was over a ten lane bowling alley which had been closed for as long as I could remember. "It's big and might make a good disco."

My cousin Joe arrived and came over to say hello. He knew Dick and shook hands with Sonny. He excused himself and went into the kitchen.

"I'll get the keys and show you the basement…be right back."

I went into the kitchen and Joe said, "Do you know who that guy Sonny is?"

"He's a friend of Dick's."

"Yeah, but he's Sonny Franzese. I know him from Little Italy. Nobody fucks with him. He is very bad."

"Well, I know I never met anybody like him."

Buddy came into the kitchen. "Who are those guys?"

"You don't want to know. Stay in the kitchen till they leave."

I got the keys and showed them the basement. I explained that you couldn't use it for a disco because there were not enough exits and the occupancy was only seventy-five people. I pointed out every negative aspect of the space that I could come up with. It worked and they were convinced that it would also take too much money to fix it up. After we finished looking at the basement I said, "By the way, do you know a Vito Catrone from the neighborhood?" I described him and told Dick what happened.

"Fucking bastard! Never heard of him. You know I don't go for that shit. You did right. Kick the shit out of any body that sells that shit."

Sonny, who had been silent all the while, exploded like Mount Vesuvius. "Kill the cocksucker!" as he slammed his huge fist on the table. "I'll take a chain and break their heads!" Saliva was flying from his mouth and his eyes seemed to shoot sparks. I have been around many violent people in my life but nothing like this. I grew up in the Red Hook section of Brooklyn with more than half the young men ending up in prison many for physical violence but never have I felt the anger and fury this man exuded. He was on my side and he had me shaking.

"You did right. If they come again, tell Dick, and I will come and crack their heads."

"Well, thanks," I said. "That's nice to know."

"Thanks Frankie, be sure to call me if you have any trouble or if those bastards come back."

"Well thanks and I'll see you soon. Bye now." They were gone.

Buddy came over to the door. "Wow, that was something. Who were those guys?"

"The older guy is related to our landlord, the younger one is his friend. They were upset about last night, but they said we did the right thing and they would be glad to help if anything like that happened again."

"Why?" Buddy asked.

"This is their neighborhood and they want to keep drugs out.

They have families like everyone else and they know what drugs can do."

"You know Frank, I'm not much good at this kind of stuff. Sorry I left so fast last night. I just had to get out."

"No problem. I understand."

Many years later, during the writing of this book, I picked up the NY Post one evening and Sonny Franzese was the subject of a news article:

MOB BOSS JOHN SONNY FRANZESE
FOUND GUILTY

Written by Janon Fisher on July 7, 2010. Stating that a Federal jury found the 93 year old reputed under boss of the Columbo family guilty of racketeering charges. He is to face 20 years in jail which is a life sentence for someone his age. Then again, if there was ever a man that could survive 20 years in prison it would be this man.

Chapter X

The Mustard Bed

It was a busy Saturday night at the disco. Buddy had lots of new gimmicks: lights, a new DJ, two movie projectors, and a kaleidoscope that changed every thirty seconds. At about 10:30 p.m. a young girl came into the disco. She was wearing a very provocative outfit—black and silver boots, a light blouse, and a tight mini skirt. Her hair was jet black and down to her shoulders. Her lips were fire engine red and her nails were long and painted black and silver. She appeared to be well developed and her breasts pressed against her scoop-necked blouse.

Buddy, who happened to be near the door, spotted her and she gave him a big smile as she paid her admission. I lost sight of her in the crowd and continued to help with some chores at the bar. It was about 11:00 p.m. when I went to the dance floor and spotted Buddy at a table in the corner with the girl in the black boots. About fifteen minutes later I heard a commotion, thinking it might be a fight so I made my way toward the noise. I pushed people and found myself next to Joe Cinigilo, my cousin.

"What happened?" I asked.

He was laughing and pointed to the far table. Buddy was standing in a puddle of beer it came from his head down. I saw the girl with black boots storming towards the front door. Buddy was calling to her and appeared to be pleading with her. In a minute she was gone.

"Buddy, are you okay? What happened?"

"It was Linda."

"That was her?"

"She hit me with a beer and boy is she pissed."

"She arrived about a half hour ago, dressed in a mini skirt, wearing a wig and lots of makeup. She looked hot and came on to me. We danced and then she wanted to sit and have a drink, one thing lead to another, and I kissed her."

"Is that it?" I asked.

We followed him to the door but she was nowhere in sight. We went to the kitchen and he dried off.

"We were making out and she went wild. I told her I knew it was her, but she didn't believe me."

"Well, did you?" I asked.

"Sure, sure I did."

Joe laughed.

"I just went along with the act."

"Get cleaned up and go home. Joe and I will close."

"I can't believe it. I don't know why she did it, but I knew it was her. I did."

I looked at Joe and said softly, "I wonder."

He left and we finished the night.

I went to the barn early. It was Sunday and Bill Frankel was coming out to visit Buddy.

"Where's Linda?"

"Home, I think," he said. "When I arrived home she had locked herself in the bedroom, put a chest up against the door and wouldn't let me in. I noticed she made the couch for me so I decided to get some rest. When I pulled back the sheet, I couldn't believe it. She had emptied the refrigerator on the couch. There was mustard, mayonnaise, pickles, butter, honey, pancake syrup…just everything. She even spread my chopped liver all over the sheets. I was getting sick looking at it. I took a blanket and slept on the floor. I woke up early and left her a note telling her how I knew it was her. I hope she understands."

"Bill Frankel is coming with Stanley Fingerhut, maybe you can stay and give me a hand."

"Bill is bringing some bagels and stuff."

"Sure Buddy, glad to."

Bill Frankel was Buddy's number one owner. He ran his horses in his wife, Marion's, name. He was a Wall Street guy who was well respected and liked to gamble. He used to say the stock market was the biggest gamble and he was lucky. Bill was a big gambler, the Las Vegas casinos used to comp him whenever he wanted to go. They would send him gifts all year, like prime steaks, boxes of cards and dice, lighters and pens. Buddy was lucky in that Bill would, in turn, send all of the gifts he received on to him. Frankel knew Buddy tried with all of his horses. He never gave a horse a race. He wanted each horse to finish the best he could. The owner received money for the first four finishes, and he wanted the best of each horse. Jockey's knew this, trainers knew this, and the public knew this. That's why they bet on his horses so heavily.

Bill Frankel said $1,000 was his standard bet. If a horse was better than two to one, he might bet $2,000. The bigger the price, more he would bet. That's the kind of gambler he was.

Bill arrived in his limousine with Stanley. Stanley was carrying two large shopping bags. I had the coffee machine going and cleared the desk. Stanley brought a dozen bagels, two kinds of cream cheese, regular and low calorie, chopped liver, and four frankfurters with mustard and sauerkraut. They were Buddy's favorite. We all exchanged hellos and had our breakfast. We listened to Stanley tell about his job He was a stockbroker and had been on a hot roll, picking a dozen winners in a row and how he had a large glass bowl on his desk and anyone who wished to speak to him must first put money in the bowl. He then would donate it to charity. Bill Frankel told him he would help him pick a horse to buy and he was very happy. Buddy spoke privately with Bill and the meeting broke up.

He later told me Frankel was thinking of retiring and moving to California, and he asked Buddy if he would go with him. Buddy told him he would think about it, but Frankel said it would not happen this year.

Buddy called the apartment and Linda answered. He was happy, and although she wasn't sure she was giving him the benefit of the doubt, he rushed home. I called Joe Porter and had him give any leftover food to the boys in the barn. I was glad the morning was over.

Chapter XI

LeFrak

It was Tuesday morning when I returned to the barn. "I'm glad you came out," Buddy said. "Sam LeFrak called, and we have a 1:00 p.m. appointment at his office."

"You want me to come?"

"Yeah, yeah, I think it would be good."

"I'll go home and clean up and meet you at noon at the apartment."

I left and went home to get a jacket and tie. We arrived at LeFrak's office about 12:45. Mr. LeFrak was the second largest landlord in the United States. The United States Government was the largest. There were three men waiting in the office and the receptionist asked us to have a seat. The men waiting were obviously in the construction business. They were all in work clothes with one in overalls wearing a jacket with the name of his glass company on it. They were talking to each other about how long they had been waiting for payment of their bills and how long they had been sitting in the office waiting to speak to someone. In the time it took us to find our seats and pick up a magazine the receptionist called us to go in. As we rose to go in, the room was silent and you could see the questioning on the faces of the three men.

We entered a large office and Sam J. LeFrak sat behind a large mahogany desk—a very impressive figure. He was well groomed and gave off an aura of success. There were two large leather and wood chairs on our side of the desk and he greeted Buddy and asked us to have a seat. Buddy introduced me as his assistant and LeFrak was very cordial. The room was filled with many awards and a large, life-sized painting of his father was on the wall.

"Buddy, I want to tell you I'm happy we are doing well at the track. Now what can I do for you?"

"Well, I know you have lots of property, and I was interested in opening a disco in one of your buildings. I saw a closed restaurant on Queens Boulevard, and I think it would be a great location," Buddy answered.

LeFrak sat back in his chair and began to finger a watch bob. It was a small, silver track shoe. I recognized it because I had one at home. It was given at track events in place of a medal.

"Excuse me," I said. "Isn't that a track award you have?"

"Why yes, I won it at school in a track meet," he proudly said.

I didn't mention that I had one.

"It means a lot to me. You can buy lots of things, but this was earned by lots of hard work and competition. I told the mayor last week that we must emphasize to all city employees that hard work is what made this nation great and encourage it. You know, I'm going to Washington in two weeks, having lunch with the President. I think I'm getting some kind of award. Buddy, I hear what you are saying. I'll tell you what. I'd like to win a stake race in New York. Let's make a deal. You win the stake race and I'll let you have the spot for a ham sandwich. Okay?"

Buddy appeared in shock. "Okay," he said.

"Buddy, I hear there are some good horses for sale. Maybe you can get one for me."

"I'll look into it right away."

"Good, give me a call."

We said good bye and left. As we approached the car Buddy was very quiet. "Frank, what do you think he means, a ham sandwich?"

I said, "Well Buddy, he knows the place is probably very expensive, but if you can win a stake he would give it to you for a very cheap price."

"Oh, that sounds good. Let me call the barn. There's a phone on the corner. Here's the keys to the car." He made the call and returned quickly. "Let's go to the track, I think we have a filly in trouble."

We arrived at the barn twenty minutes later and found Joe Porter. "What happened?" Buddy asked Joe.

"Buddy, I called the vet but he is at Belmont Race Track and can't leave yet." We walked into the stall and found the filly lying on her side in distress. She was thrashing about and looking at her stomach.

"Colic," said Buddy. "Let's get her up." The three of us entered the stall and helped the filly to her feet. "Put a shank on her and held her head up," he said. "Joe, get the tub. We will give her some oil."

He placed the tube down her throat and poured some olive oil in. "Joe, how long since she took a crap?"

"Nothing all morning, I think." Buddy took off his coat and loosened his tie.

"Frank, you just hold her head. Joe get the kit." Joe came in with a box. Buddy took out a large jar of Vaseline and a plastic sleeve. He put the sleeve on, and it was as long as his arm. He began to put Vaseline on the glove and then on the rear end of the filly. Joe took the tail and wrapped it with an elastic bandage and began to clean the horse's rump. Buddy applied the Vaseline to the anus and slowly inserted his sleeved arm into the horse. He began to remove the manure from the filly. As he did, the gas began to escape and the smell was pungent, but this was a good sign.

Buddy was standing in horse shit. It was on his new shoes, his pants legs, and everywhere but he continued to probe for more. We worked for about fifteen minutes when the vet arrived.

"Do you want to put me out of business?" the vet asked.

"Just giving you a hand," Buddy said. "No pun intended."

The vet was "Red" Finkle and was one of the best vets around.

He did all of Buddy's work on a regular basis. Buddy liked him because he understood Buddy and only did what Buddy asked. He very rarely made suggestions and never questioned Buddy's orders.

"You guys did a good job," he said as he gave the filly a shot.

"I'll rig up a jug. She's probably dehydrated."

Buddy removed the sleeve and we walked out of the stall. I saw a different Buddy—someone who was concerned about the horse, someone who had the ability to see the situation and act. This was not the act of a callous person who saw horses as machines. That was all baloney for the public. He was deeply involved with these animals. But for some reason, it seemed he felt that to show this side of himself would be a sign of weakness. My admiration for him grew that day.

It was a sunny, Friday morning when a man I did not know came to the barn and said, "I'm looking for Buddy."

"He's at the track," I said.

"I'll wait." He was a surly looking character about fifty years old. Buddy came in and recognized him. "Hi Uky," he said. "Come into the office."

Linda was in the office making out the paychecks. It was no concern to me since I never received a check form Buddy. I earned money in my business, and I worked for free. Buddy would always pick up the dinner check or pay expenses for trips, but I was not a paid employee.

The fellow left the barn and Buddy came out of the office. "He's a horse seller, got a nice horse for LeFrak. Jimmy Conway has him. I'm going to buy him. Ask Red Finkle to check with Conway and have him vet the horse as soon as he can."

"I'll call him today. By the way, how did he know you were looking?"

"He said that a guy that works in LaFrak's office told him. He said the guy is LeFrak's nephew and likes to bet on horses. Uky gives him tips and he bets for Uky, just another schmuck."

Linda called from the office, "Buddy, the checks are ready."

"Frank, give them out will you."

I walked down shed row and gave the checks out. Buddy had a good crew. Many of the men had been with him for more than ten years. Joe Porter, his foreman, was a great horseman.

Buddy said he could easily be a top trainer, but no one would give him a chance. He was Spanish and black and there were no black trainers in New York and very few black owners. Joe spoke broken English and although he knew his business, he would never get his chance.

"Lots of assistant trainers or foremen work for trainers and when they go on their own they steal the owners, but I know I'll never have to worry about Joe," Buddy would say. And he was right, not just because of Joe's heritage but mostly because Joe was faithful and loved Buddy.

As we were leaving the barn that morning, Buddy took me aside and said, "Listen, if Linda says anything tell her we are going to see some new guys about horses at the farm tonight and we will be out late. I expect to get home about 12:30."

"Sure, but what's up?"

"Dennis called and he wants me to visit the apartment. He and his pals rigged up some two-way mirrors in the bedroom and you can watch all the action without being seen."

"That sounds creepy to me. I never liked that junk. Why do you bother with those kids? They will only cause trouble."

"Don't worry, I'm careful. He is dying to come to the track, but I won't let him but he and his friends go after the girls and have lots of parties in the apartment."

"Buddy, it's your life!"

Linda was in the car waiting, so he ran off. She never asked me anything about the plans for the evening.

About a week later a new horse arrived at the barn.

Uky came by and Buddy said, "Nice looking horse. Gave $30,000 for him and I think we can do good with him. Also bought some breeding stock for LeFrak. Uky, did a god job. I've got to get the farm going, maybe a stallion. The breeding program is going to be big in New York."

Once again Buddy was right and again ahead of the rest of the pack. Later on it turned out to be a very profitable investment and just by being the breeder of record you could sit back and collect money on any horses that win in the many New York bred races.

Chapter XII
Odd Dancer

The following week on a Friday, Buddy was very excited when he received a phone call at the barn. "Frank, big news, we're buying a stallion for the farm. Odd Dancer is the name. Arnold Winick had the horse and sold him to Jack Dreyfus, who has Hobeau Farm. Allen Jerkens is his trainer. He wants $30,000 for him. I have first option, but we have to close the deal today. Call Tom at the bank and tell him I'm going to give a check and I'll bring the money in on Monday. Make sure he honors the check."

"Do you have any money in the bank?" I asked.

"No, today is payroll, and I wrote a few checks to pay some bills, so I may be short."

"What do we have to do with the check for the horse?"

"You have to bring it to Belmont, Allen Jerken's barn."

"When?"

"Today, but maybe you can get lost and arrive at Belmont after 3:00 p.m. The bank will be closed. Call Tom and tell him not to accept the check if anyone should come with it after 3:00 p.m."

"Okay, but will you have the money by Monday?"

"I'm syndicating the horse, selling shares, $5,000 each. I'll call and have the owners bring the checks to the track tomorrow. I've got to get busy."

"How many shares will you sell?"

The total is thirty-six, but I'll keep ten to control the syndicate. I know I'll sell ten by tomorrow and that's $50,000. Get the check from Linda and make sure not to get to Jerkens barn before 3:00 p.m."

"Sorry, I'm late," I told Allen.

"No problem, I'll give Mr. Dreyfus the check later this afternoon. Tell Buddy I wish him luck and tell him I heard the horse is a rough breeder, so be careful."

Allen Jerkens was a great trainer and one of the most honorable and kindest man on the track. They were friendly rivals. Buddy won more races but Allen had better horses and won more stake races.

I called the apartment and Buddy was home. "All done," I said.

"Great, I have eight for sure and three maybes for tomorrow.

I won't be at the disco tonight. I'll see you at the barn in the morning."

"Buddy, the old owners of the disco were asking me if you applied for the new license and they hope that you are taking care of it."

"Don't worry, it's in the works. See ya."

Sure enough, by Saturday afternoon Buddy had the eight checks and told me to deposit them at 9:00 a.m. on Monday. Not a bad deal. Buddy claimed a $30,000 horse for LeFrak and that was a lot of money. As I traveled around the track an assistant trainer told me that we claimed a horse with a broken knee. This was the horse Buddy said he was going to win a stake for LeFrak with.

I spoke to a number of the jockey agents who reported they were told the same thing. "The horse will never start. Your Brooklyn cowboy bit off more than he can chew this time." This from one of the top agents. I argued they were wrong, but I didn't ask Buddy if they were right. I'd know about it soon enough.

Two weeks later the horse ran and won by eight lengths, and I laughed at all the wise guys, but he never ran again. How did he get the horse to improve so much and run so fast? I was there. I saw it, but I still can't figure it out. LeFrak was happy for the win, but he had already rented the space Buddy had asked about. Relations between him and Buddy began to cool.

"By the way, how is Linda? I have been so busy and I just can't get out to the barn as much."

"OK, I guess but she is starting to talk marriage. I don't want a divorce, but Joan knows about her and she is pushing for a divorce. Funny, I thought Catholics didn't believe in it, but I told Linda I was divorced so she thinks there will be no problem for us to marry."

"The only problem would be you go to jail for bigamy."

"Yeah, I know. By the way, next Tuesday I'm doing the Barry Gray show on radio. I have to be there at 7 p.m., in the city, and I want to take Linda. I'd like you to come along."

"Sure fine, it's a date. Why don't you take tonight off and go home?"

"No way, I've got some new films and this rotating strobe light. Got to make sure it works right."

He just loved the business and had to be involved in all aspects.

I met Buddy and Linda at 6 p.m. at his apartment on Tuesday evening.

"Linda, you have the apartment looking great."

"Thanks, just a few more things to get."

"She bought a great sofa, so you can stay over anytime."

"Thanks Bud, I'll keep it in mind."

Buddy drove us into the city and to the radio station. Barry Gray had an evening talk show and discussed various subjects. He was a tall, friendly fellow and was very respectful towards Buddy. Buddy introduced us and we took our seats in a small room where the interview was held.

Buddy was answering all his questions but was critical of the NYRA, the jockeys, and many of the owners at the track. One of his statements was that, "the horses were trained to run and that jockeys were very secondary." He also said that, "the horses could be ridden by a monkey and do just as well." This was not very complimentary to the jockeys. He then said that, "many of the owners would interfere with the trainer's decisions and when they were wrong the trainer would take the blame, and that many owners have no loyalty and changed trainers like we change socks. He said that the racing association needed to take better care of the men that worked on the backstretch and cared for the horses." I felt he didn't make too many new friends at the track. It was funny, Buddy was shy as a youth and he told me he took a course at Dale Carnegie school on "How to Win Friends and Influence People." This changed his life. If you asked him any question, he had the answer and his favorite approach was to quote statistics.

"About 98 percent of all owners lose money in the business and 12 percent of the trainers make a good living. The others survive." These statements were just what Barry Gray liked. They were controversial and caused lots of discussion about the show. When it was over, Barry invited Buddy back to do another show.

As we left the building Buddy asked, "What do you think? Was it alright?"

Linda laughed and said, "Well you spoke nice and loud and I could understand all of it, but I don't know how popular you're going to be with the NYRA."

As we reached the car he turned and looked at me.

I said, "It was a lot of fun, but I think once is enough unless you want to go back to apologize to the entire racing community."

"Boy, you guys are sure hard on a guy," Buddy replied. "Don't you know it's good to get this kind of exposure on radio. We may get some new owners."

"What are we going to do with new owners, we have no room now?"

"You never know, some millionaire might want a new trainer."

We all laughed and headed for P.J. Clark's for a burger. We were in the back room just finishing our meal when a figure crawled along the floor and leaped up yelling "Boo!"

There was a dead silence in the normally noisy room.

"Hi, Bud," he called out.

Before us was a young fellow about thirty years old. He was average height with thinning light hair, a round smiling face, and a slightly pot belly.

"Stanley?" Buddy asked.

"Yeah, Fingerhut at your service."

He was carrying a baseball glove and a ball.

"I'm here with a girl. Can we join you?"

"Sure, come on over." Buddy said as he moved over to make room.

Stanley sat down and shouted across the room, "Hey Babe, come on over."

It was dark in the restaurant but you could make out the form of a beautiful girl coming towards the table. She was much taller than Stanley and had honey blonde hair. Her skin was white and her lips were strawberry color. It was hard to see the color of her eyes, but when she sat down there was no doubt they were cat green.

"This is Antoinette. Say hi to Buddy, a famous horse trainer.

Antoinette just signed with the Ford Agency today and we are celebrating. She comes from Florida. Just here two weeks."

We all said hi and Stanley ordered Dom Perignon champagne.

Stanley continued to be loud and told lots of jokes. His date said very little. She spoke to Linda and said she was new in town and very happy to have signed with one of the best modeling agencies in New York. She had only met Stanley two days ago, and he was helping her find an apartment. As we were ready to leave Stanley announced he was paying the check.

"Buddy, I've been meaning to call you…since my visit to the track. I would love to have some horses you could train for me. I'd like to buy about six. What do you say?"

"Great Stanley, call me in the barn and we will take care of it."

"Okay, good night all."

We left Stanley in the restaurant and went to the car.

"Buddy, who is that guy?" Linda asked.

"His name is Stanley Fingerhut. He works on Wall Street. They say he is a crazy genius. He picks so many winners in the stock market he has made a fortune. He sits at his desk and swings a bat and wears a baseball cap. Sometimes, when he is thinking, he wears a football helmet. Bill Frankel brought him to the barn on Saturday and showed him the horses and tonight he wants to buy. Like I said, you never know."

"A nice looking girl," I said.

"Yes, and very sweet. I hope someone takes care of her," Linda said.

"Oh, Stanley is harmless. He's just a Jewish kid from Brooklyn who got rich overnight."

"She will probably be rich someday, I guess."

As Linda left for the ladies room he smiled and said, "You know Frank, that modeling business is very interesting. I think we should look into it."

"Buddy, what do we know about the modeling business?"

"It's a great way to meet girls."

He paid the check and we left.

The next day the track was full of talk about the radio show, and none of it was good. "Who the hell does that little shit think he is? Is he trying to ruin this business?" This was probably the mildest comment. But Buddy said he was not worried, "It will blow over in a few days." Things got quiet but the officials were very cold to the Jacobson crew.

Things at the disco were good, but he still didn't get his license.

I asked him over and over, "Don't worry. It's in the works" he said.

Buddy loved the farm and felt it was important to get it going. He hired a man for the farm. He was Joe Martin, an ex jockey and exercise boy. He was about sixty now but still did a good days work and was a fine hand with a horse. He was a great help and a good horseman.

There was an apartment on the farm, and Joe and his wife moved into it. This took a lot of pressure off Buddy, and he began to send horses to the farm. "You and I need vacations, so do horses who race all year long. A short stay of two or three weeks will be super for them."

The farm was located in Old Westbury, Long Island, New York about a fifteen minute ride from Belmont Racetrack. It was twenty-six acres of land in one of the most prestigious areas in the United States. This was before the 90214 Beverly Hills zip code took first place. This was real money...old money. The people who had land there included: The Phipps family, the Grace shipping line family; Paul Mellon, the banking family; and Alfred Vanderbilt—not a bad neighborhood. It had one of the highest incomes. I began to spend much more time there.

We shipped to Saratoga at the end of July and left a crew of men in New York with some of the horses. I stayed in New York. In the first week of the meet Buddy called and asked me to come to Saratoga for the weekend. I was to pick up his sons and bring them up. I also brought my two oldest boys, Joseph and Frank Jr. We drove up and met Linda, who made the boys feel right at home.

We had a great weekend and Buddy had the boys doing chores on the farm. They worked hard, but they loved it. In the evening we would all go to a local restaurant where the meals were served family style. It was a wonderful time, but the best was later on at home as Buddy would tell ghost stories. He and Jimmy Ferraro had rigged up bells on the floor of the house and by pulling on a kind of rope he could make them ring. Just at the right time Buddy would pull the cord and everyone would cry out, "It's the ghost!"

Jimmy was outside with a sheet on a form. He would wave it at the window when the bells would ring. The kids never forgot that night. Buddy was laughing and this was not the hardnosed person that the outside world saw.

On Monday morning we left the farm. It would be the last time we would see it. Buddy sold it that summer.

Chapter XIII
Modeling Agency

September is a beautiful time at the track, and I was working hard at a job I loved when I received a call to go to the barn.

"I was at Belmont when I got your call, what's up?"

"Let's take a walk," he said.

"I've been doing some checking, and I found out it's not hard to start a modeling agency. All we need is a person with three years experience to get the license."

"Are you serious?"

"It's a good business, and I have some ideas how to get jobs for the girls."

"What about the boys?"

"Don't be negative. This can work. I called Al, and he is looking for a small office in the city around midtown. He said he will have some spots for us to see at the end of the week. I'll put an ad in the paper for someone with experience who can get the license"

"Great, and how are you going to run it?"

"I'm going to let you do that."

"You're nuts!"

"You could go into the city about 11 a.m. and be back by 1 p.m."

"Great, be in the barn at 6 a.m., work till 10:30, shoot into the city by 11:00, leave to go to the track at 1 p.m. Maybe go to the farm for a few hours, then the disco at night? I have at least half an hour during the day to call home and check on the family and somehow find time to sleep. Thanks, but no thanks."

"Don't make it sound so bad. After a while you can go to the city just three days a week. We only race five days a week, and I'm telling you we can have a great business. You will be a partner, and I'll put up all the money. How about it?"

"Have I ever said no to you? But I think it's nuts."

That week we went to the city, Al found a beautiful small building on 72nd Street off Madison Avenue. It was an old brownstone that was a mixture of the old and new, with a small elevator and four floors—some were private apartments with a few commercial offices; Buddy chose one on the second floor, and it was perfect for us. The entrance was a beautiful large wooden door leading to a small foyer, to the left was a small kitchen area which could be hidden by closing its door, at the end of the hall was a room of good size that could be used as a reception area. There was a small bath to the right of the room and a doorway in the reception area leading into the main room which was very large and located in the front of the building. The three large windows that faced 72nd Street and the afternoon sun was bright and inviting in the room.

"This is it," Buddy said. "I'll take it."

"Do you think we should know the rent?" I asked.

"When you see the right place, it's like seeing the right horse. I've got to have it."

"Al, make the deal. Let's go Frank."

As we walked to the car he said, "It's going to be great here, look at the neighborhood, lots of beautiful shops, classy people. We are in the right spot to attract the best people in the city."

It was three weeks later that he told me to be sure I was at the barn at 10 a.m. after I finished at Belmont, so I made sure I was ready for something, but what?

"Let's go."

"Want me to drive?"

"I've got it."

His Caddy was long and black and the top was down even when it was a little cool, as it was today.

"Are we going far?"

"Into the city, I want you to see something."

We arrived in Manhattan and drove to 72nd Street. I guess he was still interested in the modeling agency, although he had not mentioned it anymore since our visit. We went to the building and up the elevator. As we approached the apartment, I saw the brass plate on the door said "Ideal Agency."

We went in. "Hi, Anna," he said. "This is Frank Pagano, who I told you about."

A small gray haired woman about sixty or so with large black rimmed glasses and a bright multicolored dress over a very thin frame got up from behind a desk and extended her hand, "Nice to know you, Frank."

"A pleasure," I answered just getting over the shock.

"I'll show you your office." Buddy said as he opened the door to the front room. It was a fully furnished office with a large wooden desk. There was a leather armchair on rollers, a telephone, a desk pad with a pen set, two large wooden chairs facing the desk, and a bronze desk lamp. But the highlight was the wall to wall, shaggy, white rug. The windows had gold colored drapes and Venetian blinds.

"This is amazing. How did you do it?"

"Well, have a seat at your desk and I'll tell you. I put an ad in the *Village Voice* newspaper and got Anna. Then we talked about the license. She has lots of experience, worked for the Ford Agency for six or seven years, then a lot of smaller agencies. So, she became my partner with 10 percent of the business, plus $300 a week, and she is good. She applied for a license and got it almost two weeks ago. Then I started to buy the furniture. Al Bierd got me his office supply company and I picked the colors, the rug, and that nice desk. We finished about two days ago and Anna has been getting supplies.

"So, what do you say?"

"Why didn't you tell me?"

"Wanted to surprise you, and I knew you would say it was a bad idea."

"Hmm, well I guess I would, but only because you have so many things going on right now."

"But Frank, this will be a winner. Anna is setting up the files. She gets the *New York Times* each day and checks the help wanted ads and then calls to tell them she has someone for the job. We get a commission from the company and sometimes from the person we place. It's easy."

"What am I supposed to do?"

"You run the joint. Come in. You can learn quick, but the most important thing is to search out some great looking chicks."

"You must be kidding. What about the track?"

"You only have to be here an hour or so a day, lots of time for the track."

He got up and we went to see Anna. She was a pleasant woman and very happy for the chance to prove herself.

"I know we will do great here," she said, and I'm sure we will work well together."

"I don't know much about this business," I answered.

"Not much to know. I'll teach you. Buddy said we start next week, so I'll get some ad's ready for the paper. You can check them when you come back."

"Okay, let's go. Frank will call you and anything you need, tell him."

He turned, we said good bye and left.

On the ride home he told me his plan. "We have lots of owners in many different businesses, but they all need people to work for them. We will supply the people. We can develop a good business and also get into the modeling business."

"Well, if you think so, I'll try."

"Thanks Frank, I knew you would."

"By the way, what did Linda say."

"Oh, now that's where you come in. It's your business and I'm helping you."

"Oh no, Bud. You know I like Linda, she is like a little sister to me. If she finds out it's all over. Is it worth it?"

"Don't worry, she won't."

We were in Queens now and close to the track, as we made a right turn off Queens Boulevard, a siren sounded. It was the police. Buddy pulled to the curb and an officer approached the car.

"License and registration, please."

"Sure officer. Is something wrong?" Bud asked.

"No right turn off Queens Boulevard at that block."

"Guess I missed it, sorry."

"Howard Jacobson, not Buddy Jacobson the horse guy, are you?"

"Guilty." Buddy laughed.

"I like to follow the horses, and you win plenty of races."

"Thanks, on my way to the track, got one in the last should do real good if I can get there in time."

"Hell Buddy, get going and good luck."

"Thanks officer." And away we went.

"Nice guy."

"I don't think he does that for everybody. You got lucky. I hope the horse in the last wins, or we will have to find the long way to the track to avoid him." We both laughed and Buddy was relaxed and happy.

Now we had to get clients for the agency. We started with Al Nat stable, there were two partners, Nathaniel "Sonny" Usdan and Al Gold, both nice guys. Sonny was a real horseplayer and a good friend. He loved to handicap the races and was very good at it. We got to meet at the races, and we both loved to bet. Sonny was very handsome and he could have been a movie star and was tan even in winter. He was a pleasure to be around.

"Buddy has this agency and wanted me to ask you if you need any help at your company." He and his partner owned Perfect Tread Company, a nice, growing family business.

"Well, we do business shows and we hire girls to work at the booths. It helps if they are pretty."

"Great, I'll have our girl call and if you also need office help, we can do that too."

He was our first client and a loyal friend to Buddy and me. We canvassed the other owners and I gave Anna their names and numbers and she did the rest. I enjoyed the agency and Anna was a good teacher. She told me she had polio as a young girl and as she got older her left leg was affected and her limp grew worse.

"I could still do the job, but I guess I made all the pretty people uncomfortable, so they let me go. Buddy gave me this chance, and I am grateful." Her last name was Komisky and she was born in Brooklyn, so we had Brooklyn in common.

I was still going to the barn every morning and Buddy said, "Frank let's walk to the track. I want to watch this horse work today."

As we spoke a young boy brought out the horse and the exercise boy mounted, "You lead him to the track," Buddy told the boy.

"Who's the new kid?" I asked.

"Oh that's Bobby Frankel, a new hot walker."

"Is he related to Bill Frankel?"

"No, his folks have a grocery and deli on Pitkin Avenue and his pop asked a friend to recommend him, so I put him to work. Nice clean cut kid, why he would want to work here I'll never know. Come on, I want to speak to you. You're doing a great job at the agency. Things are going good, and we are getting some good business."

"I think it's time to start with the model trade. I've been talking to some people and the Jockey Club is doing a film on racing and the stress on the horses. I was thinking of doing a racing film."

"Buddy, that takes a lot of work, and about making movies we really don't know a thing. Plus it's very expensive."

"How tough can it be? You know we meet so many of those movie people at the races, and I never was too impressed by any of them. I know we can do it. Let me worry about that, and you start to line up pretty girls who want to be in the movies."

Buddy started to write ads, and I would go in and interview the girls. I would arrive at noon and be gone by 1:00 p.m. If we had a horse in the first race, I would leave or just not go to the city.

There were lots of girls, and I would ask Anna to see them. Buddy would only see the exceptional ones. There were not too many of them and Buddy was getting impatient. He wrote this ad for the *Village Voice*, "Golden Girls Wanted, Our client wants young attractive women for immediate employment, Hours 11 AM to 2 PM one hour for lunch, For Modeling or Movie Work, No Experience Necessary, Must Be Free to Travel, Ideal Agency

The ad ran and the office was packed. Anna had to turn girls away. When I arrived they were standing and sitting everywhere, but the one who caught my eye was in the corner sitting on an empty wastepaper basket she had turned upside down. I went into the office and asked Anna to come in. I told her to have the girls fill out the application forms and send them in one at a time, but save the little dark haired one on the basket until last.

The girls came in, one at a time and were all very anxious to get the job, whatever it was. I checked their applications and asked a few questions. "Are you working now? Have you ever done any modeling? Do you live in the city?" Along with other things that were not very important. I marked the applications with a number one to ten according to what I thought Buddy would appreciate, then I marked from "A to Z" as to where we could place them with our clients who were looking for office help. I was amazed how some responded.

"I like to do lingerie work," she said as she raised her skirt up to reveal her legs.

"That's fine. I'll keep it in mind." She was attractive but much too young and dangerous.

"I can do anything on and off screen," said the tall blonde.

"And how old did you say you are?" I asked.

"Almost eighteen," she said but she looked fifteen.

"Thank you. We will let you know."

So it went for the next hour.

"Just one left, Frank," Anna said.

"Good, send her in."

The door opened and the little brunette came in. She was only about 5' 3" or smaller with shoulder length, jet black hair which looked even darker because of the crisp white blouse she wore. Her high cheek bones and dark piercing eyes were classic features and were almost Egyptian. Her complexion was smooth and tan as an autumn leaf. All this and a perfect body in a size six skirt.

"Please sit down, Miss Philips." She took a seat and pulled her chair closer to the desk.

"I have some head shots and a small portfolio. I've been working on more pictures and hope to have some soon."

I took the book and the head shot. I was very impressed, they were good.

"Nice. Very nice. Are you working now?"

"Not at the moment, but I'm hoping I'll start today."

We both smiled. There was not much work for short girls, all the agents were looking for girls 5' 9" or taller.

"Tell me a little about yourself."

"Well my name is Diana Philips, I'm twenty years old. I come from Detroit, Michigan. My father was an Army officer and my mom is part American Indian. I've been in New York for three months, and I live with a girlfriend on the upper east side. I want to be a model or maybe do some acting, but so far I've worked in a coffee shop and now a restaurant on 45th Street and that's about it."

"You are a very pretty girl, but you know it's hard to do much modeling if you are not five nine or taller. I have a client who is putting together a movie idea about horses. Nothing is set, but you are the right type. He may be able to use you. I know he is going to be at the racetrack today. Would you like to take a ride and see him?"

"Yes, yes of course."

"Sure you're not busy? It's not a sure thing, but you will get lunch."

"I never turn down a free lunch."

I called Buddy and he said he would meet us at the restaurant at the track so off we went.

As we drove towards the track I was hoping she would have said she couldn't make it. She was sweet and beautiful but she was also smart and maybe too smart for Buddy.

Buddy rose to greet us and was very charming. They got along fine as Buddy told us of the picture he was planning. We had our lunch and I told them I had to leave. Buddy said he would be happy to drive Diana home. She said that was fine with her, so I left. As I drove to the disco I just could not get her out of my mind. For the first time I felt guilty, and it was not a nice feeling. Something about Buddy that day made me feel uncomfortable, and that he was not on the up and up. Was I really looking to cast someone in his movie or just supplying him with a date for the evening?

The morning was crisp, and I was on my second cup of coffee when I spotted Buddy watching a horse on the track.

"Well?" I said.

"Well, what?"

"What happened with her? Did you give her the part?"

"Oh, just not my type. I took her for a drink and right home. I told her we would be in touch. By the way, I'm getting a few new horses for the farm. You should go out and see if Joe needs any help and check the feed."

"Fine, I can go today after the overnight comes out."

I felt good but sorry not to see Diana again.

For the next month or so I saw lots of girls. I was amazed to see how many were interested in modeling. Some were very attractive, but others would have no chance, although they would not believe it. I didn't want to tell Buddy how easy it was to corrupt such young girls—it seemed like a sin. I thought about my own three daughters, and I sent lots of the young hopefuls home and into another business I hope.

I had to go to SoHo to meet a friend. After the meeting, I drove uptown to the office. At about 23rd Street I stopped for a red light. A slight rain had begun to fall, and I gazed at the people waiting at the bus stop. Didn't I know that person? It was Diana.

I rolled down the window and shouted "Hi, Diana. Need a lift?"

She looked for a second then smiled and came toward the car.

I reached across and opened the door as the car behind began blowing his horn.

"Jump in."

"Thanks, you came just in time. I'm not dressed for rain."

"How've you been?"

"Fine, but I never heard from Buddy."

"Well, I don't think the project got off the ground. Where are you headed?"

"To 57th Street, I've got an appointment at the Playboy Club about a job."

"A bunny. Wow, nice going."

"Well, I don't have it yet."

"Say I was going to the office, but I haven't had lunch, hungry?"

"You know I can't refuse a free lunch."

I parked in midtown and we enjoyed a great lunch and a new friendship. I didn't mention it to Buddy, but that's a story for another time.

Buddy had a taste of the modeling business and liked it but now it was necessary to get back to work. We gave Anna a month to clean up loose ends, and she could make arrangements to take any business to another agency and maybe get a job if that's what she wanted. We had Al take the furniture and put it somewhere in one of his buildings, and just like that we closed up shop. It ended like it began in a twinkle of an eye.

"With all the expense and the income we took in I guess it cost about eight grand, but boy it was worth it. If I had more time this would be the business for me." he said.

"Well, I had some fun, but I'm glad it's over." I sighed.

Chapter XIV

The Wedding

Meantime Linda had claimed two horses and won some more races. Buddy made sure she received cash, and she started her own bank account. But money did not really interest her. She was getting too close to discovering Buddy's other life with the boys and stews.

"I'm having a dinner Friday night at Elaine's in New York. Linda likes it there, say about 6:00 p.m.? Make sure you come."

It seemed more like an order instead of a request. I arrived ten minutes early to find a party of ten. Buddy, Linda, Al Bierd, Al McPeet, Jim Ferraro, three stews, some little girl, a friend of Linda's from her home town, and me. We started with a cocktail and then lots of ordering.

Buddy had ordered mussels, clams, roasted eggplant and the dinner was served rather quickly. Buddy announced he had a surprise.

"Leave everything and follow me," he said. We all left and found two limousines waiting outside the restaurant. "Everybody in," he said.

We split up into two groups of five. Buddy was never much for champagne but there was plenty on ice. "Open them up and have a good time." Off we went. There was plenty of music and I rode with Jimmy, who was a racetrack regular and a great friend of Buddy's. He was very funny and had us laughing all through the ride. "Buddy has discovered some evil place and he's taking us there, and just on a night when I come out broke and probably won't be able to get home. Hope you guys got cab fare for me," he said. I could not wrap my head around just what Buddy was up to this time. After about a forty minute ride we slowed down in front of a large, white house in Connecticut. A sign near the front read, "Justice of the Peace."

Buddy jumped out first, "Let's go. Let's Go." He lead the way in with Linda in tow. She was like a little girl on Christmas morning seeing all the gifts under the tree. There was such excitement and wonder in her eyes. I don't think I ever saw her look more beautiful. A tall, gray haired man of about fifty answered the door. He was wearing a shirt, tie, and a dark vest. "Welcome. Come right in." He shook hands with Buddy who introduced Linda and himself. He announced he had called and made arrangements for a wedding that evening. It was 8:50 and Buddy was due at 9:00 p.m...very prompt, very Buddy.

We went from the hall into a large room with a fireplace, which was not lit because it was June. There were three baskets of flowers placed around the room and a podium at one end. There was a small desk and to the right, a record player that would play the wedding march. Jimmy was shouting for joy. The girls were excited and Linda was stunned. She clung to Buddy and was between tears and laughter. The rest of us were in shock. Buddy asked Al Bierd to act as best man and Linda's friend was her maid of honor. The minister put on his jacket and turned on the music. The ceremony was short, and being so excited and a little drunk, not very memorable. There were lots of congratulations and kissing when it was done and back into the limos. We left the scene with the minister and his wife on the porch waving good bye.

The next morning at the barn. "Buddy, are you crazy? Did you get the divorce?" I asked. "If not Joan or Linda can make it very hot for you."

"Did you see how happy Linda was? Anything that happens will be worth it. By the way, how's business been?"

It was the end of June when Buddy got word LeFrak was questioning his recent horse deals. He claimed Buddy received a commission without his authorization. Someone told him that some of the horses were in Linda's name and may have belonged to Buddy. A lawyer contacted Buddy and said there was going to be a civil lawsuit.

Buddy told Linda, but she was unconcerned since she didn't feel she had done anything wrong. But Buddy felt he should have a lawyer just in case. He said LeFrak was a very powerful man.

We were making plans to go to Saratoga and some owners were behind in paying their bills. Linda gave Buddy an envelope and said she knew he might need some money so she emptied her bank account and gave him $15,000.

He was shocked and told me, "I can't believe she did that. I'll get it back to her, but she is a special person."

Everything went well in New York and the lawyer reported LeFrak was not going ahead with the lawsuit. The lawyer said, "I guess he realized he didn't have a good case."

Thank goodness, that was over. It was funny that Uky, who had been ruled off the track was now getting his license back. He gave a statement against Buddy to the officials saying he gave Buddy a commission on the sale. He also implicated Jim Conway, but no one believed Jim would do anything wrong. Jim had years of success and a great reputation, so the case ended, we thought, but not the feelings against Buddy.

Al Bierd called the barn and asked for Buddy. I told him Buddy was still in Saratoga and he would be back next week. He acted funny on the phone and said to forget it and hung up. Buddy returned and we went back to our regular routine. It was three days later when he arrived at the barn very concerned. "Linda is not feeling well so she will not be coming in today."

"Nothing serious, I hope."

"I don't know. She went to lunch with a girlfriend and came home and went right to bed."

"Maybe she should see a doctor."

"Come home with me and we will talk to her."

"Fine."

We finished at about 10:30 and left for the apartment. "Leave your car and we can come back for it later." So we went in his car.

"Let's stop at the deli and bring in some breakfast," he said.

Breakfast was always the same, bagels, cream cheese with chives, chopped liver, and three small containers of orange juice and, of course, his favorite three hot dogs with mustard and sauerkraut. We drove to the apartment and Buddy rang the buzzer, but no one answered.

"She must be sleeping. I hope I brought my key." After a minute he found the key and opened the door.

"My God! Linda, Linda," he cried out. The apartment was in a complete disarray. Was it a robbery, an attack, where was Linda? Buddy was frantic! "She's not here. We should call the cops!" he said.

As he searched the apartment he called out, "Her suitcase is not in the closet and most of her clothes are gone." He was babbling as he waded through a pile of his clothes on the floor. The drawers from the dresser were emptied with most of the contents on the floor.

I looked in the kitchen. "Buddy, come here. A note for you." It read something like: "You lying son of a bitch. You low life bastard. Al told me what you did. I hate you. Drop dead!" There was no signature.

"What does it mean, Bud?" I asked.

"That bastard. Give me the phone." He dialed, "Al, its Buddy. What did you tell Linda?" A pause, "How could you? That's not true. Where is she? If you know, tell me. You just ruined my life." He hung up.

"Al went back to Connecticut and found the house. He checked and found there was no justice of the peace. I rented the house and the guy was an actor I hired. Al told Linda it was a farce. Says he cares about her and was looking out for her welfare. I'm ruined."

"Buddy, I can't believe it."

"What should I do? I love that girl. I didn't want to lose her, that's why I did it. I just wanted to make her happy."

"I'm sure she will call you. She can't go far. She gave you all of her money."

"I've got to find her, Frank!"

"Okay, I'll call Al and tell him I want to help. I'm sure he can get in touch with her. He probably gave her one of his apartments."

"Do it Frank. Do it."

I called Al. He was very defensive. "Look, he's my friend, but I just couldn't let this happen to Linda."

"Al, he loves her. Maybe he can explain. Anyway he wants to give her some money to help her…try to convince her to see him."

"I'm not promising anything, but if she calls me I'll tell her."

"Nothing to do now but wait," I said.

Buddy was still in a panic. "I'll help you clean up, maybe we should have some breakfast? I'll bet she calls." We began to clean up and ate our hot dogs.

It was two days before we heard from John O'Hara, the lawyer for Linda. "We represent Linda and if Mr. Jacobson would like to see her I can arrange a meeting at our office. He can bring his lawyer if he wishes."

"Fine, we would like to do it as soon as possible."

"We can do it this evening at 6:30 in our office." He proceeded to give me the address and directions.

Buddy was anxious and at 6:00 p.m. we were outside the office.

"Just take it easy Buddy, don't be upset. Just let her know how much you care."

The meeting was in the conference room and Linda was accompanied by her lawyer and his assistant. Buddy and I were across the table. Linda just shook her head, she never said hello. I got the feeling she felt I was in on the deception. Buddy tried to speak to Linda but the lawyer kept interrupting saying Linda was leaving Buddy. She did not want any contact and no money except what she had given him. She would not expect the money all at once but would accept whatever he was able to pay until it was satisfied. Buddy didn't appear to hear anything. He just kept pleading. Linda never answered.

After almost ten minutes of this, the lawyer announced the meeting was over. Buddy asked if he could speak privately to Linda and his request was denied. He pleaded with Linda, but she never responded.

Buddy turned to me. "Frank, the checkbook is in the car. Bring up a blank check." I told the lawyer I'd be right back and went for the check. "Write it for $5,000, and I'll sign it," he handed it to the lawyer.

"This is for you Babe. I'll get you the rest. You take a trip and when you are ready, I'll be waiting. Please call me soon."

She turned away and began to cry softly. He turned and we walked out. I never saw Linda after that. I heard she was pregnant and had a girl. Buddy never spoke of it again but when he was arrested many years later she came to New York and gave him her support. She called all of his friends and asked each and everyone to give him all the help possible. It could not have been easy for her with everyone knowing the story of her departure. He was right, she was one of a kind and very special.

Chapter XV

Breeding at the Farm

Now Buddy was alone. He missed Linda, but he never spoke of her and never said if he tried to reach her. He asked me to spend more time at the track with him. He gave up their apartment and moved back to the one he kept before she ever came. The boys, Dennis and his pals, had to find a new home but they were around to gofer and get new girls.

The disco was in trouble. Buddy never applied for a license and the old partners would not get the renewal. "Let's close. I've had it. My heart is not in it right now," he said.

"I'll look for a new place. I've got to make a living."

"Wait now. Hook up with me…start now."

"Are you sure?"

"You started."

About two weeks later as we finished training he called me to the office. "I know you like the business and have been spending every day here and doing a good job. I was thinking, Tony Garramone is my jockey. He had a serious fall and is just about ready to ride, but it is not easy getting started. He still has a weight allowance and any horse he rides will carry five pounds less, so that's an advantage. He has no agent right now. How would you like the job?"

"Well, it sounds good, but do you think I can do it?"

"Sure, why not? I'll ride him on all my horses so you know you will make a good living. You can still be in the barn every morning."

"Do you think it will be okay with Tony?"

"Let's ask him, he is in the barn. Call him."

I found Tony and we went to the office. Buddy explained and Tony agreed. "Sure, I like Frank and he is smart. I know he knows a lot of people. We will do good." We shook hands, and I started a new career.

Part of this new job was being at the barn every morning and doing the books and payroll, then going to see the trainers and trying to book rides for Tony. Our first ride was with an Irish trainer, Murty Houry. He liked Tony and kept telling me how honest he was. When I told Buddy he said, "All you have to do is to go to three barns every day...Frank Martin's, P.G. Johnson's, and Alan Jerkens'. At 8:00 a.m. they list the scratches for the day. You get the list and deliver it to those three. They win most of the races and like the weight advantage." He was right and Tony won lots of races, and I spent more time at his barn.

Now I started to spend much more time with Buddy. Linda didn't come back, so almost every day we would leave the barn at about 10:00 a.m., pick up breakfast at the deli, go to the apartment and take a nap. If Buddy had a horse racing we would go to the races and often to the farm in Old Westbury.

Buddy was working at the farm and would have a working party on weekends. He would invite many of his owners, some newspaper people he was close to, and lots of girls from the old apartment. He would sleep there but loved the farm and would spend all the time he could with the horses. The farm was only a half hour from New York city, right off the Long Island Expressway. Everyone had a job, painting, cleaning stalls, walking the horses and even driving the tractor. It was like seeing Tom Sawyer come to life and everyone wanted a chance to paint the fence. At about 4:00 in the afternoon he would send for Chinese food or start a large wood fire and roast frankfurters and chicken. Sometimes during the good weather we would play softball or football in the main paddock.

Buddy decided to do some breeding at the farm. Our stallion was Odd Dancer, a very strong gray horse. He was very hard to handle but Buddy, all of 5' 8" and 155 pounds of him never showed any fear of this monster. When you entered his stall the horse would rear up on his hind legs and try and strike you with his front legs. Buddy was one of the few people who could handle him. In the beginning we would do the breeding ourselves. I would handle the mare and Buddy the stallion.

One day we had a horse running in the first race at Belmont Park. After the race he said, "Let's go."

I followed him to the car and said, "Buddy, we have a horse in the eighth race. Where are we going?"

"To the farm, we have a mare to breed." We arrived about fifteen minutes later, and I got the mare ready while he got Odd Dancer. Twenty minutes later, while I was holding the mare he brought in the stallion. We completed the mating and I walked the mare for about a half hour while he cleaned up the stallion.

As we drove back, I noticed that our shoes and jackets were rather shabby looking. "Well, I guess we look like horse people," he laughed. We returned to the track and that day we won the eighth race.

With all this action he decided Joe Martin needed some help, so he hired a black fellow, Rocky Raines. I knew the Parker brothers from the track, they were six brothers who worked around the track and were at the races every day. We would talk horses and became friends. They were black and had a good reputation as honest and hard working. I asked if they wanted to work on the farm. They recommended their older brother, Rocky.

Rocky was about fifty-five, six feet tall, 260 pounds, and a born worker. We used him as a night watchman as we began to get more mares for the breeding program. I gave him a room on the farm and he loved living there. He learned about the horses and was a very valued employee.

Chapter XVI

Wendell P. Rosso

We went to the city more often especially to Mr. Laff's. Sarah Hall, a girl we had met before, was there often and since she loved horses and betting, Buddy enjoyed talking to her. The three of us became friends and laughed a lot. Buddy liked her as a person, something that did not happen often. August was coming again and Saratoga was here. We got a call from Jimmy Ferraro. I spoke to him and he said, "Frank, I have some hot news. Tell Buddy I was in Kentucky and met a very rich guy named Wendell Rosso. Mr. Rosso just purchased a Sea Bird filly at the Keeneland July sale."

I said, "Wow Jimmy, that's great. What did she go for?"

"Son of a bitch topped the sale by paying $405,000. Frankie, this was a worldwide record and he out bid billionaire, Charles Engelhard."

I turned to Buddy and said, "Bud, you gotta hear this."

After I repeated the story to Buddy he asked, "How well does he know this guy?"

I said, "Jim, how well do you know this guy? Is he for real?"

"I met him at the track and every hustler here is trying to get into his pocket. He loves to bet and I gave him a few winners…he seems to really like me."

"That sounds great, Jim. Is he coming to New York?"

"Better than that, I am trying to get him to go to Saratoga."

"He has a local trainer in Virginia but does not really have anyone in New York."

Buddy immediately took the phone, "Jimmy, if he comes to Saratoga, does he have a place to stay?"

"Buddy, this guy is a cheap bastard. He eats frankfurters and pizza at the races and never picks up a check. But he will bet $2,000 a race and buys lots of horses. He would be great for you."

"Jimmy, I rented a big house in Saratoga. You get him to come and stay with us."

"I'll try and as long as it's free, he just might go."

"Don't try, Jimmy. Do it," Buddy said.

"Buddy, we don't have a place in Saratoga yet," I told him.

"I know Frank, that's why we are going there tomorrow."

"Call Molly Doyle at the local real estate office and tell her we want to see some of her top properties. If we leave here after training tomorrow morning we can fly to Albany and then rent a car. This is important."

"But Buddy, what if Jimmy cannot get the guy to come?"

"From what Jimmy said, he's cheap and it's free."

The next day we took a plane to Albany, rented a car and drove the thirty-five miles to Saratoga. We went directly to meet Molly Doyle. He rented one of the best houses in town— a large four bedroom home with a pool. He had sold his farm in Saratoga but normally would not rent a $5,000 house. We moved into the house and Buddy had invited Sarah Hall to come for a visit so she helped us stock the house with food, wine, and flowers. Sarah was a genius when it came to making a house a home. Funny, all of the things a man would never think of getting, yet the little extra touches were exactly what we needed to make the right impression.

That weekend Wendell P. Rosso arrived very late. He was a pleasant fellow with a round face and was slightly balding. We hit it off right away. He was very impressed with Sarah and Buddy. It appeared this might be a successful trip. Wendell apologized for arriving so late and told us that he had gotten a little lost. We asked if he had stopped for dinner or if he wanted us to make a little something. He proudly produced a little brown sack with some sandwiches inside and told us that if we had a beer he would be all set. Sarah being the perfect hostess took the brown paper bag from him and returned a few minutes later with a freshly made roast beef sandwich on a beautiful plate served with kosher dills and potato salad. His ice cold beer with the sandwich was looking very good to me but I resisted. We talked a little about the town of Saratoga, the history of the track and congratulated him on his winning bid while he ate his sandwich. When he finished his dinner he told us about his long exhausting trip and then excused himself and retired to his bedroom for the night. Buddy had given him the master bedroom and Sarah had placed a beautiful bouquet of flowers on the desk in his room along with a silver tray holding a water pitcher, bucket of ice, and a couple of crystal glasses. We had pulled out all of the stops!

Buddy was up exceptionally early the following morning. "Kinda early, isn't it Buddy?" I said.

"Yeah, but I want to get back as soon as we can. I think this guy can be good for us."

We rushed out of the house and left Sarah and Wendell fast asleep. Saratoga is the most beautiful early in the morning. The mountain air is fresh and clean. There is a carnival atmosphere on the backstretch, an openness in the barn area, and a strange comradely that does not happen anywhere else in the New York racing community. Saratoga is famous for many things including its corn, unsurpassed tomatoes, and its unique hand melons, which are not found anywhere else in New York. The grooms set up fifty gallon drums over wooden fires, heating the fresh spring water for cooking the sweet corn.

By 10:00 everyone is consuming the mouthwatering corn which needs nothing but a dash of salt to compliment it's natural sweetness. The local vendors come in small trucks and quickly sell their produce.

"Frank," Buddy said, "pick up six ears of that corn and a bunch of those tomatoes and whatever else he has fresh today. I will be ready to leave in five minutes."

I bought the items and met Buddy in the car. We were not running any horses that day so he just left instructions with the crew as to how to handle the horses.

Sarah looked radiant even this early in the day. Her beautiful blond hair was tied with a blue ribbon and she was wearing a flirty apron. She was preparing a lunch/brunch.

"You guys are early. Wendell has not even gotten up yet," Sarah said. I have been as quiet as possible so he could rest. He seems like a nice guy and you would never know he has so much money."

Wendell told us last night that he had over forty food markets in Virginia and some shopping centers. He was rather low key but not shy about talking about his rise from his father's tailor shop. How even as a young boy he felt the entrepreneur spirit.

Buddy and I had a cup of coffee and then he went up for his shower. I had another cup with Sarah and resisted nibbling on the goodies she was preparing. She was an amazing girl and could be as tough as a man when it came to gambling, but the Southern Belle would appear in a blink of an eye and she would turn into Betty Crocker. This week she was completely into her Betty Crocker role. The house was bursting with the aroma of baked Smithfield ham, buttermilk biscuits, red eye gravy, grits, and she was holding off on the eggs and other last minutes dishes until Wendell was up and we were all showered and ready to eat. She knew that Wendell was from Virginia and so she wanted to make him a real Southern, horse country breakfast. It was truly a feast to behold. With Sarah in our corner, how could he resist and how could we miss?

Rosso came down in a bright colored Chinese kimono type robe, fresh from his morning shower. Sarah greeted him with his choice of a bloody Mary or mimosa and we began our wonderful brunch/lunch of Southern treats.

Wendell was an easy guy to be around—no airs and kept referring to himself as "a banana salesman." He asked us what we thought was the best selling item in a fruit and vegetable store. I thought apples. Sarah guessed tomatoes, and Buddy answered potatoes. "Bananas, bananas," I buy them by the carload. I sell more bananas than any other item in the store, but it's not just me and my stores…it is nationwide. The markup is in pennies, but I learned years ago, if you watch your pennies, they grow into dollars." As we continued to enjoy our meal I felt more and more comfortable and asked Rosso why he bought such an expensive horse. "Well, Frank, I'll tell you. My standard answer has been I was sitting there and this beautiful filly came into the ring and Engelhard, the billionaire horseman, began to bid and I said to myself, why should he have that horse? So I began to bid, and I decided not to stop."

Everyone at the table began to laugh. We knew he was the largest grocer in Virginia. but this was a great deal of money to spend.

"Now, I'll tell you the real story. In 1965 I went to Paris to watch the "Arc." I was backing Tom Rolfe and in the stretch I thought I had a sure thing when a beautiful chestnut came roaring out of the pack and destroyed the field. His name was Sea Bird. Although he cost me a lot of money that day when he beat Tom Rolfe, I fell in love with him and his performance. I followed his progress and decided one day I would own a Sea Bird fold. Sitting with you today is a man that owns four. You can mark my words, within the next three years you will see Sea Birds flying all over the world."

We were amazed that Wendell had beaten Charles Engelhard, who was a member of the established racing elite. In previous years he had purchased the two half brothers to the filly and had done very well with both of them. Therefore he went into the sale determined to go home with their sister. A wealthy mining magnate who was a very aggressive bidder and rarely lost a bidding war, now found himself outbid by an Italian banana salesman.

As we finished lunch, the phone began to ring. I answered it, "Mr. Rosso, the call is for you," I said. He took the phone and I returned to the table. Buddy was saying we better get ready to go to the races even though we were not running anything today, we can show Wendell around. Suddenly Rosso returned to the table. He was white as a sheet.

"I have to leave," he was in a panic. "The horse, the horse, she's been injured. A groom stuck her with a pitchfork. I've got to go!" and he went to his room.

We sat there shocked. "What happened," Buddy said.

"I'll call Jimmy, he may know," I said. I left a messages for Jimmy to call and tried some other people but no luck.

Rosso was dressed and asked if we could call a car service so he could get to the airport. We did. In a few minutes, he said good bye and he was gone.

Later that day Jimmy called and we got the story. It seems that after Rosso got the horse in the sale he shipped it to a local farm and before he left Kentucky to come to Saratoga he arranged to send the horse to a farm in Florida. While loading the horse on the van the groom asked for $20 for traveling money. Rosso heard him and gave him $10 and told him that was enough. The groom got drunk on the trip and attacked the horse with a pitchfork, jabbing it in the knees, a very sensitive place in a young horse. So injured, it was possible the horse would never run, a disaster for Rosso and the horse. We were all in shock and the rest of the meet was overshadowed by the event.

Rosso named the filly "Reine Enchanteur" and two years later the horse ran three times, finishing third and never winning. She was retired and became a broodmare. We never heard much of Mr. Rosso again.

Sarah Hall was a good sport about it all, "Well so much for Mr Rosso. Now what?"

"You stay as long as you like and you can go racing every day,"

Buddy said.

"Thanks. I'll stay a few days, then head back to the city."

She was a beautiful girl and rather petit with a nice figure, blonde hair and a peaches and cream complexion. She was born in a small town in Mississippi and left home at sixteen, married a young boy and divorced soon after. She went to Hollywood and tried her hand at acting but spent most of her time fighting off agents and casting guys and girls. A girlfriend was going with a jockey and she introduced her to Dean Hall, a very good jockey who enjoyed success in the game. She was married after a short courtship and found herself at the track almost every day and loved the horses and the gambling. The lifestyle was fast and furious. The racing, the parties, and the gambling turned out to be too much and so she split with her husband and after a quickie divorce found her way to New York. She liked Buddy because he was in such an exciting business, he had charm, was good looking and never hit on her. We had spent some time with her at Mr. Laff's in the city and Buddy would always ask her to dinner. Sarah and I would spend lots of time talking and she was a good handicapper. We both loved horses.

"I like guys," she would say to me, "but they want to get you to bed and then brag about it to their friends as if they bagged a lion. I don't have many male friends, just lots of guys on the make. You and Buddy treat me like a lady.

"Thanks Sarah, you're a beautiful girl and I love betting horses with you." We laughed and she pressed my hand, "You know I'm beginning to know a lot of people in the town. I may get a horse or get a new owner for you and Buddy."

This she did sooner than I imagined.

We spent the weekend at the track and had some winners. I left Sunday night and drove Sarah back to her apartment.

Chapter XVII

Unrest at the Track

We returned to New York at the end of August when Saratoga closed and got back to the racing scene. Buddy had an idea to make a school at the farm for training young people to work on horses and others to learn how to become riders. There was a shortage of experienced help at the racetrack and many undocumented workers were being employed. Buddy had been elected as president of the Horseman's Benevolent Protective Association. HBPA was made up of about 75 percent of the trainers and horsemen at the track. The HBPA was a national organization and Buddy was president of the New York group.

The idea for a school was a good one, but Buddy plunged into it and just didn't have enough good people to help and he was too busy to give it the time it deserved. He installed fire exits, classrooms and had it approved by the department of education; "I think I'll put the kid Dennis out here," he said.

"Buddy, why would you do that? He's not qualified?"

"We can teach him and anybody who can bullshit like he does with those young girls can handle the kids. Besides, he lost his job and we can get him a place to stay at the farm."

"I think it's a mistake," I said, but he went ahead with it.

I refused to spend time on this project and after a few months Buddy closed the school, "Too much paper work, and I was not happy with Dennis."

At the track there was a great deal of unrest over the long hours the stable help would work with no overtime, no vacation, no pension and no health care. Buddy's uncle, Hirsh Jacobs, had a pension plan for his help, the only such plan on the track. Buddy wanted the same and approached NYRA. His plan was thought to be too radical and would increase the cost of keeping a horse for the owner. He wanted the track to pay this and not put the burden on the owners or the trainers. He began to get publicity and he was involved in controversy.

Two small owners left the stable but Buddy continued to win. We went to dinner and were celebrating a nice win that day. The horse was owned by an Italian auto dealer who loved to bet. He was at the races with his entire family and after the race were in the winner's circle to take pictures.

"You know I can't imagine why we lost those two guys, they were having a winning season. I just can't figure it out. I know one thing we will never lose Vito. He was so happy today and I've won three races for him in the last two weeks."

"I know Buddy, but I heard that the owners are worried about the NYRA being upset over the trouble with the backstretch and you being a leader."

"Don't be silly, as long as I win that's what it's all about."

"Well, I guess you're right, but be careful."

The next day I made my rounds of the barns and went back to Buddy's barn at about 8:30. There was lots of activity.

"What's up?" I asked.

Joe Porter said, "Frank, we lost six horses!"

"Which owners?"

"The guy who won yesterday."

"What, Vito? Where's Buddy?"

"In the office," he said as he began to move a horse towards the track.

"Buddy, what happened?" He was sitting behind the desk holding a check.

"I just don't know. Vito sent a guy with a check paid in full and he is moving his horses."

"Did he say why?"

"NO, no, not a thing. I just can't figure it out."

"Buddy, there's something fishy about this. We should cool it with the NYRA. They are just too powerful, take it slow for a while."

He didn't answer, just left the check on the desk and went out to the track. At 10 a.m. I gathered up the books and told him we should go home. As we were leaving the office the phone rang.

"Don't answer it," he said.

"Buddy, its 10 a.m. You told the owners not to call while you were training but to call after 10:00. I should answer it."

"I know what I said. That's why we don't answer it. Come on lets go." And we did.

We picked up our breakfast and went to the apartment. As we arrived Dennis was already in the apartment.

"What's up?" he said. I said hello and Buddy asked him to join us for breakfast.

"I'm going to look for a ski lodge, and spend more time skiing.

Frank can look after things here, so I'll take you with me."

"That sounds good, Bud. I don't have a job and I can help drive."

"Can you leave today?"

"You bet. Boy was that a time last night, Buddy. That little stew is crazy for you and what an ass. I'll bet you enjoyed that." Dennis laughed as he dug into the breakfast.

"She's all right, but once was enough for me. She has a funny smell about her. I hate that in a girl. But I must say Dennis hunts up the best young broads."

"Just make sure they are not too young," I said.

Dennis finished and said he had to go to get ready.

"Buddy, that guy gives me the creeps!"

"He's okay, don't worry. He knows lots of guys in Queens and can get you anything you want."

"Buddy, I hope you are not getting into any shit!"

"You know me better than that, it's just these broads want stuff and he gets it."

"Buddy, you know how I feel. I won't be around junk and neither should you."

"Frank, I swear to you I could never do that."

"I believe you, but those young kids cause trouble, and I heard this kid is hanging out on Queens Boulevard—in all the joints that have bad reputations. I hope you don't go with them."

Buddy was away for two days. He had no success with the lodge but had a great time skiing. I made preparations to go to Bowie for the winter racing, and I roomed with Tony Garramone in a very nice apartment and had good times while Buddy was enjoying skiing in Vermont. He would call everyday and tell me what to do with the horses, but it was so cold and often we couldn't even get to the track due to the snow. So I would always agree with him and then do what we could and it worked well.

A young fellow who worked for John Campo, a very close friend of mine, was Nick Zito. Nick would later became a Kentucky Derby winner and an outstanding trainer. He would spend lots of time with us and came with me often to the races. One day he came running up to me and said, "Frank, we've got to leave quick!"

"Why?" I asked.

"Well, I gave a guy a tip on a horse, and he ran last."

"So what's the big deal?"

"He is J. Edger Hoover, the FBI guy!"

I laughed, "Boy you sure aim high. It's getting cold so let's go home."

We went back often but never saw Mr. Hoover again.

We had great fun at Bowie. I spent a lot of time with John Campo a fine trainer and a great guy.

Chapter XVIII

The Mystery Horse

Two days later I was in the barn early and the phone rang. The caller asked for Mr. Jacobson. I told him I was his assistant and he was not available now.

"Well maybe you can help me. My name is Charles O'Brian. I live in Boston, and I would like to send you a horse to race in New York." Normally, I would refuse but we had some empty stalls, and I was anxious to get a new owner. I told him the cost and expenses and he agreed.

I told him our barn number and he said he would send a billing address and all of the necessary papers and that the horse would ship in two days. I felt good about the new owner and when Buddy returned to the office I told him.

"What kind of a horse? When do we run him? For how much?"

All the questions, I never asked.

"Buddy, I only figured we could use a new owner. Sorry, I goofed."

He laughed, "Don't sweat it, we will see what happens when he arrives. You did say he was a colt, right?"

"Yes, of course!" I was emphatic, even though I had forgotten to ask.

It was about three days later when I was in the barn and the phone rang. I picked it up and it was the receiving gate at Aqueduct Race Track.

"Hi, is this Jacobson's barn?"

"Yes," I said. "What can I do for you?"

"We have a horse here, the van just arrived and it is a delivery for Jacobson."

"Who is the consigner?"

"It is from Suffolk Downs, a guy named O'Brian."

"Okay, we will accept the horse. I'll send someone over right away to pick up the horse. Thank you, bye."

I called Joe Porter

"Oh yes Frank, you want me?"

"Yes Joe, a new horse coming in. He is down by the gate. Send one of the boys over to pick him up, will you?"

"Okay, you know the name?"

"No, I don't know his name but he's the only horse there I think, so you shouldn't have any trouble. Make sure he brings the shank with him."

"Of course. I'll send him now."

"Thanks, Joe."

Buddy was at the track watching some horses and I was finishing up some work. He came walking back into the barn.

"Bud, the new horse is here."

"Huh?"

"You know, the one from that guy at Suffolk downs."

"Okay, I'll take a look at him when he comes in."

One of the boys brought in the new horse. He was wearing a shipping blanket and had four bandages on. He walked well, was an average sized horse, a bay with no particular markings, except for a very small, white star on his forehead. Buddy came walking down the shed row.

"Ah, so that's the new guy, huh? Mm, stop right there sonny," he said to the hot walker.

Buddy felt his knees and said to the boy, "Take the bandages off."

I held the horse for the boy as he began to take the bandages off.

"Not bad," he said. "They look clean, feel cool. Take the back ones off too, will you?" He did. "And the blanket too. Hmm."

Good or bad, he looked fine to me, but I knew he had the trained eye; so when he said "Not bad, not bad. Ordinary looking horse but give him a couple of turns and let me know Frank, when he comes back, and I want to check him again."

He went into the office and began to fumble with some papers that he had brought in from home. I waited out in the shed row as the horse walked. He walked and took one turn and then another. On the third turn I told the boy to stop and told Buddy, "He is here now, do you want to look at him?" He came out and checked him again. Looked in his mouth, felt his rump, ran his hands down his sides. Checked his hocks.

"Looks pretty sound," he said.

"Okay Joe, put him in sixteen, and mark him to walk the next two days."

From that day on he became number sixteen.

The horse reacted very well and did not appear to have any problems. On the third day we took him to the track. The rider said he just felt very good and looked like he had been in some kind of training.

"You know what? We will breeze him on Saturday and see what he looks like. Give him a slow three eighths just to try him."

Saturday morning came and Buddy put on one of his better exercise boys and said "Just take him three eighths and when you finish at the finish line just gallop out an extra furlong or so."

"Okay, Buddy."

"But don't push him too hard. I don't know what he's got right now."

We went into the shack overlooking the racetrack on this cool, fall morning. Many of the other trainers were gathered there having coffee and watching their horses go and exchanging hellos. Buddy just nodded to everyone. He very rarely spoke to anyone, especially during training hours. Everyone knew this and no one seemed to bother him.

Our horse went down and the clocker yelled down, "Buddy, are you working that horse?"

"No, no just give him a light canter."

"Oh, okay."

It is the clocker's responsibility to find out the names of the horses, and to put the workouts in the public papers so that there will be a record every time a horse does serious work. We watched number sixteen go by and the boy was almost standing up in the saddle as the horse appeared to want to go on. He passed the finish line and just jogged another quarter of a mile.

"Not a bad move," Buddy said.

"Bud, I caught that horse in forty. Do you want that in there?"

"No, no, he's just playing around today. I'll let you have a work as soon as I get him ready."

"Okay, Bud." The clocker said.

And we left the shack and went back to the barn.

Buddy said, "That horse went pretty good. Let's see how he comes back." We got back to the barn and Buddy checked him from head to toe and saw that he was not laboring. His breathing was almost normal as if he had not done very much. I was surprised he was spending so much time with this horse.

"This horse is pretty fit," he said. "I'll work him again and we will try him with number twenty. He is about the same kind of class. That was a horse worth about $20,000."

"Okay," I said, "that sounds great."

"Maybe you did the right thing taking this horse. You never know."

For the next two weeks Buddy trained the horse along with his other twenty-five or so and was very happy with the way he was going.

"You know," he said, "I breezed him the other day with number twenty and he kept up with him very well. I wonder what his record looks like. Do we have a copy?"

"No, Bud. We didn't get any."

"What's his name anyhow?"

"His name is Buck's Break".

"That's an odd name. Well okay, Buck's Break. We'll enter him on Monday's card, get a look at his past performances, and then decide whether we are going to run or not."

"Sounds good. What are you going to enter him for?"

"Oh, I don't know we will try him for about fifteen and see what happens."

"$15,000 claimer?"

"Okay."

I was anxious Sunday night to get the racing form so I could see what this horse had done in previous meets. The record was printed in the entry form. I was shocked when I saw his last ten races were horrible. He finished tenth, twelfth, and almost pulled up in one race. He had also run for the bottom of the barrel, the lowest claiming prices in Suffolk Downs. "My God, what kind of a horse did I get here?"

The next morning Buddy scratched the horse. He was thirty to one on the morning line for $15,000.

"This is crazy," he said. "I cannot believe the horse ran that kind of time."

"Well," I said, "maybe you found something special about him and turned him around."

"In three weeks? You saw what we did. Cleaned him up, fed him a few vitamins, a jug, checked his teeth, and put new shoes on him. You know what we'll do? We'll just run him down at the bottom of the barrel ourselves. There is a $5,000 claimer coming up in about ten days and that's where we'll put him in. I'll get him ready and see what happens."

"Oh boy, I wonder what the owners got to say?"

"What's he got to say? The horse is running in a similar kind of race and if there is any kind of chance to get a win out of him we might as well try. Maybe he is just a bad performer in the afternoon—a morning glory. A horse that does so well in the mornings and then won't perform in the afternoons. That's the only explanation I can think of."

"Okay, we'll try it. Sounds good."

Buddy entered the horse and it was a twelve horse field. His horse was fifteen to one in the morning line. In all the time I knew Buddy, I never knew him to have a horse in a race with that sort of price. His horses were favorites or close to it and six to one was a huge price for him.

"Wow," I said, "look at this. What if he could win?"

"I don't know, Frank. We've got to be careful. He could be a morning glory, but I never had a horse train this good and not perform in the afternoon."

"Did you hear from the owner?"

"No, but I have his number. I'm going to give him a call."

I looked up in the Rolodex and found his number and called and said, "Hello Mr. O'Brian, Frank Pagano from Buddy's barn."

"Oh yes Frank, well nice to speak to you. And how is that little guy doing over there?"

"Better than we thought."

"Really?"

"Yeah, Buddy found a few things and worked on it, and I don't know he's in tomorrow and the price in the morning line was fifteen to one. If we had him longer, I would really be encouraged. But we don't know him that well. I feel he will run real good for us. You know we will try hard to win."

"Good, Frank, good. Just tell Buddy I said good luck, let him run and I know he will do the best he can."

"He sure will. Talk to you later. Bye."

He seemed like a real nice fellow. He had a New England accent and was a very soft spoken man. Oh well, he probably just liked animals and kept this one even though his form was so bad.

We went to the races the following day. It was a cool autumn day. I wore a light top coat that day and Buddy didn't even bother getting dressed. When people see us in that style they imagine we are not really confidant in winning. It's odd at the race track, but when owners, trainers, and so forth think they have a real good shot to win the race they usually dress up so they will look good in pictures. Little by little trainers were getting away from this idea because they felt that those who follow their movements at the track and detect their pattern would take a chance betting on their horses. And when they did the prices would be lowered of course. I sat up in the box and Buddy saddled the horse. I was reading the daily newspaper when Sydney approached me. Sydney and I had become good friends and though he was the king of the worms, we had the agreement that if I gave him a horse it was for him and maybe one or two of his real good clients who would bet $10 or $20.

The worms were a group of older guys who were old-time horse players. They lived for horse racing and never missed a day. They knew what every trainer and owner was betting and would follow them to the betting windows. They would bet on what they thought was a big move by the person. If they usually bet $5 but today bet $50 or more that was a tip they liked their horse. After a while they knew the people who were right more times than wrong.

"Frank, Frank," he said, "What kind of horse is this? It's twelve to one."

"Twelve to one?" I said. "It's kinda high, I think."

"Yeah, but can he run at all?"

"Sydney, you see the form. He's coming from New England, though he has had him for quite a while. But I never saw a horse of Buddy's go off at this price that I wouldn't bet on him. Keep it to yourself and bet $10 and maybe you'll get lucky."

"Thanks, Frank. Thanks."

And away he went. I waited until the clock was on one minute to post and made my bet. Buddy did not bet. "When I run a horse my reputation is my bet," that is what he would always say, but I loved the excitement of the race and the bet. I liked the price. You could never get this price on any horse he was running, most of them were two to one or less, so this was too good to pass up.

The race was six furlongs and number sixteen did his job, third until the turn and won by three lengths, paying $28.60 for every $2 bet. I had a big smile and Sydney came by to give me a wink, I guess he did fine too.

Buddy did not take a picture but called me to hurry. We had to leave so off we went, I still had my tickets which I would cash another day.

"What do you think of that?" I said.

"Well either I'm a genius or someone was doing a very bad job with that horse."

"I'll let you know after the next race."

We went back to the apartment and as always never talked about horses when girls were around.

Just ten days later a race came up for the horse, the price was a $10,000 claiming—the same distance, six furlongs. Buddy entered the horse.

"Now, we will see if that last race was a fluke," he said. "Call up your man and let him know."

I called and left a message with a woman who answered telling her that Mr. O'Brian's horse would run in about ten days in a better race, but he was still in good shape and we had high hopes. This time the price was six to one, the betters were not sure either about how good this horse was. My pal, Sydney, was in attendance and waiting for some word. "It's a go," I said. "What the hell, you have to take a chance sometime and this was as good as any."

The gate opened and Bob Ussery, our rider, sent him right to the lead. He left the field behind and coasted to a two length win. A nice $15 payoff.

"You know, I'm beginning to like this horse," Buddy said,

"Well, I love him," I answered as we left the track.

Back at the barn Buddy looked him over and he was sound and happy.

"You know, I wonder if they knew how good this horse was when they sent him to us?"

"Well, if they did why would they send him to us?"

"That's the question Frank, but what's the answer?"

I called Boston and spoke to Mr. O'Brian. He was overjoyed. "Never thought we could have so much success. Tell Buddy thanks and do what he wants with the horse, and thank you Frank, for all your help."

"Thank you for sending the horse, and if you have any more we would be happy to have them here, bye."

Things were going well, and I was spending more time on the farm and back in the barn. I became friendly with the new boy, Bobby Frankel, and his friend, Herbie Nadler. Nadler's father had some horses with another trainer and Herbie wanted to be a trainer, but his father was not helping him as he felt he was too young. Both boys spent lots of time at the barn but Bobby was everyone's favorite. He was quiet, polite, and very good looking.

Buddy liked him and invited him to the apartment, but he did not get along with the other guys, especially Dennis. Bobby spoke to me and said he only went to the apartment to be around Buddy. He had a girlfriend at the track, her name was Bernadette but he called her Bonnie. Bonnie was young and still in high school, and her dad was an exercise rider and a white cap in the afternoon. Her father was very strict and did not want her to date a race tracker, which I understood because I had three daughters and never brought them to the track although four of my sons were licensed at age fourteen. She was in Catholic school and Bobby was Jewish, same situation Buddy had with Joan, his wife. I think these are some of the reasons Buddy tried to help him.

Buddy gave the horse three weeks off. He put him on two pills of "Bute" which is Butazolidin, an analgesic used to treat pain in horses but very dangerous and not used with dogs or other small animals. A horse can't run on this medication but can train on it as long as it is out of his system before the race. He changed the training schedule and would send the horse to the track with a pony and no rider on his back, only light workouts and cut back on his feed slightly.

"He has had two good races, but I think he is developing a suspicious suspenseory" he said. This was a term he used when a horse was not right but no one could tell what was wrong. He was never questioned about it. It's like the story of the emperor's new clothes in the fable—no one wants to tell him he was naked. So he got him ready for the next race

"We will put him in for a $15,000 claiming, if they want him they can have him, and with any luck he will get the job done."

And he was right, the public made him favorite at five to two and in a hard race he did not disappoint them.

"He did a good job, but I think he needs a nice rest now," Buddy said as we checked over the horse. You could see he was very tired and stopped to drink every time he walked past his bucket. Buddy had done a good job getting him ready but knowing when to stop was a very important part of training.

"You can call the owner and tell him I want to stop on him and he can take him back or I'll send him to the farm for a few weeks."

"Ok, Bud."

The next day I called the owner. "Hi Mr. O'Brian, just wanted to let you know your horse is fine but Buddy thinks he needs a rest after the last race. You can pick him up or we can send him to a local farm. Buddy says he is a nice horse and has lots of racing left in him, but he should be handled carefully. You can think about it and let us know."

"Frank I wanted to congratulate you and that team for such a fine job. Buddy sure did the best for me. I'll let you know."

I was sorry to think of the horse leaving. He was so honest and easy to work around. He wasn't the most expensive but he sure was one of the favorites.

It was less than a week since I called Mr. O'Brian in Boston when a Pinkerton guard came to the barn, "Your phone has been busy so I walked over. There's a guy at the gate to see you says he is an owner but he did not have his pass, name is O'Brian."

"Sure, thanks. Let him in."

I walked to the barn door and saw the long black limo approach. The driver stopped the car and went to open the door for the passenger. A tall, well dressed man with red hair and a ruddy complexion walked towards the gate. I waved and he responded.

"Frank?"

"Yes, hi."

He came closer and extended his hand. "Charlie O'Brian, nice to meet you."

"Welcome. Buddy will be happy to see you."

He was six feet tall and slim, looked like a basketball player to me and about fifty years old with a shock of red hair.

"Nice barn. We don't have it as nice in Boston."

Buddy was in the shed row and turned to shake hands.

"It's a pleasure to see you Buddy. Wonderful job you have done, thank you."

"Just our job things worked out right, you have a nice horse. Now he needs a rest."

"I'm making arrangements to send him to a farm near my home in Boston. I wanted to come and see you before I did. Can we go in your office?"

"Sure, this way."

Buddy led the way, and I waited outside.

A few minutes later they both came out smiling and saying their good-byes.

"Frank, will you show Mr. O'Brian his horse? I've got to get to the track. Bye and thank you," he was off.

"Your horse is in stall sixteen. Right this way."

"My, he looks so good," he said as he placed his hand on the horse's neck. The groom, Pappy, came to the front of the stall and said, "We gonna miss the Mister. Buddy says he needs a rest. I hope he comes back soon."

"Thank you for all your work and this is a little something for you." Then he handed Pappy a $100 bill.

"Well, thank you sir," Pappy said with a grin.

We left the barn, and I walked him to the car.

"Frank, this is for you," I was surprised as he handed me a white envelope.

"Thanks, very nice of you."

"I can't leave without telling you my story. I am a stockbroker and a horseplayer. I've had a few horses, never much. I began to bet and used money I shouldn't have, and I got in debt to the bookmakers and used more money that did not belong to me. I couldn't see any way out. I have a family and a nice home but the situation could change so I decided to buy this horse who was doing well in training. I borrowed the money on my house and began to run him. I guess now you see that all those races on the form were just workouts. I guess it wasn't fair not to tell you, but I knew Buddy's reputation and I was afraid he would not want to be a part of this. I also know he always tries to win and will not hold a horse. So I sent you the horse, and I bet all I could the first time he ran. The bookies were happy to take my action as I had lost so much to them. When he won, I won a little over $50,000, a lot but not enough to pay everything. I took a big chance the second time and cleared up all my losses. The third time I bet the profit I had left over and now I'm respectable again. You might wonder why I'm telling you all this, but being in the business I think you know half the fun of a big win is to share the story with someone and I haven't been able to talk about it to anyone else. I think you will appreciate it and keep it quiet...nobody would believe you weren't in on it, okay?"

As I stood there with my mouth opened he broke into a great smile. I began to shake my head and laugh, "Great story, Charlie. I'll tell my kids one day. I hope they believe me." He shut the door and drove off. I never heard from him again. Buddy came out of the barn and called me to come quick.

"Look at this, $5,000 cash! He gave it to me."

"He gave me an envelope, too. I didn't look. Wow, $2,000 all green. Now that's an owner." We laughed all the way back to the barn and decided to take off early to go for a good breakfast.

Barbara Jo Rubin

Chapter XIX

First Woman Rider in New York

"Come on, come on," the roar of the crowd was deafening as the horses turned into the stretch, this sunny, Friday afternoon in March. I was seated next to Buddy in box 6E, overlooking the finish line.

"Nice day for a race," he said as he turned to me.

I said, "Are you kidding me? This crowd will tear us apart if this broad doesn't ride well today."

"Don't worry," he said. "We've accomplished our purpose. Look at these fans. Look at the publicity we're going to get."

"I know Buddy, but shit, what if the broad can't ride?"

He turned with a slight smile and said to me, "What are you worried about? I told you when this all started, the whole thing is just an idea to get public sympathy on our side. I'm doing something no one ever did, riding a broad, in a race like this, in New York. Do you realize what that means?"

"Yeah," I said with a frown. "I guess I do, Buddy. Another one of your genius tricks."

"Come on, don't say that. It's not a trick. It's a good public relations thing. You always have to keep the image alive."

Buddy was right, you do have to keep the image alive. He sat there with his blue blazer, dark tie, white shirt and grey slacks. he looked more like a businessman than the leading trainer he was.

We had come here today to watch Barbara Jo Rubin, a girl from Maryland, ride in a betting race in New York—the first woman to ever do this. A lot of people had spoken about it, but there was a great resentment among trainers, jocks, and especially the NYRA. The racing association was steep in tradition and the old guard had no desire to see women come into racing. I thought back to a month or so ago when this all began.

We were in Buddy's apartment when the phone rang. I picked it up and a voice on the other end said, "Hi, I'm looking for Buddy Jacobson. Is he there?"

"Who's calling?"

"Just tell him Brian, Brian Webb. He'll know."

"Hold on, I'll see if he's here." I answered. I covered the receiver with my hand and screamed out to Buddy. "Buddy, some fellow named Brian Webb. You want to speak to him?"

Buddy was lying in the corner of the room, drinking a coke and listening to the music playing from the reel to reel tape and in deep conversation with some little blonde who had wandered in from an apartment somewhere in the building. It seemed he was making good progress. She was in awe, looking into his eyes as he explained to her all of the things she had to know if she wanted to be a success while she was working as a stew here in New York.

He turned quickly, "Brian...Brian Webb? Oh yeah, I know him.

Maybe he's got a horse to sell. I'll be right there."

I spoke back into the phone. "Brian, he'll be with you in a minute."

"Thanks," said the voice on the other end.

Buddy came walking over to the phone and picked it up nonchalantly as I went over to the bar to make a drink. I heard him speaking to Brian, but I could only hear half of the conversation.

"Yeah sure, Brian", he said. "It sounds interesting, but I'm not sure if I would be interested. Yeah, well, I mean, I don't know, a woman in New York...maybe, you're right. Can she ride? Well, I don't know Brian, most of my owners wouldn't want to put her on a horse. What? Oh, you would send a horse, huh. Well, let me think about it." He grabbed a pencil from the desk nearby and began to scribble a number.

"Huh..huh, I've got it...I've got it Brian. I'll be in touch within a day or two. Yeah, I understand. I've got to go now, Brian. I've got some people here, big business deal, you know. See you later," and he hung up. Buddy left the number on the pad and went back over to the corner where he had been sitting and started the conversation all over again. It was a long night and Buddy didn't miss any opportunity. Later that evening when everyone had gone home and we were cleaning up I mentioned to him.

"Buddy, what happened to this fellow Brian. Who is he?"

"Oh yes," he answered as he washed one of the dishes in the sink. "Well, I tell you Frank, this guy Brian Webb, I've known him for a long time, pretty good trainer you know. A gambler, had some problems in New York. I think he was ruled off, wrote some bad checks or something. Can't bring any horses in. You know what I mean?"

"Yeah Buddy, but what does he want with you?"

"He's got an idea. He's got a new broad...some young kid, said she used to ride in the show circuit. Wants her to come to New York and ride."

"What, are you crazy? A broad in New York? Why should you ride her?"

"Well, there's more to it than that. Women are going to have their day, you know. They are into their own and it's going to be fashionable sometime to support their causes."

"What the hell are you talking about Buddy?"

"Well, times are changing, Frank. You just don't understand."

"I understand one thing, you are in a fucking lot of trouble all over the place, and if you take the cause of some broad and ride her here and she rides like hell, how is it going to look?"

"Take it easy! You know half the population is made up of women."

"Yeah, sure."

"And they pack quite a blow."

"But Buddy, women?"

"Listen Frank, every guy that owns a horse at the track has got a girlfriend or wife or both."

"I know Buddy, but they don't want them messing around with broads."

"Well, there may come a time when they would like to see a woman represented here. After all, look how big they are becoming in tennis, golf, and swimming. Christ, that Babe Zaharias, she played baseball and all that shit! I'm telling you Frank, women have got to come to New York. Why shouldn't I be the first guy to help give a broad a shot? I don't care much about jocks anyway and this guy Brian said he'd send a horse. I'm sure he wouldn't send a piece of crap. I've got to think about it."

"I think you are nuts, Buddy. All you do is create more controversy."

"I'll think about it Frank, I'm telling you."

And that was it. The next thing I know, a week or so later, Buddy is on the phone from the barn making arrangements, talking to some girl. He hangs up and says, "That was Barbara, Barbra Jo Rubin, that's her name. She's going to come up here in about two weeks and ride a horse for us."

"What, are you crazy?"

"I'm telling you she is going to ride a horse for us. Come on, get the books, we're leaving."

As we left instead of going towards Queens Boulevard which was our usual route, I noticed that Buddy was taking a detour.

"Bud, you're going the wrong way, aren't you?"

"Wrong way? No. I forgot to tell you we're going to Maryland."

"Maryland? What are we going to Maryland for?"

"Oh, I did forget to tell you. I've got an appointment with Brian. We've got to firm up this deal before the girl rides in New York. Oh, by the way, are you feeling tired?"

"No Bud, I'm not tired. Why?"

"Well, I thought you might like to drive and I'd just take a couple of winks."

"Okay Buddy, pull over."

We pulled over and I switched places, and I began the long drive. This trip we were going to Pimlico, which is where Brian had some horses. It took us about four and a half to five hours and I was tired by the time we arrived. Buddy slept most of the way and we approached the Pimlico Hotel.

"Shall we pull into the Pimlico?"

"No, I don't think so. Let's just stop at a phone booth and I'll make a call."

We pulled by a phone so Buddy could make his call and I turned off the motor and closed my eyes to take a few winks myself.

"Well, we have a few hours to kill. I arranged to meet Brian about 7:00 p.m. in Little Italy."

"Little Italy? That's in New York city!" I said.

"No, there's a Little Italy down here in Maryland. Come on, I'll take you around and show you." We drove through sections I was not familiar with but Buddy seemed to know his way around quite well and we ended up in a section that reminded me a great deal of the Little Italy section in Manhattan. It was filled with restaurants, large neon signs and was quite busy by the time we arrived.

"It's quite early you see but this is a pretty busy area, very similar to the one in New York. They have some good food here."

"Great," I said, "but Buddy, by the way, what are you going to see Brian about?"

"Well, I just want to get the conditions straight. After all I'm not running a horse in New York for the glory you know."

"I see."

"There's a space to park," he said.

"The place was something like the Luna, something with a moon," he said. "I don't remember, but he said this to…yeah, right on that corner. There it is!"

It was a restaurant on the corner of a narrow street with a large neon sign and some of the bulbs were missing and when it lit you could only see half the word. It looked as if it was a Luna. And there was an image of a half moon above the sign.

"Come on; let's go in and have a drink while we're waiting."

I followed Buddy into the restaurant as he spoke to the waiter.

"Hi," he said. "I'm looking for Brian Webb. Does he have a table here?"

"Oh yes," The waiter said, "but he is not due for about an hour."

"I know, but we'll just sit and wait."

He took us to the back of the room and in the alcove was a little table set for six.

"Sit right here and we'll set you up and you can wait."

"Fine," said Buddy. "Let's have a couple of cokes, will ya?"

"Right away!"

"Do you want some appetizers or something while you wait?"

"Whatever you say, Buddy," I said being more tired than hungry.

We sat down and began to wait and Buddy ordered a few of his favorite appetizers: mozzarella, tomatoes, and fried zucchini. About half an hour later the restaurant began to fill up and there was quite a bit of noise, but the alcove was quiet and secluded. At that point the waiter came over and pointed to the table and right behind him I got my first glimpse of Brian Webb.

Brian was a nice looking individual—his hair neatly combed, white shirt with striped tie, a blazer, and a pair of light gray slacks. You might say he was a fashion plate—very neat looking compared to what Buddy looked like. Buddy's hair was disheveled. He had on an open work shirt, his old jacket was half on the back of his chair and half lying across the floor. His looks were dirty and mucky from the stalls. The pants he wore were black and old and hadn't been pressed or cleaned in about a month.

Buddy greeted Brian as if he was an old friend. "Hi Brian, come on in."

"Hi Buddy, sorry to keep you waiting. I didn't know you would get here so early," said Brian.

"Well, say hello to my friend, Frank Pagano."

We made the introductions all around. A short time later a stocky, gray haired individual followed and Brian said "This is a friend of mine, Pete."

"Pete, say hello to Buddy Jacobson. You know him."

"Sure do," he said, "great trainer…nice to meet you, Mr. Jacobson."

"And this is his friend and assistant, Frank Pagano."

"Hi, how are you?"

Pete and I sat next to each other while Brian sat next to Buddy.

There was an empty chair next to Brian. I wasn't sure exactly who that was for.

"Well, let's order something right away," said Brian very briskly. "Do you care for anything special?"

"Order whatever you like," Buddy said.

Brian proceeded to place an order and ordered a bottle of fine red wine. He then began to talk very quietly to Buddy while Pete and I engaged in pleasantries about who's going to win what, when, and where—not really caring what we were talking about and every once in a while catching a bit of the action. As I turned one time to pick up a piece of bread I noticed Brian reaching into his inside jacket pocket and taking out a large white envelope and giving it to Buddy. Buddy stuffed it into his pants pocket, shook his head, nodded, and smiled broadly. Two or three minutes after that the head waiter returned to the table escorting a young lady.

"Well, well," said Brian, "here she is…come on in."

We all rose and said hello to Barbara Jo Rubin. This was our first meeting. Barbara Jo was a comely girl, rather tall and very thin. She smiled and had an appealing way about her and had long dark hair. She sat down and after a few pleasantries she remained rather quiet the rest of the evening. Brian continued to tell Buddy how she had done so well in the show circuit and how she had ridden in Maryland and had showed she was a capable rider. He said it would be great for the game to have a woman like this involved and Barbara Jo expected to make this her career. She smiled and agreed with Brian and hung on his every word. After a very pleasant dinner we waited for the coffee to come.

Buddy just stood right up. "Well, Brian, Barbara, I guess I'll see you guys in New York. We've got to head back."

"But Buddy," said Brian, "we're waiting for the coffee and dessert."

"No, not us. We don't take that. We're on the road...time to leave."

It was his curt, normal way. Before you could say another word, Buddy had begun to shake hands with both the men and just waved to Barbara Jo as we walked out. I felt rather embarrassed to leave so quickly. I apologized and said that Buddy was tired and we had a long way to go. Brian said he understood and we left the restaurant. It was now about 10:15 p.m.

"What do you say, Buddy? Should we get a room and stay over?"

"What, are you crazy?" We've got to get back. Let's go!"

"But Buddy, it'll take five or six hours," I protested.

"What's the difference? You're not tired are you? You know what I always tell you, you never get tired at the racetrack. Come on, you want me to drive for a while?"

"Well, I shuddered...maybe."

"Okay, you start off then I'll pick it up! Okay? Get behind the wheel, let's get going."

I jumped behind the wheel. I was tired, but something about the way Buddy spoke to you, made you reach down and give a little something extra. I drove the rest of the night. He didn't mention the envelope but when we got about an hour from New York he perked up.

"Want me to drive a little, do ya?"

"No, Buddy, that's quite all right. I'm wide awake now and there's not much traffic."

"Okay, good. Let me see what this guy gave me here," he looked through the envelope. As he opened it I saw a number of bills, tens and twenties.

"A lot of chicken feed," he said. "A lot of chicken feed."

"But Buddy?"

"Ah.. a kind of a fee, you know? Two thousand he gave me. Said it was a little fee, that maybe I should bet it...screw him. It's going right into the bank. We've got to buy some new equipment, you know? I can use it."

He stuffed it back into his pocket and we drove on.

"Does that mean we don't get paid for the horse?"

"Ah, we get paid a commission, if she wins," he said, "but the horse is not going to be here very long. She's only going to run and then go back. He said she's a nice filly. He owns her I think. He's got her in somebody else's name. You never know about Brian, he might be just conning this broad, maybe she's got money. I don't know. Who cares? It'll serve the purpose just as well," he said. As we continued down the road he fell asleep.

Three days before the horse was to run, that was on a Wednesday, the horse arrived at Aqueduct Race Track in Buddy Jacobson's barn. She was a medium sized, chestnut filly with a white blaze. She had a rather odd way of going when she got off the van. We looked at each other, Buddy and I and wondered if this was normal. Or was this a slight condition she might be suffering from having traveled this great distance? The groom took her out and removed the bandages from her legs and walked her for about fifteen minutes, gave her a little water, and put her in a stall.

"She'll be fine in the morning," Buddy said. "I'm sure she will be fine in the morning."

The following day Buddy planned to train her and put his best exercise boy on her back and had them go to the track.

"Now, once around easy, just want to watch her go. Brian said she's ready to go and doesn't need much. So just once around easy. Got me?"

The boy nodded. There was very little communication between Buddy and the rider. According to Buddy's system, "I'll tell you what to do, you just listen, but make sure you do it."

"I am the trainer, don't give me any advice or any information. Anything you can give me I can see." And that was the rule he followed around the barn and anyone who wanted to work there knew that they had better comply with that rule.

The exercise boy took the horse out and galloped her once around. She seemed to go quite easily and when she returned to the barn she was not in any sort of distress and hadn't worked up too much of a lather.

"Seems fit, doesn't she?" he said.

"Yeah," I said, "she sure does, Bud."

He was very quiet as he watched her walk. "We'll check her again in the morning."

The following day was Thursday, the day before the race. As we took the horse out of the stall we noticed that she appeared to stumble but no one said a word about it. Buddy just watched her. He had the boy give her a couple of turns, just walk her around the shed row, then he had her stopped and checked her from stem to stern. He checked her knees, feeling every little bone. He checked her ankles, flexed her leg, went up into the shoulder, lifted her tail and looked at her behind to make sure she wasn't in heat, looked into her eyes, then opened her mouth and checked her teeth to see if her bite was fine. It had been a long time since I'd seen Buddy take this much time and interest in a horse. He was acting as though he really didn't care, but it appeared that he was concerned and didn't want this incident to backfire.

The newspaper people were around taking pictures, doing interviews. The NYRA had expressed secret displeasure with the fact that Buddy was breaking one of their rules—a *men's only* club was being invaded by some woman. The jocks were disgruntled. "Why should we have girls?" they said. "There is not enough work for us as it is. Some of the trainers will get hung up on a broad and we'll never get a chance to ride." Others were complaining, "It's too dangerous. I'm telling you these broads have no guts. When they get in too tight they may drop somebody, hit your horse, knock you over. It's too dangerous. Who wants them here?" But Buddy didn't seem to care. At least outwardly he didn't. But noticing his mannerisms I was sure he was concerned.

Friday morning approached, the day of the race. The papers had been filled with articles about what a great thing Buddy Jacobson was doing for the sport...for women in general, for just everybody.

Then there were a couple of detractors claiming that Buddy was a publicity hound. How could he take this untried girl that had only won a few races out of town and bring her in against champion riders, with champion horses? Buddy seemed to enjoy all of controversy.

Friday morning we left the apartment very early. Buddy turned to me and said we have to get there very early. "I want to make sure this filly is fine for the race."

I said fine, and away we went. As the filly walked that morning Buddy had a keen eye on her. Almost everyone in the barn could see that she was nodding. That means every time she would take a step her head would raise and lower, raise and lower. When a horse is perfectly sound the head usually stays firm and erect. This was an indication that something was amiss. No one said a word about it. The atmosphere in the barn was somber and quiet all though different people were calling, reporters were coming by, and camera's were flashing all around. Buddy kept his cool.

About a half hour after we arrived Dr. Manuel Gilman, a state veterinarian came by the barn. It was his job to examine all the horses running that day. Dr. Gilman was notoriously scrupulous and careful about examining horses. But it had come to my attention that he seemed to have a soft stop in his heart for Buddy. Although he was part of the association, he was one of the only Jews to have an important position in the association. He came in and checked the horse. He also didn't appear to like the way the horse was traveling.

"Let's take the horse outside and jog her," he said to Buddy.

This is not customary, normally a veterinarian just examines a horse in the shed row and lets you know whether or not the horse is going to run. But there was a question in his mind about this horse, as there was in all our minds.

"Oh Christ," I said under my breath. Buddy never said a word.

He walked out with Gilman and watched as the groom led the horse out.

"Come on, let me have that horse. I'll show you how to walk her." Buddy took the lead shank from the groom and began to walk the horse back and forth. When he got further away from the veterinarian who was watching him, he turned the horse sharply started to break into a slight jog coming towards the vet. The horse began to move quickly with Buddy, and her head began to nod. Buddy put his hand under her jaw as close to the bridle as he could, almost pushing her head up into the air.

"She's fine Doc! See, she's just fine." he said, as he ran past the veterinarian.

The doc kind of shook his head and looked around. Buddy then gave the horse to the groom.

"Take her back and put her in the stall."

"Okay, Doc. Are we all set?"

"I don't know," said Dr. Gilmore. "She doesn't look that great to me, Buddy. Have you had that horse long?"

"Well, not really, Doc, but I know her. She's a nice filly and she's okay."

"Well, you know Buddy... I don't know that I would okay her for anyone else, but if you say she's all right..."

"Trust me, Doc. I know what I am doing. Besides with the crowd we're going to get today, can you imagine what it would be like if we had to scratch her?"

"Well, I guess you're right," said Doc Gilman. "I'm going on your word, Buddy. I know you know what you're doing. Anybody else and I'd scratch this filly."

"Thanks, Doc. You won't regret it." The doc turned and walked away.

"Boy, that was okay, Buddy. I'm glad she's fine."

"Fine, shit!" he said, "doesn't look good at all to me."

"But, you just told him..."

"Ah, what else am I going to do? All these people coming out, and this bitch is off. We had better put her in ice before we take her over, Frank. You stay here and make sure she gets taken care of. Will you?"

"Sure, sure, Bud. I'll get here early, don't worry about a thing."

"Make sure Joe Porter puts on the cold water bandages too, that might help taking her over to the paddock."

That afternoon I came back to the barn early. Joe Porter already had the filly in ice. He anticipated what was going on and knew almost better than anyone that she was slightly off.

"Joe, I'm going back over to the main track."

"You go Frank, you go. I'll take care of the filly," he said. "You don't worry. I'll take care of her."

"Okay, Joe. You make sure she comes over with the cold water bandages on."

"All right, no problem...she'll be there, you go."

"You tell Buddy, no worry."

"Thank you, Joe!" I said, as I left and went over.

I met Buddy in the clubhouse on the second floor. He was walking towards the box. "Hi Frank, let's go sit in the box and watch some races."

He didn't show any sign of nervousness or any sign of the pressure that he was under. People stopped him, and came running up, "Hi Buddy, what do you think? Has she got a shot? Can she win?" He just nodded and smiled and kept right on going.

"Don't look around, Frank, just keep on walking," he said as we walked through the gate and the white cap said hello as he let us into the enclosed area that was reserved for owners, trainers, and other people who had use of the boxes. The boxes were rented by the NYRA and there were a limited number. Once you got a box you very rarely let it go unless you left the business. Even then you might continue to pay for the box.

We sat down in the box and Buddy opened his program to glance at the horses running. Buddy studied the racing form for hours at a time but would never have one in his possession when he got to the race track. Another one of his rules, was "We don't carry the paper at the track, Frank. It gives the wrong appearance. People will think that we are gambling and no matter what we do, we don't want them to think that we are gambling. Even if we are gambling!"

The racing form is a horseplayer's bible, And no horseplayer worth his salt would try to make a bet without first conferring with the racing form.

"What do you think, Frank? Does the track look fast today?"

"Christ, Buddy, does it matter?" I said.

"Sure it matters," he said as he glanced back down at his program. "Let's see how these horses run. We'll get a good indication what we should do with our horse."

"What do you mean, what you should do with your horse? You told me the horse was sore!"

"Frank, always remember, it doesn't matter what the horse is like in the morning. It's what she's like in the afternoon."

"But, Buddy, we didn't do anything to her, you didn't give her anything special…a little B-12 or something."

"Don't worry Frank, that ice might help her." I looked at him, I knew he didn't really believe it. It helped a little but the way she nodded in the morning it wasn't going to help that.

As we sat in the box two or three jock's agents came by, nodded to Buddy and kept on going. Very few would stop and talk to Buddy. They knew when he was at the races he didn't acknowledge many people. He might talk to a potential new client, if he was assured that they had a lot of money, and that they were willing to put it up. He always said, "It's not how much money a guys has Frank, but how much he's willing to spend and half of these guys aren't willing to spend." Another of Buddy's rules.

The first race that day was for maiden three year olds. Tartan Stables was trained by John A. Nerud and he sent out a real wiz—a horse called Quick Blink who went to the lead, lead by two or three and finally won by five.

"A lot of speed today," Buddy said. "Looks like the track is good. Probably that's what we'll do with our filly."

"What are you talking about?" I said. "You always send the horses on the lead, but you don't know anything about this horse. You haven't had her long enough."

"Don't worry, I know plenty about her."

I looked at him. He smiled a wiry little smile, and I knew he was kidding—always claiming to know everything about everything, even when he had no idea what was going on.

"Let's watch the second race. These horses are cheap but we'll see what's going on." It was a distance race. We watched as the speed horse made a good pace but toward the wire he tired and a horse called Something Rare came on and won the race.

"Hmm," Buddy said. "So much for the speed track, huh?"

"But," he said, "that was a distance. I think our little filly will run much better. I'm going to the paddock. Do you want to come down?"

"No Buddy, I think I'll sit in the box for a while. I'll see you down there." I knew he was nervous and wanted to be alone.

"Okay, see you after the race. We're going to leave right after the race," he said. "Now, don't forget, there is a party back at the house. I've got three new broads coming, just flying in. I think they are on Pan Am or something and the flight gets in about four o'clock. I want to be home in time. Okay, so don't get lost."

"Don't worry Buddy, I'll see you right outside the paddock and we'll take off," he got up and nonchalantly walked to the platform leading to the stairway down into the enclosure.

A little later I saw Buddy shaking hands with an owner and two or three officials as he went down. The people had now rushed over to the rail to see and get a glimpse of the first woman to ride in New York. This nineteen-year-old Miami Beach girl who was coming into New York's first pari-mutual betting race which included a woman. Could she do it? Would she do it? She had won five or six races out of town but mostly on very small tracks, the last one at Pimlico. So this was the real test. Here it was Friday afternoon, March 14, 1969... history in the making, and Buddy involved again. Some people were skeptic thinking that Buddy was just trying to win a bet.

It figured no one would bet on a girl and he might have been right because the broad showed the horse at thirteen to one, completely overlooked. How can a woman ride a first time starter, especially a filly that is so skittish. This girl does not have enough experience thought many of the handicappers. It's all a game, Jacobson is looking for publicity, said some of his distracters. Why else would he put a broad on the horse? It was possible. The jocks and many of the jock's agents whispered about the fact that Buddy was causing too many problems in racing by having a woman come in. "She'll probably get nervous around the turn, bear out, maybe kill somebody," said one of the Spanish riders, who made sure Buddy didn't know about it, because he always hoped that he might be riding some of Buddy's horses at a later date.

As Buddy walked into the paddock I could see the flash of cameras. People were clicking in all directions. It was a little overcast so some of them had their flashbulbs out. He just smiled and walked right to the center. He always stayed in the center field, waiting for the horse. When the horses come in they paraded by him and went into individual stalls where he would go and put the saddle on the horse. He went over and Joe Porter brought the horse to him. The horse looked excellent and didn't appear to be in any sort of distress. The bay filly had a small white blaze on the nose and carried herself with a certain determination and class. Maybe we had the right horse, I thought, better make a small wager even though we're not too happy about it. I got up and went to the betting window and was followed by a group of people who knew that I was close to Buddy. They saw me go to the $10 window and I bet $60 to win on the filly. The filly was number four. I saw people disperse quite quickly and run in different directions. I was approached by Sydney, the head worm.

"Frank, can we win today?" I told Sydney the truth, he was a friend. "I'm making a small bet, but I don't know. We always have a chance."

"Got you, you don't like her." We both laughed.

"Well Sydney, let's just say we're not trying hard," and I walked back to the box—my standard answer to Sydney when I was in doubt.

I watched Buddy, his horse now saddled and walking around the ring. Barbara Jo Rubin came out, people were cheering. There were a few boo's too but mostly applause. She smiled. She was tall and very thin and had her hair done up and in pig tails under her helmet. They spoke briefly in the paddock. Buddy telling her, "Barbara, just go out and do what you think you can and just be careful." She smiled again and told him not to worry.

The cry came from the paddock judge, "Riders up". Buddy walked to the horse, put his hand out. Barbara put her leg in Buddy's hand and he gave her a lift up. They circled and he said, "Good luck." I noticed he didn't come back upstairs. He went through the tunnel, which led under the stands and into the horsemen's room to watch the race. I immediately went down the back stairway and met him below. The horses were now on the track and galloping around.

"Buddy, don't you want to watch upstairs?"

"No way," he said. "We'll watch on TV because if this filly breaks down or runs badly we're out the door and gone!"

"Oh, I thought you told me not to worry!"

"An ounce of prevention, Frank. Let's not look stupid."

"Okay, Buddy."

A number of horsemen were gathering by the TV to watch Buddy's horse. He stood there very quietly. It's funny they were all grouped together but Buddy was almost in isolation—all by himself, no one crowded him no one came near him and no one even asked any questions. They knew how he was before a race. I stayed about two steps behind on his right-hand side, just watching the board. We watched them load in the gate and Barbara seemed quite up and so did the horse.

In a minute the announcer was ready. "And they're off," he said. "And out of the gate like a bullet darted number four, Braver Galaxy. Braver Galaxy on the inside, moving away to a length lead."

Everyone laughed and looked around. They watched Buddy. He smiled just a little but then his expression went back to deadpan and he never changed his expression. "Around the far turn it's Braver Galaxy in front by two and maintaining the lead."

Other horses were beginning to make their move. This was a short race and speed was important. Barbara Jo kept her hands closely cocked on the horse's neck, never making a move. Her seat was good and her stick was in her right hand folded across the neck of the filly. It seemed that she was well in control; The horses made the turn and Braver Galaxy never drifted off the rail. She was about five or six inches away from the rail and skimming it. She was on her way home, in the lead. The crowd was in a frenzy.

"Come on!" everyone in the horseman's room began to cheer. Somehow everybody got caught up in the idea that this woman was doing something that had never been done before...riding in New York, and winning.

"She's going to win. She's going to win. Come on Barbara!" You could hear them screaming and yelling.

"Keep her going."

"You've got it. You've got it!"

Sure enough, she had it…across the finish line. People cheered, throwing programs in the air. It was like a 4th of July celebration. What happened? Buddy even broke into a smile!

"That a boy, Buddy. You showed 'em. You did it."

People were still cheering. Buddy ran out, down the companion way, and down the long hallway. I was standing there stunned. Thirteen to one and me with a $60 bet and Buddy not even betting a quarter.

"What are we, crazy?"

"You must have cleaned up," everybody said. People thought I had bet for Buddy, and I was the bag man. You had to have cleaned up. Boy, you guys pulled a fast one. That filly is dynamite, can she run. And the girl, she's great!

There were photographers out there. I walked back upstairs. People congratulated me. My friend Sydney came running over, "God damn, I only bet $6 on her," he said. "I would have bet a lot more Frank, but I know you, when you only bet sixty bucks something's wrong. You must have bet off the track, right? I know you guys!"

"Yeah, Sydney. We bet off the track." I said, a very hollow answer. What could I tell him, we're dummies?

Buddy went into the paddock, pictures were being taken.

Barbara Jo came back and dismounted. When she saw Buddy she screamed, "Hi Buddy, give me a kiss," she ran over and gave him a big hug and a kiss. He looked embarrassed but he smiled. He loved all of the publicity, he loved to be a winner, and right now he was a big winner. People wanted to interview him but he just shook them off. Barbara was the center of attention and he left it to her. He came down the end of the ramp and up the stairway and met me by the gate going to the parking lot.

"Come on, let's go!"

"Okay," I said. I never told him about my tickets. I tucked them in my pocket. Tomorrow is another day. I can cash them then. No sense worrying about it now. Let's see, twenty eight and change. Not a bad price for a horse we didn't even like. $28.20 for every two dollar ticket. For every twenty dollar ticket, that would be $280. And I had three, it wasn't a bad day's pay.

Looking back, Barbara Jo was the first woman to ride and win in New York and I feel this was the first major breakthrough for women riders. In 1969 there was only one *major* track in America and that was New York. Everything else was second string. Of course there was the Kentucky Derby at Churchill Downs, the Preakness at Pimlico, and the Belmont at Belmont Park, but the first two tracks were really hot only one day a year as it hosted that particular leg of the Triple Crown. The rest of the year the best horses were raced in New York and primarily because the purses at out of town tracks did not hold a candle to the purses paid out at the New York tracks. As Frank Sinatra said, "If you make it there, you'll make it anywhere, New York, New York."

Chapter XX

Lake Delaware and Whitey Ford

"It's good to be back," said Buddy. "I did a lot of skiing and I like it. I never did much sports. My game was ping pong and I was damn good at it."

"I never went skiing. We didn't have lots of hills in Brooklyn and who could afford skis and boots, that was a rich man's sport. I loved baseball, football, and games you could play in the street."

"You sound like a snob, looking down on the rich. You might be one of them someday."

"Well, I'll let you know how I feel when I get there," I said.

As we walked to the track from the parking area we saw a group of people around two men going to the owners and trainers entrance. Someone said, "That's Whitey Ford, the New York Yankees pitching star." Buddy loved baseball and I never saw him get excited about anything, but he seemed so now. "Let's say hi. I know he runs a horse today," he said.

So we got close, "Hi Whitey." Buddy said.

I never knew if he heard him, but he gave a half wave and just went on.

Buddy was shocked, "Was that a snub?"

I could see he was not happy

"I don't think he heard you. I'll speak to him inside and maybe bring him to the paddock."

"Forget it, it's not important. Get me a paper and meet me in the box."

"You want a racing form?"

"Yep."

Well, this was a first, and I was in shock.

I bought a form and brought it to the box. He checked the form and after about five minutes he turned to me and said, "Go down to the office and call the barn and tell Joe to bring a shank. We're claiming a horse in the sixth race."

"Shall I bring up a slip?"

"Yep."

I didn't ask what horse. He never did this before... something was up. I went to the office and got the claim slip. A few of the jockey agents saw me and asked if there was "some action today." I told them this was for the next time. Claiming is like a poker game, you never know for sure what the other guy is holding and you never reveal your hand.

Back up to the box where Buddy filled out the slip, he signed it and handed it to me.

"Lake Delaware," I said.

"Don't you like him?"

"For $15,000 you may be able to claim something a lot better."

"Yes, but I want this one."

I waited for the sixth race and without even looking at the horse went to the office and deposited the claim slip in the box. The race ran and the horse was third, beat by about two lengths.

"Not a bad race, but I'll bet he can go a lot further," he said as we watched from the box.

As the horses returned to the paddock I watched as Joe Porter gave the slip to the judge. He then handed it to the groom of the horse we claimed. The trainer looked shocked. He took the slip and came to the box area where Whitey Ford and the other men were standing. He began talking to them but we were too far away to hear them. "Looks like they are shocked to lose the horse," I said.

"I think he knows us now." Buddy smiled.

Back at the barn Buddy checked the new horse from head to tail, "Okay, put him in seven, Joe."

"Let's go to the apartment. I'm having a new group tonight and it should be fun," he said.

He was happy and after a few minutes in the car started to talk about his new idea for a toga party, the first in New York.

"You see everyone comes dressed in a sheet...no clothes. It's like a Roman party."

"An orgy you mean!"

"No, not a lot of food."

"You think I'm going to wear a sheet over this body with no clothes?"

"It will be fun and after a few drinks no one will care what you look like."

We laughed and forgot about it, for now.

The spring came and went and then the summer approached.

"Saratoga again," I said. "You act like you are looking forward to it this year."

"I may have a surprise for them this year."

"What's that?"

"Lake Delaware."

I knew he had sent the horse to a farm to rest and re-train, but I just thought he was not doing well, so I never asked about him.

"I sent him to a farm and a very good friend has been working with me to get him ready. He doesn't want anyone to know or he would lose lots of friends in the jumping game. He still rides and between us, I think the horse is ready."

"Boy, that's swell but there may not be a lot of races for him, not too many claiming races at Saratoga."

"No Frank, I have a special race picked out for him. I want you to go to Saratoga as soon as it opens this year and I'll tell you what to do with him every day. I don't want to go early because we don't want any attention while he finishes training."

Buddy never told me who the trainer was that helped him but I had a good idea. About ten days before the meet started I was in Saratoga with a few horses and a good crew. Our job was to give this horse long slow gallops every day and to report to Buddy each night for instructions. I drove down to the city and we met midtown for dinner and more instructions. He mapped out a plan down to the shoes to be put on the day before the race. Then he hit me with the news the race was to be the Lovely Nights Handicap, a prestigious hurdle race.

"Buddy, are you joking?" I asked but I knew better. I thought back to the day we claimed the horse, he had a plan and this was it. If he said he could do it I knew he could. Jumping races were important, especially at Saratoga. The oldest and most respected families came to this town each year to celebrate the traditions of years gone by...a connection with their past glory days, when the divide between the classes was much larger. The jumping race was a continuation of the English and European traditions and the claiming trainers and even the trainers of the best horses tended to stay out of that part of racing.

Buddy took full charge of his horse and, as in the past, his hands did their magic. When the entries for the race were announced a laugh was heard in the racing secretary's office. In this meeting place of horsemen, trainers, owners, jockeys, and others, "Do you believe the Brooklyn cowboy from claimer to stakes in one jump?"

"I always knew he was nuts and this proves it."

"I guess Whitey will have the last laugh." There were many other comments that were not repeatable.

On the Morning of August 7,1969, Buddy left the barn and we went back to the rented house outside of town to have breakfast.

"Nice day for a race." I said.

"Frank, when you make the eggs, make a little extra bacon. I'm hungry today."

He never answered and never mentioned the horse. We finished breakfast and he went to shower and dress. He came down ready for the races dressed in a shirt and tie with his blue jacket and gray slacks. I didn't say a word, we had been together long enough that I knew when to be quiet and respect his feelings.

We arrived at the track and walked by the group of horsemen standing near the walking ring, "Good luck today," some said and some of the older claiming trainers meant it. They resented the second class status that the elite trainers had relegated them to. Maybe Buddy could show them that the little guys could slay the dragons. Others just shook their heads. Many just watched as we went to the box area.

"Look around," he said. "Reminds me of a wax museum." The box area at Saratoga is a large wooden structure with about ten rows of boxes, which contain from four to six chairs. These boxes are purchased by owners, trainers, and sometimes corporations. They are very hard to come by. Families buy the box and hand them down to the next generation. The atmosphere is like a Kentucky horse party at Derby time. Women in fine dresses, many with hats and the men always with jackets and ties and some with their straw hats. It appeared that the average age was about sixty-five to death. I felt that this group of not very attractive people had maybe intermarried often and needed an infusion of some new blood. This was not a very nice attitude on my part but their attitude about those who they "kept in their place" like us, was just as bad. There was plenty of chatter and lots of plans being made for dinner or an upcoming party.

Buddy had an owner with a box and we would use it. The funny part is that sometimes it would get very hot and there was no ventilation other than a breeze that did not exist. Then the president of the NYRA might go into his box and if he removed his coat it was okay to relax the regulation for the day, this was not one of those days.

Buddy went into the walking ring and saddled his horse. The stands were alive with people going to the betting windows and standing to watch the horses go to the track. Loud cheers would go up when a favorite horse or rider would appear. Buddy came back to the box to watch the race.

"They're off!" Lake Delaware jumped well and was third coming into the stretch, the crowd was on its feet and the sound was deafening. His last jump, he was now second, he gained and pulled away to win! I cheered. Buddy had a slight smile and I heard him take a deep breath, there was a wall of silence as many checked the program to see just who the number eight horse was.

"Great work, Bud." I said as I extended my hand. He took my hand and said, "Thanks." He turned and walked to the stairway and down to the winners circle. I watched as no one turned to congratulate him. The horse returned to the winners circle and the photo was taken. This was the first time in two years that I saw him take a picture. He had won many races during that time but this one he wanted to record! The crowd on the ground gave him a huge cheer when the winning horse was announced, but dead silence in the box area. The little people loved him and bet his horse. They knew they would always get an honest chance with a Jacobson horse.

We returned to New York and the Belmont Meet. The weather was mild and the horses were doing well. Bud asked me to spend more time in the barn and not to worry about the jockey so much.

"I need you here, and you can make a good living without all the hassle of being an agent. You know I hate book work and you are doing the payroll anyway."

"Sounds good, but I do like being an agent, and also training."

"Get that training out of your mind. I told you only a small number of trainers make money, the game is very hard. Look, an owner comes into the game and knows nothing about horses. He is in the hands of a trainer who is just about earning a living. What happens? He is told that the claiming game is for the slobs, you should run in all those big races, but then you must have very good horses which means they have to cost lots of money. Why? Because there is no commission when you claim but if you buy everyone makes a buck. I don't buy very often and I don't push to buy. I love the claiming game. Some trainers work for owners who breed their own horses like Allen Jerkens, he almost never buys. He wins with any kind of horse but he is a special person, one of the best. I tell you this because it's not peaches and cream out there, and I want you to stay here."

"I understand, and I am happy here. I'll do the office work, and for now, I'll keep the jockey until I can do more of the training."

I began to realize, as Buddy said, that only the top 10 percent of trainers make an exceptionally good living. About the next 40 percent make a decent living and the rest struggle every day to meet their obligations. But all of those who train horses must love the business. The excitement, the frustration, the challenges and of course the victory.

There are so many great families that keep the sport alive: Allen Jerkens and his sons, John Campo and his sons, Frank Martin with his sons and grandsons, Tommy Gullo and his son, Las Barrera and his brothers, Tommy Kelly and his fine young sons, D. Wayne Lukas and his son, Gill Puentes and his son, Dom Imperio and his brother Lenny, Max Hirsh and his son and grandsons, the Laurens, the great Preston Burch and his son, Moody and LeRoy Jolley, Harold Snowden and his sons, and one of the most outstanding men I ever met, Angel Penna and his son. There are hundreds of others but the list is just too long to mention now. They are dedicated, hard working people, and I felt it a privilege to be among this fine group of people that have made horses and racing their life and consider many to be long time friends as well as colleagues.

Chapter XXI

Sarah Hall, The Mississippi Belle

"Fine, now let's go home we have a date with Sarah tonight. She wants to meet us in the city about 7 p.m."

We met in Kenny's Steak Pub and Sarah had reserved a table. The restaurant was owned by Kenny Soretsky, a fellow of about forty-five who was a great host and a huge gambler. He was slim, handsome and always well dressed. His wife was a very pretty red head and a good friend of Sarah's and would come to the races often.

"I love this restaurant, no better steaks in New York." I said as we were seated.

"So good to see you two, and welcome back to the real world," was her greeting.

"Andre', bring the boys a drink."

"Just two cokes for now," Buddy answered.

"God, you should grow up and let lose a little," she yelled across the table. We all laughed.

We enjoyed a great meal and Kenny came by for a drink. We spoke about horses, but he said he wanted to get home to watch a ball game. As the desert was being served Sarah told us why she wanted to meet.

"I've got a new friend and he is a great guy. The day I met him we had lunch, and he bet me I couldn't name the capitol of Mississippi. It was funny because he knew that was my home state. Well anyway, after lunch we went to 7th Ave to a large fur shop, you know where they make the coats? He said, 'you won the bet, pick a coat.' The fellow brought out lots of coats and I got down to two. They are both so beautiful I just can't decide, you choose for me. He called over the owner of the shop, who he knew well, and spoke to him. They checked the coats and the owner left with them over his arm. Which did you decide on, I asked? And before he could answer the owner came back with two garment bags, which he handed to me. He said, 'Wear them in good health and when you are ready I have some others to show you.' I was speechless, and that's something for me."

"That sounds great," I said.

"Very nice for you Sarah, but what's the point?" Buddy asked.

"I have a birthday coming up and I was thinking of a special present, maybe a horse. Would you like to train for me if I get him to buy one?"

"For you? Anytime."

"Great, that's what I wanted to tell you. We are coming to the track on Saturday, can you meet us there?"

"I'll try but Frank can make it and he will take you to lunch."

"Sure Sarah. I love Saturday at the races, so many people who don't know what they're doing you can always get a good price on your horse. I'll get there early and have a table in the main dining room."

"We have to go so I'll speak to you before that. Frank ask the waiter for the check, will you?"

"It's on me, I have a house charge and my friend Bill, will be happy to treat you," she laughed.

"Thanks, can we drop you somewhere?"

"No, I'll just have my coffee at the bar. Night guys."

The ride home was quiet, both of us in deep thought. I broke the silence, "What do you think?"

"I like Sarah, she is a good sport but sometimes she just gets carried away. You go meet the guy on Saturday and let me know what you think. He may be a blank or a one horse deal, let's see."

I arrived early to be sure to get a quiet table in a corner of the dining room. Tony, the head waiter greeted me and said he would be on the lookout for Sarah and would show her to the table. I began to read my racing form and try to pick some winners for the day.

It was a very short time later when Sarah arrived. Her entrance into the large restaurant was a major event. She was a fashion plate in a special dress which was covered by a matching coat of rich mohair and wool in a blue color that was almost green and her bright blonde hair was a topping of spun gold. The total package had even the diehard horseplayers gawking. I rose to meet them and she took my hand and kissed my cheek, "very continental you know," she laughed. "This is Bill, say hi to Frank." He extended his hand which was about as large and firm as a lumberjack.

"Nice to meet you," he said.

Bill was William A. Levin, a textile manufacturer about forty-five or so. He is a very tall guy and about 225 pounds with a pleasant face set off by wide rimmed glasses. He had a slight eye problem that was not very noticeable. He smiled and was very quiet. He wore the uniform of the day, dark blue blazer, white dress shirt, dark tie, gray slacks, and loafers but these had tassels which were considered preppy by some, but only penny loafers minus the pennies by others. No matter how Jewish or how Catholic one was, they all wanted to look preppy and waspy to fit in. He was neat and polite, not what I expected. We made some small talk and Sarah ordered wine for lunch.

"I'm not much of a drinker," he said, "so Sarah is in charge of the drink selection. She is trying to teach me about fine wine and fast horses."

"Well I must say you have a good teacher." I laughed.

"Yes, but that's why I want you to show us how to pick the winners. I told Bill that you and Buddy are the best at it." she said.

"Wow, that's nice but Buddy is the trainer and I do agree he is the best. I like to handicap and make some bets but I don't guarantee success in that area. My first lesson would be to tell you this is gambling and we study the horses, the trainers, the track conditions and make a judgment call which means we guess, but it's an educated guess, and sometimes we do get lucky."

"I like that explanation, sounds true. I don't like sure things that fail, but I'll take a chance on a good guess." Bill laughed.

"Good, then let's have some fun," as I picked up my program and began to mark the races I would bet.

We ordered our lunch and spent a good day talking horses and trying to show them why I would back certain horses.

Bill seemed to enjoy the action and Sarah was all over, betting and saying hi to lots of people she knew.

"Bill, I want you to meet Lenny Goodman, he is the agent for Braulio Baeza, the leading jockey in New York. He likes his horse in the sixth race. We should bet, and also bet $20 for him," she said as she took some cash from her purse.

"Fine, here is $200 bet for us and $20 for him."

Sarah was off with her friend the agent.

"What do you think, Frank?"

"The horse has a good chance, and he will be the favorite, but I like the three horse, and I like the price, six to one. That's my bet."

The race ran and as luck would have it Lenny's horse was in a photo finish with the three horse. Sarah was all excited and Bill was silent. I didn't say a word.

It's not proper to root against the guy whose paying for lunch, unless you know him well.

"Number 3, Oh no, rats," she said.

"Bad luck, he just had bad luck around the turn," I remarked.

Bill didn't say a word. I got up and went to collect my winnings.

Lenny was an easy going guy who was considered the *Dean* of the jockey's association. He was never loud or abusive. He knew his business well and was highly respected and liked. It was not necessary for him to be as aggressive as many other jockey agents had to be. He always represented outstanding riders who's services were in demand. His job was to select the best mounts for them and he was very good at this task. Lenny was one of the few jockey agents who was very friendly with Buddy and before I began to work for Buddy his jockeys would ride many of his horses.

When I returned to the table Sarah said, "Do you like anything in this race?"

"No, but in the eighth race I like the seven horse."

At the end of the day we said our goodbyes.

The horse in the eighth won and they recouped their losses and expenses for the day. "Nice day we should do it again," Bill said as he extended his hand to offer me some bills.

"Thanks, but that's not necessary," I said, "Sarah is a dear friend and I appreciate the lunch. Besides I told you it's gambling and next time you may have to pay for lunch and go home a loser."

We all laughed as we walked to the exit. Bill thanked me again and gave me a warm handshake. "Boy you have a big hand," I said.

"It came in handy at football. I was a wide receiver at Tufts."

Hope to see you again."

Sarah waved and we parted, all in all a good day at the races and one of the few days Buddy did not have a horse in. He loved to run on Saturday because of the big crowds and the exposure, but he missed this one.

I called him at the apartment and told him we had a nice time and this guy could be for real. He said he was having a party, and I should come over. I declined and said I had a business appointment, but I was exhausted and went home to sleep.

The following week Sarah and Bill came to the races every afternoon. I had lunch with them and picked some winners. On Thursday I went to the barn and while sitting in the office the phone rang. Normally, I would let it ring because it was only 9 a.m. Buddy told all his owners to call him at 10 a.m. since he was very busy training before that, but we would leave at 10 a.m. and that way he would not have to speak to them. He thought it was clever and no matter how I tried to tell him it was not right he would smile and say, "just let it ring." But I was waiting for an answer to a call I had made to the track office about the arrival of a new horse, so I picked up the phone.

"Jacobson Stable, good morning."

"Hi, I'd like to speak to Mr. Jacobson, this is Bill Levin."

"Hi Bill, this is Frank. Hold on I'll get him for you."

I ran into the barn to find Buddy.

"It's Levin, he wants to speak to you."

"I'll be right there."

He went into the office and spoke on the phone. "Frank, I need you."

I went in and he was smiling and sitting at the desk. "He wants a horse, a present for Sarah. A claimer by the name Peddoole, it's running on Saturday. Go to the office today and get the cut from the paper and let's see what it looks like."

"Don't think I know that horse."

"He said she has a poodle with that name so she wants the horse for a birthday present. I'm going home and take a nap, call me when you get the cut."

The "cut" is a copy of the horse's racing form as printed in the Daily Racing Form. It shows the horse's recent races and how he ran and finished.

I left the barn and met some friends in the kitchen for breakfast. I had breakfast at Belmont because Liz, the black lady who ran the kitchen was the best damn cook in Jamaica, Long Island. I know cause she told me so. She was a legend at the track. Petite in height but about 180 pounds with a smile that could charm, and a temper that could tame a lion. She had known Buddy since he started and loved "that boy" as she would say and "I win plenty of money on his horses." She would tell me this often and if I was going back to the barn she would always send a special sandwich for him. Buddy said when she started she had a small chicken stand and made the best southern fried chicken in the world. Many times she would feed him and give him credit when cash was in short supply. Many a horseman would find a hot coffee or egg sandwich even if he "forgot his money in the barn" and although she had now come to a time when she had five or six other ladies working the counter she knew every one of her "boys." I know Buddy cared for her more than he would say, but he said the only thing I miss by not training at Belmont is Liz's kitchen. For me this was a highlight of the day. We would meet in the back room and talk horses, baseball, or sports in general. I asked about the horse Peedoodle and found out it was trained by a young boy named Dominick Imperio. He only had one horse and was struggling to stay in the game. I didn't know him, but it was an unwritten rule not to claim a man's last horse. The horse was running in a claiming race for between $5,000 and $7,000. I called Buddy and told him. He said he would call Sarah.

I got to the barn very early and Buddy was there. "I spoke to Sarah, and she wants the horse. I told her about the man not having any horses, but she said she had given Bill a long story about why she wanted this horse because of the name and he might change his mind. So we should take the horse. I spoke to Bill and he said for you to go to the city and he will give you the money today. I'll meet you at the races and we can put the money in the account so we can claim tomorrow. I wrote the address for you. It's in the city. I told him you would be in about 10 a.m. He handed me the address and walked into the barn.

At 10 a.m. I was in Manhattan at Levin's office. He met me and took me to a small room, "Morris, give Frank the bag," he told the older gentleman who I learned was his cashier. Morris handed me a brown paper grocery bag and smiled. Bill and I walked out of the room.

"I won't be at the races tomorrow but Sarah will. I'll see you next week, good luck." We shook hands and I left.

Buddy was waiting in the horsemen's room when I arrived, "That your lunch?" he asked.

"Happy birthday to you," I said as I passed him the bag.

"Look at this. We better count it." It was $6,500 in stacks of small bills. The horse was in the race for $6,000 plus tax.

"Well I guess we will have a new owner tomorrow, wonder how far he will go? Frank take this to the bookkeeper and deposit it and come to the apartment. I'm having a party, and you should come."

"Ok Bud, I'll see you later."

Chapter XXII

Ecstasy in the Soup

I arrived a little early. I was hoping to leave early as I was working so many hours, and I just needed sleep. The gofers were on duty but Buddy had invited some race trackers, Bobby Frankel, Buddy Gerco and agent, Jimmy Farraro, and Billy King an owner.

"We have some special girls from Norway and Germany tonight.

Dennis lined them up. He met them in a pub on Queens Boulevard and says they are hot and beautiful. I found a spot in the corner on my favorite large black pillow and began to watch the action.

The gofers, led by Dennis, were making drinks and bringing the girls in. There were some very beautiful girls, and I was impressed. Bobby Frankel came over and sat next to me.

"Hi Frank, having a good time?" he asked.

"I'm only here cause Bud asked me special."

"Tell you the truth I'm not much for parties, but I know Buddy told me to come and have fun."

"Don't you like girls, Bob?"

"Sure, sure but I've got a girl and I'm not good at this stuff. Do you think Buddy would be mad if I slipped out?"

"You go with Veterosa's daughter, Bonnie, don't you?"

"Yes, but he doesn't like her to date race trackers, says she is too young."

"I know. She is very pretty and a little young, but you two must make a nice couple. You leave and if Buddy asks I'll tell him you were feeling sick."

"Thanks Frank, I'd like to make a call before I go but it is so noisy here.

"Take the phone, Buddy has a very long cord on it and sneak into the kitchen, no one will ever notice."

"Thanks Frank, I'll do that."

I saw him pick up the phone and go into the kitchen area. I later went into the kitchen to check on the pasta sauce and didn't see Bobby. A moment later I saw two legs sticking out from under the kitchen table. I bent down and looked under the table to see Bobby lying in the corner with his hand over the mouthpiece trying to have a private conversation. I laughed and thought to myself, this guy is really in love. I returned to the living room and the party and a few minutes later Bobby came out of the kitchen with a big smile on his face. "Thanks Frank, I have a date...see you."

I shot back, "Don't let her dad catch you."

He was on his way out of the door then turned and said, "If you get a chance, tell him I'm getting a horse soon, and I sure would like to train if I could get a stall."

I laughed. "Sure, I'll tell him."

He was a shy guy and I liked him even more after tonight. As the night wore on the music was getting softer and the food was being served. One of the gofers, Roy, a young, very slim, blonde boy was passing out soup in paper cups. "Hot soup anyone? Mary made it, homemade," he shouted.

"Thanks, no," I said. "I'm getting ready to leave." Just then the jockey agent, Buddy Gerco, came over and sat down "Hey, didn't see you dancing or anything, you okay?"

"Hi Buddy, just fine, but I'm tired and getting ready to go home. How you doing?"

"Not too good. I lost my jockey, he left for Florida. Says he has an outfit that will give him some work there, so I'm unemployed."

"That's too bad, but I'm sure you will get another rider soon"

As we spoke a very tall blonde danced into the center of the room. She was one of the girls from Norway, very beautiful. She whirled around the room and began to sing in a very loud voice. The crowd became quiet and we watched as she danced and began to remove her blouse and wave it above her head. Next she unhooked her skirt and let it fall to the floor. All this stunned the place and her girlfriends began to chatter and looked as shocked as the rest of us. Soon she slipped out of her bra and panties and was completely nude. One of the girls tried to cover her but she bolted towards the door which was open and out into the hall. Buddy Gerco ran out and tried to restrain her, but she fought him. Two of the girls reached her and with the aid of another fellow tried to hold her down.

"Better call 911," someone said. "I think she is overdosing."

Buddy closed the door while the girls and two of the fellows stayed with her in the hall holding her. When the emergency people arrived they put her in restraints and took her to the hospital. The party quickly broke up and a few of the people were complaining about dizziness. I stayed with Buddy and someone said all she had was two cups of soup.

"Where did that soup come from?" Buddy asked.

"That's the soup little Mary from the fourth floor brought," Roy answered.

"Buddy, that's the broad you had last week and she has been coming back every night, but you never paid any attention to her," Dennis said.

The room was quiet, about one hour later we received a phone call from the boys at the hospital. The girl would be fine, they pumped her stomach and she would be staying in the hospital overnight and confirmed that she had an overdose of Ecstasy.

"Dump that soup quick," said Buddy. "Everybody go home!"

"Buddy, do you know how dangerous this is, you have everything you need. You don't need this.

"You are right Frank, I'll cut it out." And he did for about a week.

Chapter XXIII

My New Car and Skiing

The next day we went to the races and claimed the horse Peedoodle and Sarah was in business. Lots of agents and trainers said Buddy was heartless to take the man's last horse but he did try to talk Sarah out of it, but she said, "I want the horse."

Now she had a reason to come to the races every day to look for more horses and Bill came with her. I sat with them and we had a good share of winners. I never asked how much they bet, but knowing Sarah, it had to be a good amount or there would be no thrill.

It was about one week later I was to meet Sarah at the races to watch a horse someone told her to claim. I met Bill and Sarah coming into the track and she took my hand and walked me over to a quiet spot.

"Frank," she said, "Bill and I have had such fun here and you have helped us with some good bets and we never gave you anything."

I interrupted her, "Now Sarah, you supply the lunch and we are friends so…"

"Wait now Frank, Bill and I want to give you a present. We know you have a large family…all those kids so, William…" she turned and called Bill who was a few feet away, "give him the keys." He handed me a key ring with what looked like car keys.

"We left a new station wagon in the parking lot for you."
I was in shock, "What, for me? A car?"

"It's yellow. I picked the color, hope you like it."

I shook hands with Bill and gave Sarah a kiss on the cheek. "What can I say? Thank you! I never got such a present. It's just overwhelming thanks again. Would you excuse me while I pinch myself to see if it's real?" Bill took me to the side as Sarah walked ahead, "I may not be able to come to the track as often due to business so I would appreciate you keeping an eye on Sarah and taking care of her. She trusts everybody, and I think you will look out for her."

"Bill, thanks again, and don't worry about her. I'll take care of her."

At the end of the day I went to the trainers parking lot. Vito, the white cap, showed me the new Plymouth station wagon "She's a beauty Frank and only sixty miles, must have just come out of the showroom."

I thanked him and made arrangement to get my new car home. I guess this was a lot better than asking for a $20 bet.

Buddy laughed when I told him about the car. "This guy may be for real, in about a week I'll run his horse and we should get him out to the races and let him win one then maybe we can move him to get some more. I like your new car, one day next week we can take it for a ride."

"Anytime Bud, anytime."

The following week we received a message that Harry Hatcher was trying to reach us on the phone. Harry was a jump rider from Maryland and a good friend, so I called the number he left.

"Buddy, Harry is coming to New York tomorrow for a few days. He is getting some horses together to take to New England to train. He wants to know if you have any you want to send? Also he will be staying for about three or four days."

"Tell him he can stay at the apartment, and I'll come up with a few for him."

We liked Harry. He had success with the horses and trouble with the girls. He was always smiling and never cross. It was easy to see why his laidback, Southern style could charm the birds from the trees.

When Harry arrived he looked great, and was accompanied by two young girls, one of whom was in almost a full upper body cast. Her arm was in a cast in an extended position, and her upper torso was covered. She was Mary Ryan, a young jump rider who was hurt in a jumping race in Maryland. The other girl was her sister. Harry was teaching her to ride and after her accident he helped her get proper rehab. She was pretty and very upbeat with a beautiful smile and was still talking about future riding when she would come out of her cast.

"Hi Frank," Harry said, "we arrived last night and I took a motel room for me, and one for the girls, figured it would be too much for the apartment."

"Great to see you. You're looking great, doing much riding?"

"I retired, getting tired and want to train some,"

"Well Bud says he has some for you to take to New England, let's go and find him."

We found Buddy on the phone in the office and after introductions all around he invited us to breakfast.

At the diner we spoke to Harry about the horses, he expected to have Mary and her sister help him but things had changed since her spill. Now she would remain in New York for further care and her sister would stay with her. He would leave in two or three days, and would be looking for some good help. Buddy said we had to leave and would see him the next day in the barn.

The following morning was cool and bright at 6 a.m. as I walked to the track with Buddy.

"You got anything special to do today?" he asked.

"No, why?"

"Meet me back here at 10 a.m."

"Okay."

He never said anything else, so I finished work and came back to the barn at ten. Buddy was leaving the office, carrying the books and looking anxious.

"Everything okay?" I asked.

"Yes, but I want to hurry. I'll leave my car and go in your car. I'll drive."

"Okay by me." We were off. He was quiet and I wondered where we were headed. We drove a short distance to the entrance of the belt parkway and he parked the car.

"Are we waiting for something?"

"There they are," he said. Harry Hatcher and Dennis were walking towards the car.

"Hi guys, great day," and they jumped in the car.

"Nice wagon," Harry said.

Buddy laughed and told him how I got it.

"Boy, that's the kind of owner I want to get. We don't have many like that in Maryland. You like to ski, Frank?" he asked.

"Don't know, never tried."

"Well it's a swell day for it."

I looked at Buddy who was driving towards the Verrazano bridge to New Jersey. "Where we going?" I asked.

"Big Bolder, in Pennsylvania," Buddy replied, "and I don't want to miss this beautiful day. They say they had fresh snow and the conditions are fine, so hold tight and let's go."

He was like a kid playing hooky from school, happy and excited. I knew he was doing some skiing and he liked it but he was more excited than when he won a race or had a new date. This was another Buddy.

After about an hour or so we approached a cut off to Big Bolder, the road was narrow and covered with about a foot of snow. There was a single lane where many cars must have passed and a snow covered lane to the left that appeared too deep to drive in. Buddy stayed in the middle lane and there didn't appear to be any cars in front of us. He was driving fast and said that was the only sure way to drive in snow to avoid getting stuck. In an instant a large truck appeared as if from nowhere. He was coming right at us, Buddy turned as hard as possible to the right and the left side of the car hit the left side of the truck. We bounced around. I hit the dashboard, Harry and Dennis were in the back and were dumped to the floor, Buddy seemed okay. The left side of my new wagon was gone, the fender was ripped away, the door smashed, and the rear fender demolished. The truck suffered slight damage. My heart was broken…my new car.

"Frank, give him all the information so we can get out of here," Buddy shouted.

The truck driver appeared in shock. "So sorry," he said, "anyone hurt? It's my first accident in twenty years of driving. I tried to stop, but it's hard on the ice and snow."

"I think I'm fine," I said, "how about you guys?"

"Frank, hurry will you? We are missing the day."

"But Bud, look at the car. I don't know if we can even drive it."

"The car, the car, it's a machine, a damn machine, we will get another one. Are you worried about a machine, when we are losing the day?"

He wrecked the car, could have gotten us killed, and I was wrong because we might lose the day. So I gave the driver my information for the insurance company while Buddy and the rest tried to push the fender in so we could drive the car. The whole thing took about ten minutes and we were off again. Nobody seemed upset, except me. We laughed about it and I cried inside.

We arrived at the mountain, and it was very big! We rented our boots and skis and went off to the mountain. The trio were all good skiers. I went to a beginner's tow line and tried to learn. I found it was not too hard and after a few falls I was able to stand and get around, slowly. After about one hour Buddy appeared.

"I've been looking for you, how you doing?"

"Not bad, it's fun but I've got a lot to learn."

"Come with me," he said.

"Hey, Bud I'm not going up there."

"Just take a ride on the chair. I want you to see the view, you can get coffee up there and come back down."

While he was talking we were mounting the moving chair, and I was enjoying the ride. When we reached the top we jumped off and I saw a sign, "Expert Slope."

"Buddy, what's that?" I asked as I pointed to the sign.

"That's around the corner, don't worry."

And in a second he was gone. I went around the front of the ledge and my heart leaped in my chest. I was on the highest mountain in the world, or so it seemed. The large house which served as the restaurant and lounge had a huge glass window which wasn't even visible from up here, there was no way I could make it down. Then in an instant Harry and Dennis appeared, "Come on, it's the best," and they were on their way down. Now I'm a kid from Brooklyn, we grew up never refusing a dare or a challenge and though we are older we are still kids. I'll try, I told myself but I don't know how to stop or slow down...I never got to that lesson. I began and after a few yards I saw I could go parallel to the ground and not aim straight ahead. It worked for a few feet and then I fell. I fell many times, and almost impaled myself trying to get up. The guys passed me three times as I continued. On my trip, halfway down, I looked like a snowman covered from my many falls. Finally, as I was brushing off the snow, a young man in an official looking jacket came by, "Hi, I'm the ski patrol. Do you need some help?" he asked.

"No, thank you."

"Have you been skiing long?" he asked

"No, not too long," I said.

"Well, it's okay to just take off the skis and walk down. Lots of people do it, and there is no shame in that." he answered.

Boy I wanted to but I just said, "Thanks, I'll be fine." So he left.

I made up my mind this has got to stop. I was a little more than halfway down. I could do it. I pointed towards the bottom of the hill and began to glide slowly, than I crouched down like a baseball catcher, which I was on my school team, and began to fly. This is easy, no problem. But wait, I'm going so fast, passing lots of people, the window in the lodge is now looking larger and larger. I could not slow down and the window was now the size of a barn door. I made my decision, I lunged forward like a dive into a pool. Big mistake, the snow went into my face, up my nose, and down my shirt. I slid for about thirty feet, both skis broke loose. One went to the left the other to the right. I came to a stop and people just rode right past me. I took a few minutes and got up. Now I truly was a snowman but that was much better than being part of the building.

I searched for the skis and checked in at the lodge and returned my equipment. I found the car and curled up in the back and took a nap. I was bruised and in pain. Buddy returned with the guys and joked about my adventure. I never went into detail. I didn't want to give them the satisfaction.

That evening we returned to the motel, and I excused myself early and immediately went into a hot shower. I found at that point I was completely unable to lift my left arm. I must have torn ligaments or something in my arm or shoulder and had to wash myself with my one hand. It was sore but still able to move. I found that drying oneself with only one good arm is a very difficult feat. I skipped dinner and went straight to bed. When I woke in the morning I searched the room to try and find the truck that must have hit me. With great effort I dressed and made my way to work.

Chapter XXIV

Robin Smith Comes to New York

I limped into the barn at about 8 a.m. still sore from the day before and driving a wreck of a car. "Frank, Frank, come to the office."

"Good morning," I said.

"Did you see that girl in the barn, walking the horse?" he asked.

"No, who is she?"

"Her name is Robin Smith, she is from California. She sent me a headshot and she looked beautiful. She said she was a rider and wanted to come to New York. She read I gave girls a chance to ride in New York and asked for a job. She arrived last night and I had Dennis pick her up at the airport. She came with two rats, well she says they are pets…one is black and one is white, she even has names for them. She said she has a snake in California but had trouble getting it on the plane so she left it there.

"She slept on the couch last night. I say slept…she never stopped talking. I sent her to a motel this morning."

"So are you going to put her on the payroll?"

"No! God she has got to go. She looks like a boy. Very pretty face but flat as a board, not my type."

"The girl came all the way from California, what are you going to do with her?"

"Send her to New England with Harry Hatcher. He needs help and it will be good experience for her."

"Boy, I hope she likes coming from California and going to New England. New York is one thing, New England is another."

"Well, you tell her."

"Me, I don't even know her, and what if Harry doesn't want her?"

"Tell Harry she goes with the horses I'm sending. It's a package deal."

I called the office and left a message for Harry to call us. Then I went to meet Robin. She was walking a horse to cool him down after he returned from the track.

Robin was attractive about 5' 7" with short cropped hair of light brown…a very pretty face with sharp features and high cheek bones. She wore well pressed, slim jeans with black boots and a white starched blouse, denim jacket, and a white riding helmet. Yes, a very nice looking girl I thought. She could do some modeling if she wanted, but I have found that girls that work around the track, no matter how beautiful, have one thing on their mind and that is horses.

I sometimes think they are more obsessed with horses than the men that work with them. I introduced myself and started to tell her Buddy's plan. It did not go over well.

"Shit no," she said. "I came to ride in New York. I want to speak to Buddy. This is bullshit. I don't even know you. Why are you doing this?"

I tried to explain, but she was like a storm that came on a sunny day without warning. I excused myself and told her I would speak to Buddy. I returned to the office and Buddy was hanging up the phone.

"I just spoke to Harry, and it's all set. He leaves tomorrow. Give her a check for expenses and Harry will pay her and let her work with him."

"Buddy, I don't think she wants to go."

"There's no job here. You tell her I'm leaving. Come to the apartment for breakfast. I'll stop and pick it up, see you."

I returned to Robin who was standing by the barn door with the sun at her back. I could see she would make a model if she wanted, but she wanted to ride.

"Robin, Harry is a great guy, and a good rider, I know he will teach you and this will be good for you. He will send you back in a few months and there will be plenty of horses to ride. I'm giving you a check for expenses and Harry will put you on the payroll. Buddy is sending five horses and you will ride them all, it's great experience." She took the check and never spoke to me. She said it was all my fault and for two years she seemed to hold a grudge.

Later when she did come back to New York and rode, we became friends and she rode lots of horses for us. She also enjoyed a long relationship as a rider and friend with Alfred G. Vanderbilt, the president of the New York Racing Association. He believed in her ability as a jockey and approached me on several occasions to use her as a rider for a particular horse he thought might win for her. Our biggest problem with using Robin or any other female riders was that the wives or girlfriends of several of our owners did not want a beautiful young girl getting too close to their guy, especially when they could engage in conversation that was close to their man's heart. A beautiful woman that knows all about your passion could prove to be quite dangerous, especially for an insecure woman.

It took a long time for the racing world to recognize the ability of a female jockey. I still feel they must work twice as hard as a man to reach their goal, even today. Robin was one of the pioneers and helped promote their cause. In June of 1980, Robin married Fred Astaire the great dancer and actor that Alfred had introduced her to years earlier. Robin left the track and the horses that she loved and devoted herself to her husband and their life together. Despite the almost forty six year age difference they seemed to have a good marriage and they lived together in Astaire's Beverly Hills home until his death in 1987.

Sarah Hall and Joe Porter

Chapter XXV

The Stable Expands, Rapidly

Sarah called me and said she heard about the car, "That Buddy is wacky," she said. "I spoke to William, and if you have the car at the track Friday, he will have it picked up and leave you a loner car while they repair this one. I'm going to the races can you meet me?"

"Sure, I'll get a table and we can have lunch."

We met later on and had a good day, my friend John Campo ran a horse and came by to tell us. "Stud, this horse will win and remember the fat man told you."

"He calls himself the fat man?" she said.

"He's a great guy and I like him. His wife Peggy and his kids are his life but the horses are his passion, and he knows them, so let's bet this one."

We did and it won by three lengths.

"Frank, Bill loves the game and he is ready to buy some good horses. Tell Buddy to hunt up some good ones, but no crap. I want him to get his money's worth and they will run in my name. You know I love Buddy, but he won't spend enough time with Bill. Tell him to get on the ball."

"Sarah you know how Buddy is. He loves you guys, but he is a private person and just worries about the horses."

"Frank, you can charm the world, but not Sarah. Darling we understand each other, just tell him to take care of Bill and I'll make sure Bill takes care of him." Sarah was as smart as she was beautiful.

I told Buddy what she said.

"Sounds good but you know how I hate the bullshit of talking these owners into buying horses."

"Just have lunch and I'm sure he will bring up the horses. Sarah knows what to do."

"Okay, I'll line some up and give him a choice. Set it up for when we run some good ones. By the way, my sister called and said there is a movie in New York down in the village where she lives and it's eight hours long. The whole thing is some guy sleeping, the whole movie."

"You got to be kidding."

"No his name is Andy Warhol or something like that. You think we should go see it?"

"Eight hours in a movie? No thanks."

"Well, she said people just go in for awhile, an hour or so, the best part is when a fly lands on the guy's nose."

"Sounds crazy to me."

"Well living in the village she goes for all that art stuff. She is a nice person. She and my mom are the only people I talk to. The others just say hi sometimes. My uncles are good to my mother so that's good." And he turned and walked away. That was more than I had ever heard him say about his family. I knew his sister was Rita Costello, her married name, and he would call her sometime, but his calls to his mother were always very private.

It was the end of the week when we met Sarah and Bill at the track for lunch. Bill was very happy to sit and talk to Buddy, and both Sarah and I were happy that Buddy seemed to be responding to Bill.

"I have some good prospects in mind," he told Bill. "Woody Stephens has two horses for sale, and I like them both. Then the Murty Brothers have a filly for sale that will run in an upcoming stake race. Also there are some nice two-year-olds that are a good price. We will have to make our choice."

"Do you like them all?" Bill asked.

"Well sure, but it's hard to choose."

"Who said we have to choose?" Bill said to a shocked Buddy. "If you like them, we should take them all."

"Well, Mongolia is for sale for $30,000 and Poso is $25,000… those belong to Woody. Cherry Jubilee is $100,000, but we may get him a little cheaper if we have some cash. The Murty brothers will do business. Woody is a world class trainer and the checks must go to his owner, no cash. The two-year-olds belong to a regular guy and we can deal with him together, with cash."

"Great, when do you want to go pick them up?"

Sarah smiled, I held my breath and Buddy was cool and matter of fact. We can go out on Saturday and see them. I'll arrange to go to the Belmont where they are stabled."

"Fine, I'll bring the checks and cash. Can we get them that day?" he asked.

"Well, I have a six horse van we could take it and bring back anything we buy."

"Okay, then it's set. Let's have a drink on it."

As we left the track we were on cloud nine.

"Frank, I've waited all my life for a guy like this. I just don't believe it. I know we will do great for this guy. Go to Belmont in the morning and see everybody and make sure we can get the horses on Saturday. Tell them I stand behind any checks and see if the cash will bring down the prices. You know the horses."

"Do you want me to have the vet check them out?"

"No way, I'll do it myself. Vets turn down lots of good horses, they don't like to take chances. If we can't tell what's good we should be in another business."

Saturday was a big day for us. Would he show? Did he change his mind? Is this for real? Lots of questions, let's hope for the right answers. These were the thoughts swirling around in our heads.

"Hey Frank, that new guy is here," Joe Porter called out. I left the office and saw Bill and Sarah coming down the shed row.

"Good morning, nice to see you," I said as I approached and extended my hand.

Bill smiled and gave me a strong hand shake. "Well is everything ready?" he asked.

"Yes, Buddy is on the track with the last horse, and we can have some coffee if you like. Come on in to the office and have a seat."

Sarah had on a beautiful coat dress of yellow and tan. It was a real pretty dress which she later told me cost $2,000, not exactly what we would see in the barn this early in the morning. Her high heel shoes were perfect for the disco, but not for the shed row. Buddy came in and greeted everyone, "The van is here, and we can leave in about five minutes. I told the people at Belmont we would be there before noon so we have lots of time. Bill do you have any special thoughts about the horses?"

"If you like them we will buy them."

"Sounds good, let's go."

Sarah, Bill, Buddy, and I went in the limo and the van followed. Our first stop was at Woody's barn. It was located in the best part of the backstretch at Belmont Park. His barn was picture perfect. He was an outstanding trainer...a Kentucky Hard Boot. Every horse in the barn looked like a champion, not a blade of grass or patch of earth was out of place. Bill was in awe, "Now this is a showplace."

Woody greeted us as old friends. He was a man Mark Twain would have loved to write about, tall and slim, with a face that was quick to smile and never revealed the genius inside. He trained many champions and in later years he established a record which I am sure will never be broken. He won the Belmont Stakes, which is the third leg of the Triple Crown, five years in a row. He was proud and humble at the same time.

"This horse will do fine for you, Buddy. I've just got to make some room for the new ones coming in," he said. Buddy looked him over and had the boy walk him round, "Looks good Woody, I'll take him."

The horse was Mongolia, a big, strong looking animal who appeared to have a rather long pastern. That is the part of the leg from the ankle to the hoof. The ideal horse would have a forty-five degree angle of the pastern to the foot, but this horse had a much longer angle. We also took Poso and left. We continued and bought the other horses. The van was full. Bill paid for all the horses and gave lots of extra to the help in each barn, this at Sarah's instruction.

"It's the custom," she would say.

We returned to the barn and Bill invited us to have lunch at the track. At lunch he had two drinks and was very happy.

He told us we would all have a great time, win or lose. It was the beginning of another great ride.

At Belmont a few days later, I was having coffee when Lenny Goodman, the jockey agent, came into the kitchen. He was one of the best agents in New York and he liked Buddy.

"Guess you know their saying the Brooklyn cowboy was taken by Woody?"

"How's that?"

"Mongolia, he's rundown. Woody says he will never win, lucky if you get him to the races."

"I like Woody, the old fox, but I'll make you a bet Buddy wins with the sucker before the meet is over."

"A dinner at Don Peps sounds good to me," Lenny said.

"You're on."

"You know I don't like to lose, but it might be nice if Buddy could do it."

"Lenny, he will, he will."

Buddy knew the problem and worked on it. He tried patches behind the ankle, elastic bandages, and poultice, but did not meet with much success. The day of the race approached. Buddy entered for the grass course but it rained very hard and the race was transferred to the main track, which was completely mud.

"Don't know if this guy can handle this kinda track but not much we can do about it," he said as we went to the paddock. Bill and Sarah were in the box and were coming down to watch the saddling. This was the first of the new horses to run so we wanted to do good, but the track was so off.

"Well, I don't like excuses but the horse has no off track races. He has a grass foot. It's wide as a saucer. We could get lucky."

We both hoped, but I was glad he was the trainer. They get all the praise when they win, but when they lose they're the ones the house falls on.

We returned to the box to watch the race. Sarah was excited to have the horse run in her name and her colors. She was wearing her new raincoat which was lined with mink and had a matching collar. She was hoping to take a picture. Bill was very quiet and watched everything through his binoculars. I sat behind them and Buddy sat next to me.

"Good luck Buddy," Sarah said. He just nodded. I just sat very still.

"They're off!" the announcer cried. Mongolia was in the middle of the pack but after the first turn he began to improve. Fourth, third, second, and closing fast. There were three furlongs to go. Would he stop? Would the patch hold? Just two furlongs to go he began to pull ahead. Sarah was shouting and Bill was jumping up and down. Buddy was his normal, cool self. I'm in disbelief. Mongolia by six lengths, a winner! Everyone hugged and congratulated each other.

"Frank, take them down for the picture."

"What about you, Bud?"

"I'll see you when you come up. Check the patch."

Sarah stepped onto the track and almost lost one of her shoes in the mud. The horse came back blowing hard but otherwise fine, just covered in mud. The jockey said, "I tried to hold him, but he loved the going. He will run all day and can win next time easy. Tell Buddy I want to ride him back and thanks."

The patch was fine and the ankle showed no sign of burns or damage, the soft mud was the key.

After that day, things looked good for the barn. Bill would claim or buy lots of horses and he always paid his bills on time.

Sarah Hall and William Levin

Chapter XXVI

Winter Racing, Again

The fall meet was good and as the weather turned cold once again we would be leaving New York for winter racing. We would send some of the better horses to the farm for a needed rest and hope to have them ready for our return to New York in March. This year, Buddy decided on Liberty Bell, in Pennsylvania. We had raced there before with good success. We shipped early and Buddy took some of Sarah's horses, but only a few as winter racing is hard on the horse and he wanted fresh horses for our return to New York.

I took a room in the Penn Motel and Buddy said he would commute. Since it was a two hour ride I thought it was odd. We arrived and Buddy had us set up the office.

"Frank, make sure you have a phone in the office and one at your motel."

"Sure, but don't you think it will be hard to travel from New York every day?"

"Look, I'll get you set and I may take a little time off." And that's what he did.

We won some quick races and claimed some nice horses. Sarah came down just two or three times.

"I'm not much for these small town tracks," she would say. I think the small town feel was too close to home for Sarah. She was from a very small town in Mississippi named Sturgis. On top of that she was not from the right side of the track and in a town as small as Sturgis there is no crossing over. She never wanted to look back and found her happiness in the big city lights, especially now that Bill or William as she always called him was giving her New York all wrapped up in a big red ribbon.

Buddy would call and we would go over what to do with the horses. I had Joe Porter and a great crew. They were good guys and hard working. The crew knew what to do and the barn was no trouble.

I claimed eight horses while Buddy was not there, but Buddy would call the night before and tell me which ones to claim as long as they looked okay before the race. I received a call from Sarah and told her one of her horses was due to race on the upcoming Friday and she told me she and Bill would be coming for lunch and to see the race. Buddy called and I told him.

"I'll be there and try to run something that can win."

I checked the book and we decided Mayberry would be our best horse to enter. He said he would come down and spend the day and perhaps claim a horse. He and his friend had a plan and would fly down with three other people. He told me to make reservations for his friends and for Sarah and try to put the tables as far apart as possible.

Sarah and Bill arrived by helicopter and landed on the infield, right in the middle of the track. The groundskeepers had quickly prepared a wooden walkway for them, since there had been rain earlier and would be too muddy for her to walk on. I was standing at the rail waiting for them to disembark from the helicopter, which was one of the highlights of the day for most of the spectators at this little track.

I took them to the table and told them Buddy would be joining them soon. He arrived with his group and asked me to take them to their table so he could go to the barn and check the horses. It was like a Marx brothers movie. I was a nervous wreck while he was his regular self, very calm.

"Frank, get me a claim slip for the third race and tell Joe to be at the finish line to pick up our new horse, if we get him."

It seems his friend was new to racing and Buddy wanted to show him how claiming worked. I got the slip which he filled out and placed in the claim box. The race ran and the horse won. We were the only claim, so the horse should be ours.

"Frank, I don't get the horse, Joe told me."

"Why?" I asked, and before he could speak, an announcement came over the loud speaker for Buddy to report to the track office. I went to the office as Buddy arrived from the dining room.

"What's up?" he asked.

"I don't know. Joe said they wouldn't give him the horse."

"Wait for me here," his face was taut. About fifteen minutes later he came out.

"So, what now?"

"They said I didn't sign the claim slip."

"That's crazy, I saw you sign."

"Yes, but they have eight other slips and they said the signature on today's was not the same."

"Oh hell, I signed the others."

"Yes, but they don't know that, and I told them I would hire the best handwriting expert and prove I signed that slip, and then I would sue them for a great deal of money."

"What did they say?"

"They are thinking about it and will let me know after this race."

We waited and the officials decided to give us the horse, but they were not happy about the situation. Buddy left after the last race and Bill and Sarah left after her horse ran and won. Someone from the office told me the officials felt we did something wrong but were not sure what. Buddy said we would be leaving early so we could get a good start back home and said he had been skiing a great deal and this was one of his best winters, but he never said any of us did a good job. I mentioned it to him and his response was, "You don't have to thank or praise guys for doing their jobs, and I expect everyone to be good at what they do or they wouldn't be with me." For Buddy that was the end of story, cut and dried.

Chapter XXVII

NYRA Backstretch Strike

Everything was just the same when we returned to Barn ten at Aqueduct in New York. It looked like we would be in for a good year, then it began.

"Frank we have a HBPA meeting today at the track. Doctor Star and some guys want me to talk about conditions on the track, so let's get there early and go over the books with Ron."

Ron was Ron Moony, he was the only paid employee of the organization and his title was secretary, but in fact he ran the office and took care of the real work. Buddy was president and didn't have much to do. It was a job of representing the horsemen when there was a problem between the track or the state government and the horsemen. Ron was the nephew of Cal Raine, the steward at the track.

Buddy's Uncle Hirsh was the first trainer to have a pension plan for the people in his barn. He owned most of the horses he trained and wanted to do something for his workers. Buddy admired his uncle and he often spoke of doing the same for his crew.

We met with Dr. Star, who was a horse owner and breeder, and about five other horsemen. Dr. Star was the owner of the hospital at JFK airport, the old Idlewild airport. He owned and operated a horse farm in Montauk, located on the tip of Long Island, and he was very interested in the New York breeding program. Buddy also supported the program which would give extra purse money to horses born and raised in the state.

The group wanted Buddy to push for more funding for the breeding program and help with the tax situation to encourage more breeding in the state. Governor Nelson Rockefeller had appointed Joseph A. Gimma as head of the State Racing Commission and he was well known by the horsemen. They felt we could make real progress with these two people who appeared friendly to the industry. Also the state dairy industry was in trouble and many farmers were abandoning large farms which were off the tax rolls.

The group proposed that a part of the legislation was to be presented to the state. The meeting went well and Buddy agreed to follow up and speak to the proper people and draft some suggestions which he would present to Dr. Star's group at the next meeting.

"Buddy, things are so good now, are you going to get involved in this thing now?"

"You know this would be a good time for me to present the pension plan for the guys," he smiled.

"Bud, I know you mean well but it's lots of work. Are you sure?"

"I'm sure."

After about four or five meetings Buddy was sure the state would do something for the horsemen, "Hell, we bring in more tax money than most big corporations. They can't be so stupid and cut off that money," he said

"Bud, you are a great horse trainer but you are so naïve when it comes to things off the track. These people don't think the way you do. They are only interested in votes and how many of them do you think they will get from the race trackers?" I pleaded.

"Look, this is our chance, and I always wanted to push for the pension plan and the owners and trainers will have to support us if they want the money for the purses and the breeding plan. I know it can work."

Dr. Star continued to push Buddy, "If you can't get this done we can get someone else to take over," he said at the last meeting and this upset Buddy.

So with the support of many, Buddy began to form a committee to submit a proposal to the state. It would include a pension for the backstretch people, money to fund the breeding program, and extra money for the New York bred horses in special restricted races. The program would be funded by extra races and even an extra day of racing if necessary. The governor rejected the entire plan and would not even meet and sent a representative to discuss the requests.

People on the track were outraged. A large meeting was called and Dr. Star was the most vocal. "Buddy, you must lead or leave your post. I call for action. We must act, even a strike if necessary," he yelled out.

There were many trainers at the meeting, Tom Gullo, Al Scotti, John Parisella, Gill Punetes, Marvin Cohn, Tom Kelly, Las Barrera, John Jacobs, Dominick Imperio and lots more. Also owners like Murray Garren, Frank Ferri and Neil Hellman. Some were great support but others were dead set against any action against the state or the track

"I'm going to do this and win one for the guys that carry this show," Buddy vowed.

He knew that behind the manure, hay and horses were hope, expectations, fantasy, reality, delusion, and a way of life that we all loved. But he was naïve to think that the establishment would be easy to defeat.

After two more rowdy meetings the final vote was to strike. This had never been done and was a huge step against the establishment. The backstretch workers were elated. They gathered and hoped for a new way of life.

On Thursday April 24,1969 the strike began. The trainers did not enter any horses to race, so the track had to cancel racing. But the NYRA quickly called and asked for entries, a few responded, but not enough to fill the races. Then the jockeys refused to ride, the grooms and backstretch workers set up a picket line and the tracks were closed.

The NYRA then tried to get stable riders to ride races, even willing to issue state licenses to people without proper training. The officials met with groups of horsemen but to no avail.

Cal Reine called a meeting of the jockey agents and gave a talk on why we should return to work. Since I had a license, I was at the meeting and we were shocked when he made the statement, "We don't need these cloak and suitors here." This of course was a reference to the Jewish trainers and owners who made up a great part of the racing community. There was immediate silence in the room and he and everyone else knew he uttered a bombshell. When the word spread of the meeting the backlash was strong, even Buddy's Uncle Hirsh, who was against the strike changed his position and refused to enter horses.

The track issued a blurb that the statement was never made and the agents were approached and many said they did not hear any such comment. But there were others that would confirm the statement.

Buddy held an emergency meeting at his apartment about four days into the strike and the reaction was still positive, but there were some signs of weakness.

"Buddy, my owner says he thinks we should go back to work. He can't pay his bills, if we don't race," was the common complaint.

"Look, we are close. We have to stick together. I'm sure the state needs racing. They are losing lots of tax dollars. It will end soon."

But it didn't. The NYRA tried to run limited races and even offered full purses to four horse fields, meaning you'd get a check for every horse. Some owners entered, but the races did not go.

At one point they tried to run races, but the workers would not bring the horses to the track for the races. Tommy Trotter was the racing secretary and a well respected man. He was always fair and honest, a tall handsome man of about fifty, always well dressed and proper, he tried to lead a horse over to the paddocks for a race and he was struck in the head by a rock. The police had to be called and many of the men were arrested.

A group of horsemen asked Buddy for a meeting at his Apartment. The same fellows who said, "Lead or leave," now said "enough." And after ten days, the strike was over. Buddy was devastated. He did not believe it. "That's it for me. I'm a marked man. How could those guys do that to me?"

"Buddy, you did your best. They have owners who pay the bills but don't care about the backstretch. Your Uncle Hirsh has the only pension plan and helps in lots of ways. Maybe others will follow. You did your best." My words didn't help but after a few days he was back to himself.

Chapter XXVIII

Just Julie

Buddy's Cadillac spit up stones as he wheeled it toward the paved Belmont Park paddock area. Other drivers had their credentials checked, but I knew we wouldn't be stopped. Buddy had a sticker on the car, which guaranteed access to the back areas. It had a T on it. Horsemen and owners got a sticker with an H on it. Everyone knew his car anyway. Buddy liked to stand out, and he always arrived with a flourish. He was not particularly happy that day because we had to head out to Saratoga soon. He didn't like that track, or the town because there was no way to escape from the horsemen, owners, and public. Everything happened within ten square miles up there, unlike the city tracks, and it was like living in a glass house for the summer. I told him it didn't matter, but knew I could not change the way he felt.

In truth, Buddy seemed restless around this time. The usual pressures of work were always there, of course, but perhaps he was distracted by other things and needed a change. He had started the game very young. Three of his uncles were horse trainers: Hirsch, Sidney, and Eugene. Hirsch was the most famous trainer of all time, though it was Gene who took Buddy under his wing and got him a job walking horses down in Florida when Buddy was just eleven years old. He worked around the track when he was not in Midwood High in Brooklyn. Then he did a short stint with the Merchant Marines and was back to the track. He got a job with Dave Schinder and when Dave took sick, Buddy took over the barn. Within two weeks he won three races with horses that until that point, were not doing well. Everyone was talking about him, and Dave got well fast and returned to the barn. Then, Buddy started training, and never looked back. So he had already been in the game a long time. For most of the 1960s, he was New York's most successful trainer.

A good breakfast of franks and sauerkraut, chopped liver, bagels with cream cheese, lox and two orange juices hadn't improved his mood. Neither did this warm, sunny June morning. I would have thought coming to Belmont would have brightened his mood, but it didn't help. While he stabled his horses at Aqueduct because it was closer to the apartment, he actually preferred Belmont, which resembled a real park with trees and wide, grassy areas. Folks even liked to picnic there on race days. It was also much bigger than Aqueduct, which was closer to the city and was crammed into less space. The barns at Aqueduct could accommodate approximately 1,500 horses, while Belmont had room for more than 2,000 horses along with two training tracks. Ironically, Buddy preferred to train at Aqueduct because more races were held there. He thought running his horses on the busier, more compact track gave him an edge.

He steered the Cadillac into the parking lot reserved for trainers. When we got out, we made the usual tour to check on Buddy's horses. He had entries in the second, fifth and seventh races this day. We chatted with a few friends along the way, including a white cap named Nolan. White caps actually do wear white caps, hence the nickname for those people who work at the track and check credentials. They must have once been identified by their hats. Like Nolan, many were exercise boys, ex-jockeys and the like who worked part time at the race track after completing their horse-related chores. Nolan had broken his leg after years as an exercise boy and now worked solely for the New York Racing Association.

In the paddock, Buddy also chatted with Joe Porter, who made sure all the equipment was on hand for the horses among his other chores. There's a ton of gear needed to run races, including special bits that go in the mouth of the horses. Some of the animals like a leather bit, some like a ring bit, which is wider. Others tend to veer to the left or right during a race and would be equipped with a bit called a run out bit. Quite a few of Buddy's horses used blinkers, a hood that went over the horse's head so his eyes would be partially covered or guarded by the cups on the hood. Blinkers are open at different degrees. Full blinkers are for horses that are nervous and don't want to see too much. Other choices include open blinkers, three-quarter blinkers and various blinkers, depending on how a particular horse responds. Buddy was lucky to have Joe as an employee. Joe was a black, Puerto Rican who loved horses, but faced open discrimination because of his color. He was a great trainer but just couldn't get a chance. Instead, he worked for Buddy. My secret weapon, Buddy called him.

They talked for a few minutes. Their horse in the second race was owned by a new client, Mrs. Janet Greenberg, and Buddy wanted her to taste some early success. It would help ensure her purse stayed open to him. While Joe and Buddy conferred, I saw a few valets busily rushing from one place to another as the first race neared. Each one is assigned saddle equipment, and he brings it to the walking ring and helps the trainer with the horse. He puts on the saddle and makes sure the saddle weights that go underneath are in place. He then helps secure the girdle, which is the strap attaching the saddle under the horse's belly, and finally adjusts the saddle to preferred tightness.

The Judge was there, too. A big man, standing maybe 6' 2" and 250 pounds. He was hard to overlook, immaculately dressed, always neat and proper, and wearing a hat all winter. On very warm days, he'd be bare headed. This particular day, he was dressed in a blue blazer, a striped tie and grey slacks. He carried a program in his hand where he would mark off the different things he wanted to remember about the horses or the equipment. In a moment, he wandered off in pursuit of more infractions. Judges work for the racing association and are in charge of overseeing all the operations in the paddock, making sure the horses are properly saddled and that only people with horses in the race, or guests of the trainer are in the paddock area. No agents are allowed in the paddock, and other trainers who do not have horses in the race are excluded from the paddock except on special occasions when they are guests of another trainer. As a result, there was always plenty to keep a judge occupied. The same guy seemingly had been there forever.

Buddy and I spent the morning traipsing around and had about thirty minutes to kill before the first race. He wore tan slacks and a navy blazer tie and clean shaven…his trademark look. I wore the same thing I would wear for the next thirty years: pressed khaki pants, a blazer and loafers, with my own hair cut short. I was a product of Brooklyn's Catholic schools and Buddy was the dropout from Woody Allen's high school in another section of the borough. We were both short, Napoleonic types, and we moved with energy.

I watched Buddy grow more somber as the morning progressed. We checked on our horses first and then stopped by the bar for a coke while Buddy continued to grouse the fact that we'd soon be in Saratoga. I didn't say anything. There was no point. On the other hand, I wasn't looking forward to driving with him while he stayed in this funk. But part of being his friend and confidante was dealing with his moods. We had just started back to the paddock area when Buddy simply stopped. I had no idea what caught his attention.

"Look at that," he faintly breathed the words, almost speechless. I followed his gaze. For a moment, I thought he had finally noticed the great white pine tree that Belmont had preserved in the paddock area. Immortalized on the Belmont logo, the tree is more than 300 years old and it towers over the paddock. But I quickly realized I was looking at the wrong foliage.

He was riveted on a young woman, probably in her late twenties, seated on the bench. She had two of the longest, most beautiful legs I had ever seen. They were topped by a one-piece violet-purple miniskirt that was extremely short. It was closer to a bathing suit than a dress. Demurely, she crossed her legs, and that movement and that extraordinary bit of flesh had Buddy momentarily stupefied. She was holding a daily racing form, fanning her face with it.

"Look at those legs," Buddy whispered to me.

They were magnificent—but then I noticed her feet, too. She wore flat, open, brown sandals with a leather strap across the top so her toes were exposed. On each toe was a ring. I nodded my head at Buddy, slowly.

We took a step or two towards her, and as we did, she lowered the racing form. She was stunning, with dark, long, black hair framing her face. Black bangs hung across her forehead. Her skin was like porcelain. Even from our distance, which was narrowing by the second, I could see her eyes were bright, almost violet rather than blue. She wore very little makeup only light, glossy lipstick.

We continued walking. I didn't want to stare but she invited interest. She calmly folded her paper and put it down beside her as though she were acting in a play. Each movement was slow and deliberate...rehearsed, stylized. That drew attention to her fingers, each of which also had rings that reflected in the sunlight.

She was not alone, however. A young man sat next to her, leaning forward in direct contrast to her upright pose. He looked about thirty with blondish hair and ordinary features. He wore an earring, something unusual in that day. It dangled down from his left lobe. He also seemed oblivious to her, as if he were more concerned about the races that day and could care less about anyone or anything else.

We walked past her. She followed us with her eyes and then resumed staring into the distance as if disinterested. As we got a few yards beyond her, Buddy asked me to bring her into the paddock area. Maybe she would like to watch the horses getting saddled, he suggested.

I understood Buddy's attraction, but the outlook didn't look promising. She was with someone else, I told him. But Buddy wasn't interested in my reservations. He knew what he wanted and wasn't about to let a little thing like a boyfriend stand in his way. He nodded at the woman and then hurried away, insisting he had horses to check on. "See you inside," he called.

I turned back. She was still watching us, but surreptitiously. She would look away and then back at us. That seemed like an invitation. The guy next to her seemed just as disinterested in her as before, anyway.

I walked over to her and said, "Hi."

"Hi, yourself," she said. Her voice was light, pleasant. She must have been used to strangers approaching her.

"Listen," I said, "I don't know if you are interested, but Buddy Jacobson, the trainer..."

"I know who he is," she said.

I smiled. She had been watching him. "He's got a horse in the race," I continued, trying not to get draw into the deep wells in her eyes, "and he thought you might like to watch the saddling, you know.... if you've never been in the paddock..."

"I'd love it." she said without hesitation, almost as if expecting such an invitation. When she stood up, I could see she was even more beautiful than I imagined. She was close to 5' 10" with full breasts and a stunning figure. She put the paper down on the chair. "I'll be back, Harry," she told her companion. He didn't even bother to shrug. Instead, he picked up the racing form.

She walked with a quick gait. Her skirt was barely at a legal limit, and her toenails were painted in garish silver. Later, she told us that she thought the color was lucky. Every outfit she wore always had silver somewhere.

I introduced myself, using my full name. "I'm Frank Pagano,"

I said, offering my hand.

Her name was Julie. No last name.."Just Julie," she said.

As we got to the gate, the white cap smiled and looked at me.

"Hi, Frank," he said. I put my arm around Julie's waist, and he didn't stop us.

The horses were in their stalls. Buddy was putting new blinkers on his horse. The stallion stood there calmly as he adjusted it. The valet came out carrying the saddle. The two men busied themselves with it.

I heard the sound of feet and saw the Judge. He glanced in my direction once or twice. I knew him very well because his wife was a secretary to the race stewards, and she was a very religious person. We had become friendly over a period of time, and I had great respect for both of them. She and her husband would go on long Catholic retreats, and she would

sometimes discuss with me what they'd learned. They had a
son who was working for the government—FBI or DEA.

"Frank," he called. I walked over.

"Who is that person?" the Judge asked coldly, nodding at
Julie.

"Oh," I said, "she's a friend of Mr. Jacobson..."

"She doesn't appear to be properly attired to me. Does she
own this horse?"

"No. I don't think so..."

He stiffened, "I would think that she should not be in the
paddock. I would ask you to please excuse her and remove her
from the paddock immediately. That's not proper attire for this
event..."

I agreed immediately. I was not going to argue with the
Judge.

"Julie," I told her quietly, "I think we should wait for
Buddy outside the gate because it's getting crowded in here,"
She didn't object, but just turned and followed me out. I could
see Buddy finish saddling up the horse and come out looking
for us, but we were too far away. We walked outside the gate
and stayed close to the walking area so we could look over the
fence to see the horses coming out. Buddy put the rider up very
quickly and left the paddock even before the horses had gone
onto the track.

Eventually, he joined us, and I introduced him to Julie. He
wanted to talk to me instead. Julie waited a few yards away. I
told him what happened. He asked if I'd told the Judge that
Julie was his guest. I said I did. His face hardened. He told me
to take Julie up to box 6E to watch the race. I didn't like his
expression. Buddy was upset and from his taut lips, I could tell
he was thinking it over. I tried to calm him. After battling
through legal problems already, he didn't need any more.
Besides, alienating a man who could, if he wanted, find
something wrong with a horse or pre-race preparation hardly
seemed like good politics. Besides, there was the Judge's son.
Getting on the wrong side of the FBI, DEA or whatever
seemed like a particularly bad idea. Buddy was not the least bit
interested in my reasoning.

Julie was delighted to go to the box, but said she'd join me there. In a moment, she was gone in the crowd. I figured she wanted to ditch Harry.

After a few minutes, Buddy joined me in 6E. The box was nothing more than an isolated cubicle at the top of the grandstand. Here, owners and celebrity trainers could sit together in demure rows, watching the action and trying not to gloat if their horse won. People who populated the boxes tended to be wealthier and hold themselves in check, regardless of how they felt. They didn't want to appear gauche or draw attention, as if they had never been there or won before.

Buddy watched the horses warm up before the race, staring intently through his binoculars. I doubt he put them down when Julie arrived as the horses were being loaded into the starting gate. She sat next to Buddy. He didn't say a word.

In a moment, the flag was up to indicate all the horses were ready for the six furlong race, a short event where speed is all that matters. Buddy's horse had plenty of that. The gates opened with a clang and Buddy's horse took off quickly. Starting on the outside, he was making up ground with every stride.

As they hit the turn, Buddy's stallion was a length in front and widening the gap.

"Come on. Come on!" Julie shouted, jumping to her feet. Buddy looked at her as though she were an alien who had dropped from the sky. I tapped her on the shoulder. Everyone else in the box was quiet. "Christ, aren't you excited?" she exclaimed. Her enthusiasm seemed so absurd.

The horse was now up four lengths and pulling away. He came down the stretch with Julie screaming encouragement the whole way, beating the air with her fist. She gave Buddy a hug, and Buddy seemed a little embarrassed. I cringed.

"Wow, he won," Julie screamed. The horse went off at two to one that day and returned the price of $6.60 for every $2 wagered. I don't know how much she bet—or even if she bet on him—but she was very excited. "Wow. That was super. That was great," she kept repeating. She must've felt like Christmas. I wanted to tell her that this doesn't happen all the time. Buddy was riding high right then. We all met after the last race, and Julie was happy, smiling, and counting some bills. She was giggly like a young kid, and it was obvious she'd had a couple of more vodkas while she was waiting for the day to pass. On the other hand, Buddy's face darkened. He looked at me. "Come on," he said. He told Julie to wait for us.

We took the elevator to the lower level where all the officers of the administration had offices. Buddy didn't say a word, but anxiously watched as the elevator slowly descended. He flexed his hands and set his jaw. The door was starting to open when Buddy hurried out and walked with obvious purpose toward the stewards' office in the back.

We saw the wife of the Judge behind the desk there. She offered congratulations, which Buddy basically ignored. Instead, he abruptly asked if any of the stewards were available. They weren't. They are the race officials and needed to make sure every race was run properly. The race Buddy's horse won was just declared official, but the stewards hadn't made their way back to the office. We sat down in the waiting room. Buddy was quietly seething.

Every now and then, the Judge's wife would look at us. I could see she was wondering what was going on. I wasn't sure either. The race seemed clean, nothing had happened that caught my attention. Was Buddy really going to complain about the Judge? I hoped not.

The office door opened. Cal Rainey, who was one of the stewards, invited us in. I followed Buddy. The office contained three stewards, including Cal. They were genial, congratulating Buddy. He nodded, but definitely kept aloof. He didn't sit down in one of the open chairs. I did.

Finally, one of them pleasantly asked why he wanted to meet with them.

"I had a very bad incident occur today and wanted to tell you about it before I go home for the night," Buddy started. They sat up. From his tone, they could tell something was seriously wrong, and that always grabbed official attention. After all, Buddy was an intimate in the paddock. He could have seen someone give drugs to a horse or do something else equally sinister. They waited.

"I had a guest come up to the paddock today," Buddy continued, staring at each steward in turn, "and she was asked to leave by the paddock judge who stated that she was not properly attired. She entered the racetrack, paid her admission and was considered properly attired to come into the racetrack. I don't understand why she was automatically excluded from the paddock."

The room was very quiet. I'm sure the stewarts didn't expect that kind of complaint. I really didn't either. Buddy had just met Julie, and he was already acting as though she was his girlfriend and had been insulted.

"She had on a very short skirt that the judge didn't think was appropriate," he went on while the stewards glanced at each other and tried to think of a response. "I just feel so upset that I think I'll just scratch the next two horses that I was going to run. You know, I'll just go home. It's very demeaning and very insulting." Buddy spoke sharply, making sure the stewards got the message. Personally, I thought he was acting.

One of the stewards suggested the Judge be invited in to explain what happened. Buddy instantly agreed, and we were asked to wait outside.

A few minutes later, the dapper Judge, now tight lipped, walked by us. He looked at us and nodded; we did the same. Then he opened the door and entered the closed office. Three minutes later, he emerged. He didn't acknowledge us this time. His face was red. His eyes were hot coals. He was a man of principle in a job backed by decades of tradition, and didn't take kindly to being overruled. I'm sure that's what happened.

The stewards came out. We stood up. Rainey said, "Buddy, we agree with you that there's no reason for the young lady to be excluded from the paddock. We apologize for any inconvenience."

Buddy graciously thanked the stewards and told them that he appreciated their decision. We said goodbye and left. I could feel the Judge's wife staring at us. I doubt we'd have pleasant conversations again.

In the elevator, I felt like I could breathe again. "Would you have really scratched those horses?" I asked Buddy.

"Why not?" he said, his voice quivering with emotion. "They have to understand this track has got to be open to the general public or we're going to lose everyone. Now, that girl was okay to come into the track, and they took her money. Why wasn't she okay to come into the paddock?"

Julie wasn't in the box. Buddy went off to grab a dining room table for lunch while I waited for her. She walked in a few minutes later, all smiles and all legs.

"I told my friend he could leave," she said. "I'll get a cab home." She knew better than that. I assured her we'd find some way to get her to her house.

As we walked to the dining room, Julie told me she had been Miss Seventeen and now worked in a Manhattan bar. That seemed a bit commonplace for someone as beautiful as her. She had been a model for awhile, she admitted, but quit when the life got too hectic. She was a barmaid in a local tavern, been there about a year and a half. She was supposed to work that evening, but said Harry was going by to tell them she wasn't coming in. There were a couple of other girls that filled in when Julie wasn't available.

As for Harry, he walked into her bar some eighteen months earlier and eventually asked to become her slave. Both Buddy and I sat up at that comment. Harry wanted to be with her, but not romantically. She finally agreed. Over time, he became her guardian and protector. He only had some menial job, so when he couldn't pay rent on his apartment any more, she let him move in. He slept in a corner, Julie said. His reward was even more bizarre, she would give him a couple of swats with a small whip.

Harry was now spending his days selling hotdogs from a small cart she fixed up. I start him off with enough money to make change and give him enough so he can buy two packs of cigarettes a day. He brings home every penny, and I check it out and restock him. Since I had this extra money, I've been hanging around the track Julie explained.

Once we were seated at Buddy's table, I excused myself. Buddy had no interest in my hanging around. Besides, I had plenty to do in the paddock. I could hear Julie order a vodka on the rocks as I left.

Once outside, I was able to get a racing form and handicap the upcoming races. Buddy always frowned on that. He said patrons shouldn't know that we bet; they'll think there's something crooked about the races. The owners didn't like it either. They want to believe we're here to improve the breed, he said. I disagreed. While I worked with him, I abided. Out of sight, I read the racing form.

That evening, Buddy invited us to dinner. Julie didn't want to. She had a canary at home to take care of, she said, but finally agreed that Harry could handle the chore.

By the time we reached dessert and had enjoyed enough drinks, she had moved really close to Buddy. Their legs touched; their bodies were almost together. Her head was drooping wearily. She ended up putting her head on his shoulder, and he had his arm around her. I was struck by the image. Buddy had never showed any kind of emotion in public. However, by then, he had two or three rum and cokes, and was feeling mellow. As we were waiting for the coffee, she turned to him, put her hand on his side of his face and gave him a very loving, sweet kiss.

"I better get going," she said. "I've got a long way to go to the city."

"I've got an extra bedroom. Why don't you stay over?" Buddy asked. "Nothing physical," he said. "Just stay over." She easily agreed. I don't know what happened that night, but he had put her in a cab the next day and sent her home. That was the beginning of the wildest two months I've ever seen Buddy in a relationship.

I was more focused on Saratoga, which was only a twenty-eight day meet. To win a race, you had to have a very good horse because the competition was so great. The major players got most of the stalls, as people from Chicago, California, and trainers from Florida came up. Everybody was trying to get a share of the jackpot. The big race was called the Travers, a famous race for three-year-olds and barely a notch below the Derby, Belmont, and Preakness. If no horse won the Triple Crown that year, the Travers was quite often the deciding race of the year. First run in 1864, it was the oldest stakes for three-year-olds in the U.S. People also came for the sales, which trailed only the July horse sales in Kentucky where horses could be sold for millions.

As a result, Saratoga was flush with European trainers, different celebrities, politicians, huge gamblers and speculators. I looked forward to that every year. Buddy dreaded it and never went to the horse sale. He went years ago and set all kinds of records buying horses, but felt the sales were rigged. The horses were given different stimulants, and no one could decipher whether or not the animal was sound. So, it was a real crapshoot. Buddy wouldn't expose a lot of his owners to that. Worse, some buyers worked out deals to cheat new owners who thought the sales were all top notch and legitimate. Unscrupulous horse people might buy horses before the sale and, without revealing the new ownership, run them through the auction and then sell them to their naïve owners. With that kind of crap going on, Buddy stayed away. Besides, he preferred to work far from the limelight.

When we drove the long 200 mile ride from New York city to Saratoga Springs a few days later, Julie naturally rode with us with her canary. We put the bags in his room, and she was all over him, hugging him and kissing him. They looked like newlyweds. Nothing demure about her now. Buddy was all business, though, and insisted on checking the barns. Joe was due there the next day. We planned a dinner at a new Italian restaurant Buddy had heard about. We headed back to the room. Buddy suggested I head back to the city the next morning. "You've got a long ride home, and we're not doing much up here. I'm just getting the horses acclimated, letting them walk around up here. After our van ride, I don't like to push them," he said. I didn't argue. I'm not much as a third wheel.

"You know," Buddy said, his face wreathed in a smile, "I think this is going to be one of the best Saratoga's I've ever had."

Chapter XXIX

Saratoga with Just Julie

While Buddy busied himself with Julie and the track, I occupied myself with work back in the city. I still had to keep Sarah and Bill happy while he was having fun. After the win with Mongolia we ran Poso and he won. Now we were two for two. We suffered a rude awakening when Cherry Jubilee ran last in a stake race.

"I knew those Murty brothers were crooks," I roared.

"Don't blame them," he said. "I got carried away and didn't do a good job checking this one. The good thing is she is a filly and can be a good mom, I'll ask Bill to breed her. I never blame other people for my mistakes. We have to take care of our own business." He believed this and lived by it. He said it was something he learned at the course he took at Dale Carnegie, "How to Make Friends and Influence People."

I told him he must have only taken half the course because he was not great on the "making friends" part, we both laughed. I thought having Julie would mellow him, but he still hated Saratoga.

Beyond the rigged sales and pretentious bigwigs floating around, here was one overriding problem with the place as far as Buddy was concerned. Unlike Belmont, this track was smack in the middle of horse country. Breeders were piled on top of each other. Everyone knew what was going on at a neighbor's farm. As a quiet person who preferred isolation, Buddy must have felt claustrophobic. Julie guaranteed he couldn't hide. She was beautiful and obvious, both in appearance and vocally. Everywhere the two of them went,

Buddy knew dozens of eyes followed him. For a guy like him, that was awful.

After two weeks, he had had enough and asked me to stay for the weekend. I joined him at the track. He went back to the barn alone while I sat with Julie. I had no interest in her romantically, no matter how pretty she was. She was Buddy's girl. I would never do anything to hurt him. Even more, I was just too darn busy to spend much time with someone like her. She commanded a lot of attention. We got along because she realized quickly I was not going to hit on her. We would just chat, but she was very guarded with her comments. Several times, she seemed ready to open up, but, then would abruptly shut down.

"Buddy is such a sincere person and so kind to me, and not demanding of anything. I'm really happy about this relationship," she told me.

"He's been much calmer and much more relaxed these last two weeks you've been with him," I noted. "Saratoga is an experience. He's exposed to a lot of people who are jealous of his success and continually take potshots at him. So, he needs your reinforcement."

She was very easy to get along with, never too difficult, but in the car, she had brought along a small package which I found later to contain two bottles of Smirnoff. She drank a lot and it seemed to be getting worse. "I have a small problem I guess," she said. "I don't hide it. I'm addicted to this alcohol. I start the morning with Smirnoff's, enter the afternoon with it, and finish off the night with it. Usually, there's a little left in the bottle by the end of the day. I find it so hard to get through the day that I can't make it without alcohol. This last two, three weeks, seeing Buddy, being at the races, you guys being so nice to me, I've tried to cut back. I'm doing a little better, but I know, I just can't stop, at least not yet."

"Do the best you can with the booze," I told her. "He's not going to ask you to stop. None of us will try to change anybody else's lifestyle. I just wish for your health that you'd consider it. Other than that, have a drink!" She laughed. I always liked her laugh.

After the last race, we headed for a restaurant to the north about thirty miles away. It was a really long restaurant, built low to the ground, the kind you'd find in a rural setting with loads of food and a rough, homey atmosphere. We walked in, and there was a long buffet table packed with a variety of appetizers.

Despite the distance from Saratoga, the place must have had a good reputation. We looked around and saw a couple of friends of ours from the track, including Ray Amato, who was the premiere blacksmith at Saratoga. His father was one of the finest blacksmiths ever and had four sons, all of whom were superior blacksmiths. Ray was with his young son, Ray Jr., and another young lad whom I didn't know. We waved at each other as we passed by. They probably stared at Julie, who was wearing one of her really short dresses for the occasion. Her silver panties flashed every time she took a step.

We sat down on the corner, and Buddy bought a round of drinks.

We both had cokes. Julie ordered a double vodka on the rocks. I began to wonder about her drinking. Back in the room she shared with Buddy, I had seen empty vodka bottles. I knew they weren't Buddy's. He didn't drink. On the other hand, Julie never seemed loaded in any way. Still, someone was emptying those bottles. I doubt they were being used to water plants.

After appetizers, Julie went back to the buffet for additional salad. Two men who looked like country boys were sitting near the table. As she sauntered by them, they were laughing and carrying on. I guess they had never seen anything like Julie before. There was one chunky kid, about 6' 2", 200 pounds. He looked like a real big farm boy in his early twenties. The other young man was a skinny looking fellow about 5' 8" with long, scraggly hair that needed to be combed and a little scruff of a beard. I was closer to them. Buddy was sitting in the corner, minding his meal. I saw the scruffy farm boy reach out to touch Julie's skirt as she walked by.

She turned and started to speak to him. Buddy hadn't noticed, but I didn't miss a thing. I quickly got up, walked over and asked the guy to watch his manners. He laughed at me and said something derogatory about the city floozy with silver panties. That was not the best choice of words. Julie flared angrily and dumped salad over his head. I was stunned watching her, but the shock passed quickly.

The guy jumped up to grab her. Having grown up in the rough-and-tumble Brooklyn streets, I just automatically swung my right hand and bashed his face. He tumbled and hit part of the buffet table, knocking down some of the plates with a loud crash as he sprawled backwards. His partner quickly stood up. He seemed to keep rising from the ground and just kept getting bigger and bigger, like a mountain. I noticed immediately that he threw a big shadow.

I caught my breath. I saw him reach his right hand back and let fly. Before he connected, I moved to the left. I could feel his fist breeze by my nose about an inch away. In my effort to get away, I stumbled into a chair near a table, knocking over whatever was there. In the meantime, Buddy finally responded. He grabbed Julie and led her away.

Pinned in by the chair and wallowing helplessly in the remains of someone's ruined meal and broken dishes, I watched him go helplessly. I knew Buddy avoided confrontations, but I really could have used some assistance. The fellow I had hit regained his feet and started to scream at me. "Let's kill this bastard! Kill him!" he shouted hoarsely. Now, both of them were aiming at me.

I tried to get to my feet, but found the traction tough. I kept slipping on lettuce and chicken bones. There really wasn't any place for me to go anyway with tables behind me. The big guy recovered from his wild swing and got himself straightened out. He put two ham-like hands on my shoulder when, all of a sudden, he seemed to take off as though flying. I saw two large hands pushing him headfirst down to the ground. He plowed into the edge of the buffet. Behind him was my friend, Ray. Years spent working on horses and holding them up had left him with more muscles than Mr. America. His son, younger but almost as big, was there, too, shouting at my two opponents.

The big guy stared up at Ray. I could see in his face that he had never encountered someone like this. Ray sneered at him and turned towards the scraggly guy. "You want a little more, buddy?" he asked coldly.

The kid didn't. Neither did his companion. They scrambled out the door as though a barnyard full of savage geese were on their heels.

Ray looked at me and smiled. "You guys from Brooklyn get in such fucking trouble," he snorted, helping me up. His hands were so strong. They were like clasping solid iron. I gave the waitress some money and spoke to the owner. He shrugged off the damages, saying it was the fault of the two farm boys. We paid for dinner, but he wouldn't take anything else.

Outside, I told Buddy that I'd be better off in New York while he stayed in Saratoga with Julie. Then next day, after thanking Ray again, I drove back to the city. I spoke to Buddy probably twice a day for a month. We never talked about the brawl in the restaurant. Julie said she just wanted to wear something nice and was saddened her skimpy dress provoked such a reaction. We both forgave her, but we didn't go back to the restaurant again.

When the season ended, Buddy asked me to take Julie home.

Maybe he had had enough. Someone like Julie can be overwhelming after awhile. That coupled with the fact that Buddy has a short attention span and that she had served her purpose and kept him past the time in Saratoga and also annoyed the established waspy element.

The evening, before we left Saratoga, Julie prepared a little dinner of roast chicken and a bottle of red wine. She naturally served plenty of vodka. After dinner, we sat around and listened to records while Julie tried to sing some songs. Her voice was light and occasionally bumped into the tune. Her little canary kept chirping. She never mentioned Harry nor had brought up his name all the time we were in Saratoga. Her slave was just enamored with her beauty and, I guess, figured that, sooner or later, she'd decide he was the only faithful one. At the moment, Julie had forgotten all about him.

"I really like it here in Saratoga," she said. "It's just nice and quiet; it reminds me of back home when I was a kid."

That comment struck me after our earlier chats. Just Julie hadn't talked about her past, limiting her comments to her current situation. I sat up. She continued, "I've been working since I was six years old. My mother thought I was pretty, and had me in ads, doing print work, and all sorts of work."

"You like modeling?" Buddy asked her.

"Your modeling business is good," Julie said softly, "but it's very hard work, and there are a lot of unscrupulous people who are out there to take advantage of you. It's hard to know the good ones from the bad. I really don't like to think much about it." That was the end of the conversation.

In the morning, we packed up. Most of the horses were already gone. We put everything into the car. Her little canary was still chirping, and we headed back to the city. Julie was very quiet the whole way. She and Buddy had become very close. I was surprised he didn't take her home himself and wondered if that was why she didn't say anything. On the other hand, there always seemed to be a tinge of sadness about her. It clung to her as tightly as her blouse. Something in her eyes spoke of pain, the way an abused dog cringes even when a friendly person raises a hand. Buddy would have never hit or hurt her. That couldn't have been the problem. It was far deeper than that. All the way back to New York, I wondered what secret festered inside her.

After I found parking, she opened the door to her apartment house, and we went up three flights to her apartment. She lived on the top floor. She had the key and opened the lock. There was only one lock, but once I got inside, I noticed there were three locks on the door. Harry was staying here, Julie said causally, but was at work and wouldn't be back for a couple of hours.

I looked around, somewhat stunned by her decorating efforts.

Julie had placed wooden shutters on all the windows in the apartment. Closing them up eliminated all light in the apartment. She had security guard gates on all the windows with a huge lock locking them all in place on each window. She had no lights on. Instead, she lit candles as we walked about.

"Come on," she said, without a hint of embarrassment. "We'll put this stuff in the bedroom." The next room might have been as large as the living room. About twelve by fourteen feet, and it was jet black in there. I couldn't see anything until she began to light candles which she had strategically placed around the apartment in all sorts of containers, which she said, kept them safe. In case they broke, there wouldn't be a fire.

I looked up in the flickering light. Her ceiling was made of the bottom part of empty Coca-Cola cans. She had cut them in half, and then glued and pushed them into the regular ceiling so all I could see was the silver bottoms of the cans. They were so close together that I couldn't see the Coca-Cola logo or anything. When the light flickered off the bottom, it reflected around the room in such strange shadows.

I had never seen any such thing in my life.

She had a floor made out of red bricks scavenged from old buildings in the neighborhood that were being torn down. Someone had filed them down flat so there was no concrete or anything on them and layered them on the floor side by side with very little space between them. I don't know if there was anything stuck between them, like a concrete, but they were very tight and very close.

The floors were covered with large rugs. The rug in front looked like a bear skin without the head, just the feet, paws and with what looked like claws stretched out. In the other corner of the room, there was a skin that looked like a tiger. Julie told me it was just cotton and rayon. They found it in Greenwich Village, but she liked the texture so she bought it.

She also had a small dresser in the corner with nothing on top. There was a large wardrobe in the other corner made of a dark mahogany, which fit right in. Without lights, I couldn't tell where it was.

The best part was her bed. It was suspended from the ceiling with four chains in each corner. They were large industrial-type silver chains that took the hand-crafted bed, which was made of what looked like pine, and suspended it at least five feet, maybe six, off the ground and maybe two feet from the ceiling. She had a wooden ladder that hooked on the side of the bed so she could climb up to it. There was no other way to just jump into that bed, which hung way over her head. The bed featured a blue comforter, which was almost wooly, and a large white pillow at the head of the bed. Next to the head of the bed and hanging from one of the chains was a small whip-like crop which she used to give Harry a few whacks. It looked really hard and dangerous. I wouldn't have wanted to be hit with it. In the corner was a blanket; apparently that was Harry's bed.

She offered me a drink. I accepted. Her manner seemed innocent. Mine certainly was. She took another rug from the corner of the room and spread it out next to the bearskin rug. She sat on the bearskin rug and took a small table, which could double as a stepping stool, and put that between the two rugs. On that, she placed two glasses and her bottle of vodka. She sat down on the bearskin rug, and I sat on the other rug, which was very thick and comfortable even over the bricks.

"I'm very comfortable here," she said. "I designed the apartment myself. I know it's very dark. I really like the dark. I think the darkness is my friend. I've always felt like that. Since I was a little girl, I used to sit in the dark." We had our drink; I sipped mine. She gulped hers down and got another.

"You know, I'm wondering what's going to happen between Buddy and me," she continued. I relaxed. She just wanted some information. We don't talk about him, I told her. There's too much other stuff to take care of. She nodded. "We just made love and said we'd see each other, but I don't know what that means," she said. There was a mournful tone in her voice. She knew exactly what Buddy meant. She must have heard the same promise before. She just didn't want to accept it.

"Buddy's a really hard guy, and right now he's kind of lost. He doesn't know what he wants," I said.

She nodded. "I feel the same way."

She poured another drink and offered me the bottle. I declined. "I'm not much of a drinker, never have been."

"This is a special occasion," Julie insisted. I relented. It was like drinking gasoline for me. However, once the vodka got past my tongue and down into the stomach, it wasn't that bad.

She gulped another two fingers worth down.

"You drink too much," I told her.

"I have a lot to drown," Julie replied.

She put down her drink and stared at me for a moment, as if thinking about what to say or if she should say anything. Then, in a torrent of words, she told me what had happened to her. She held onto the vodka bottle as she spoke, as though it were a life raft.

Her mother forced her into modeling, although, originally, she liked it. Julie went over to her wardrobe and found some large scrapbooks. They were thick and clean, as though someone had been looking at them and made sure there was no dust on the covers

"You want to see my life?" she said. "Take a look."

The photos showed her at age five or six years old, lots of outfits, playing around, growing up to maybe twelve or thirteen years old. Another album was stuffed with magazine covers she had done. The last album featured mostly the work she had done around seventeen. That year, she was named Miss Seventeen, which was quite a big contest in America at the time. Being a cover girl was a big honor. From there she got all sorts of offers.

She said, "That's the part that changed my life. I better have another drink."

She was getting a little woozy. I had never seen her consume so much alcohol in such a short period of time. With the candles flickering in the room, swaying, I was getting a little lightheaded myself.

"I was all over the place with top photographers after me," Julie continued. She was sitting back on the flood, legs crossed, swaying slightly. "Most of them were guys I didn't have to worry about because they only cared about other guys. I was new in the game, and hardly knew about sex and things like that. My mother was with me all my life, close to me, guiding me and didn't let me have a childhood. She took me to this top-flight fellow. He was young with dark hair, slim, very attractive. He told my mother he needed a couple of hours to shoot me. Mom said fine and left me there."

Julie took a deep breath and another drink. Her eyes misted over; then, she stared at the ground. Her voice lowered. "He said that we need to concentrate. We need to meditate, get in the mood. He wanted all my emotions on this camera. He had me pick out costumes from a closet. Something purple, he said. The one in purple looked like pajamas. They were light in color, very silky. The pants were wide bottoms and very loose. It was a pretty outfit. The sleeves are long, covering my arms. The top was a little short because I was tall, but it was fine. I noticed that it was so sheer. I thought I'd leave my underpants on, which I did. I came out. He told me to sit in a large velvet chair, blood red. I sat there, and he began to shoot. I had my arms up, my arms down, my legs up on the chair. We continued for almost forty-five minutes."

She paused again. "I like you, Frank," she said. "You respect me. I really haven't told this to anyone." I believed her.

"He offered me a drink," Julie continued. "I didn't drink then, but he said I should have one. He poured me a drink—my first drink—of vodka. I drank it. It burned just terrible. He told me it was good for me, to take the glass, to hold the glass on my lips, to enjoy it, to make love to that glass. He had me take it with both hands, hold it close to my mouth. He went on and on, and I was getting tired. He kept putting a little more alcohol in the glass."

The words flowed faster than vodka from the bottle, broken once or twice by a sob.

"He spread a large white mat on the floor in the corner where he was shooting the pictures. He had me lie on the ground, on my back, with my head up, then sideways. He put the vodka bottle near me, telling me to sip, to feel light headed so he could see it working in my eyes. He kept shooting. He had his legs spread over me and shot down at my face. He told me to move my lips, to lick my lips. He had me move my hand to my face, my breasts."

She stopped and finished her glass before pouring another one.

"This is enough. All I can say is he seduced me. He wanted my lips to be wet. He got down against me, and put saliva on my lips and moved my tongue. His hands were on my breasts. I can't go on." More vodka vanished.

"We were there four hours. He did things to me I couldn't tell you. I was ruined. He took those pictures. They were erotic pictures. My mother came back later. I was in the dressing room cleaning up. I couldn't tell her what happened, but when I came out, she could see something was wrong. He told her I was just exhausted from the long shoot. My mother believed him. She took me home. After that I never did another shoot ever again. I ran away. I hid in my dark room. I just completely collapsed and disappeared for awhile. I met a guy in the school bathroom and we traveled for awhile. I came back to New York. I started on my vodka."

She slurred her words now and came close to me. "I don't know what happened to me, but I've been ruined. I just can't get back. I don't know what is going to happen. I don't know." She put her head close to my shoulder and her arm around my neck. Her head fell down on my leg and she was just babbling incoherently and just seemed to go sound asleep. I put her head on the rug, blew out a few of the candles, and looked at her lying there, so beautiful, but in so much pain. I walked out the door, and noticed there were three locks on the door and large bar that went across it. She tried to keep out her demons, but they had no trouble getting in. I left just two of the candles on.

I left the building and found myself downstairs in the sunlight. It was already late afternoon. The sun was going down. I jumped in the car and drove away. Buddy never asked about her or spoke about her. He didn't even know where she lived. He never took her home, and I never went back. I have thought about her often, but I never saw Just Julie again.

Chapter XXX

The Frankel's, Bill and Bobby

The weather was still warm, but you could feel the change in the air. We were back at our barn and people were coming and going.

"It feels like we never left. It's good to get back."

"You said it, but you better check with Sarah. I have a few horses to run for her and she told me she wants to start claiming some."

"Bud, where do you think we can put them? I've got guys waiting to claim and get going and I just tell them the time is not right."

"We can send some to the farm and ship in for the race. It will work out."

"Buddy, telephone for you," cried Joe Porter.

"Who answered the phone?" Buddy asked.

"The new boy, he don't know." Joe answered in a very quiet voice.

"Frank, get rid of whoever it is and tell the kid not to go into the office or ever answer any phone calls."

"Hello, Jacobson Barn, may I help you?"

It was Bill Frankel, "Hi Mr. Frankel, it's Frank. Buddy is on the track."

"Hello Frank, just wanted to let you know I'm on my way out to the track, ask Buddy to wait for me I should be there in about an hour."

"Sure thing, see you then." I went to find Buddy and told him the message.

"Funny he never comes out on weekdays, wonder what's up?" he said. He went about his work and l had things to do.

It was about 9:30 when Bill Frankel arrived, his driver was carrying a shopping bag that looked like it came from the local deli.

"Hi Frank," he called out and extended his hand. He was always a gentleman and very pleasant. He never raised his voice and was quick to smile and laugh. "Have your breakfast yet?" he said.

"Even if we did I know what you brought would be hard to resist," I laughed.

We went into the office and the driver handed me the shopping bag, as he turned and said he would be in the car. I called out to Buddy and he came to the office. They exchanged warm greetings and both looked genuinely happy to see each other. It was clear that Buddy admired this man and had a very special feeling for him. They were together a long time and had great success.

I began to unpack the food: bagels, lox, cream cheese, frankfurters, orange juice, and chopped liver. It was all there.

"Buddy, let's take a walk." Bill said as he rose from the chair.

Buddy looked surprised and nodded as he exited the office. I opened the orange juice and had my breakfast. It was about fifteen or twenty minutes later when they returned.

"Well, it looks like someone enjoyed the breakfast," Bill said as he sat down.

"Don't worry I saved plenty for both of you," and I handed Buddy a glass of juice.

"You know I'm going to miss these meals with you guys, but when you come to the coast we will do it, unless of course if Buddy decides to join me and leave this rat race."

Buddy looked up and smiled. I was in shock. I even stopped eating, "Look at Frank, he can't finish his bagel. Are you okay?"

"Okay, no I don't think so," I gulped.

"Well Buddy has a week or so to make up his mind. I hope you two want to come, as for now I have to get to the market and try to earn enough money to pay this month's bill, so I'll be in touch." Bill rose quickly and Buddy followed him out. I waved good bye and thanked him for the meal.

I waited for Buddy to return, and he came in and sat behind the desk. "Close the door, Frank." I did and returned to my seat.

"That guy is closer to me than any father. He gave me my chance and always believed in me. I just never thought he would leave."

"What's it all about?" I asked.

"He is retiring and wants to move to California and race out there. He asked me to go and train for him, he has ten horses now but would get five or six more. I could still train for other clients. He would help us relocate and he wants to be near Las Vegas, he said he loves the casino action."

"Would you go?"

"For him I might, but we have too much going on here. The farm, Bill and Sarah, I'm President of the HBPA, my family is here, and I love New York. I just can't do it."

"What a shock."

"You know he is not a well guy and getting on in years, if something should happen I would have to start over and I hate California more than Saratoga." We both smiled at an inside joke.

"Wow, what now?"

"Well he asked me to recommend someone if I don't go, said he would take whoever I think can do the job and would ask me for help if necessary."

"Bud, California might not be too bad with fifteen horses a guy could make a living."

"Not you, Frank."

"I sure would like to try."

"I told you just 10 percent or less of all trainers make a good living. You have a family. You like to go home and see them. You would be alone and starting is very hard. Also I need you here, you know you will be with me as long as you want."

"I know you are right, but being in the barn and close to the horses you want to do it all. I love being with you, and I know I have a long way to go, but I also know there are plenty of guys who hire a good second man and spend the time training the owners and their girlfriends." He laughed and said he would let me do more around here.

"Well, who are you going to recommend?" I asked.

"Off the top of my head maybe, Bobby Frankel."

"The kid?"

"He worked with us and you told me he is a nice clean cut kid. You even asked me to help him get a stall in Florida when he had one horse. Don't you think he can do it?"

"Yeah, I guess he can, but I wanted it to be me."

"Frank, we can help him. He has no wife or kids. He can live in the tack room and he is not a gambler or a doper, or so you told me. I'll think about it and we will talk to him soon and see if he wants the job."

I don't know just why Buddy wanted to send Bobby, they were not close, Buddy never spent much time with him and never let him do anything special with any of the horses in the barn, but he was the first name he could think of. I liked Bobby, but I sure wanted a chance and with a great owner like Bill Frankel it would be a dream come true, but I could see it was not going to happen.

"I better call Sarah and see if we can claim some soon so we can replace the horses that will be going to California."

"Don't panic Frank, we have lots of time, but do keep in touch with her."

The next day Buddy told me he decided to send Bobby Frankel and asked him to come by the barn. "Bill Frankel is going to California and he wants me to get a trainer for his horses. I am going to tell him I think you are the guy for the job."

Bobby was speechless, he was quiet and then scratched his head in disbelief, began to laugh, and then almost cry.

"Is this a joke?" he shouted. "Are you kidding?"

"No and I guess you want the job."

"Yes, sure. What do I have to do?"

"Well you will go out soon and get set up. Hire a good crew and the most important thing is to buy the best feed and hay. Don't look for bargains. The people out there are cheap. You buy the best and treat your horses well. I know you have worked hard here, and I hope you will use what you learned to do good. I will be in touch with you if you need any help. Don't trust the other trainers, if you do good they will not be winning as many races. Run the horses where they can win, not over their heads. The better races will come. You will make a reputation with winners. Run every horse like your job depends on it and never give a horse a race. I know you will have success. Any questions?" I was impressed with the speech, Buddy summed up his creed in a few sentences.

"Buddy, I don't know what to say but thank you. I won't let you down."

"That's good because I like Bill Frankel, and I only want the best for him."

Bobby left the barn and Buddy turned to me. "I think we did the right thing, I know you could handle the job but it's not for you. Let's give him all the help we can."

"Okay Bud, we will."

I guess Buddy knew what he was doing. Bobby went on to become a Hall of Fame trainer and although he had great success he remained a nice guy, and never got too full of himself. I got over the feeling of loss when he came to me the following week and asked me to go along with him. "You can do what you do for Buddy. Be my assistant and help me run things. I know you always put in a good word for me with Buddy, and we can have a ball."

I thanked him but explained that I had a family and could not leave everything in New York, and I liked my job with Buddy. "But don't think I wouldn't have liked to be offered the job, good luck and you know I will always be here to help if I can."

"Thanks Frank, I didn't think you would go so I am going to ask Al Schweitzer to go with me. He is a good exercise rider and a good horseman, and I am sure he would love to go."

"Bob you are starting on the right foot. Al is one of the best and he has always been a great help to John Campo. You will be lucky to get him."

Sarah Hall and William Levin

Chapter XXXI

Sarah Adds to Her Stable

I called Sarah and made a date to see her at the track for lunch. We would have to fill the empty stalls. "Nice to see you again," she smiled and took a seat.

"You look beautiful Sarah. I'm glad Saratoga is over and we can get some winners here. How's Bill?"

"Everything is great and I want to build up my stable, should we buy or claim?"

"Well, we like to claim, its fast and we can do it everyday if there are good horses. But we could buy when the time is right."

"How do we do it?" she asked.

"Buddy will check the paper and call you with the name of the horse, and if you like it, we will claim it that day. All we need is the money in the account at the track."

"How much?"

"We could put it in as we need it or put some in and draw against it, just like a bank."

"I'll speak to Bill and ask him to make a good deposit so we can start this week. You better get busy and look for some good ones."

"Sounds good, now let's have lunch and pick some winners."

We spent a good day and had a few winners, but I was thinking of what kind of a check Bill was going to put in the office. I told Buddy and he was happy and began to study the form in search of some new horses. I know he missed Bill Frankel, but now it was down to business.

It was three days later when I received a call from Sarah, "Frank I'll be out today with the check. Meet me and tell Buddy I want a horse."

I met her and she handed me a check for $75,000, certified of course. "Can't take a chance he may change his mind," she laughed.

I deposited it at the track and the next day we claimed a horse.

Things were in the fast lane, watching the races, trying to pick the right horses, running every day in lots of races, and lots of winners.

"This is the way it should be," I nudged Buddy as we watched some horses go by in the early morning sunlight. But he seemed distant and out of sorts.

"Anything wrong? You feel okay?" I asked.

He stiffened and said, "I just need a change. I think I'll take a few days off."

This was not possible, not the Buddy I knew."Are you sick? This is the best of everything and you want to take off? Why?"

"I'm going to Maine or Vermont. I'll call you every day and tell you what to do. I'll sign some claim slips, and you can fill them out if we see something we like."

"Bud what will I tell Sarah and Bill?"

"They won't even know I'm gone. I'll only be gone a few days."

At ten a.m. he left me in the office and handed me five claim slips he had signed. I was in shock. I could not replace Buddy, and I didn't want to.

Sarah called and picked a horse to claim. It was trained by Frank Martin, who was a Cuban American, known for his hot temper and fine horsemanship. Buddy and he never claimed from each other. They were not close friends, but I knew Buddy had a great respect for Frank's ability with a horse, so I tried to talk her out of the claim.

"Well If Buddy doesn't want the horse tell him to call me because I have a friend who told me this is a good horse and will win today."

I was in a spot. I would never claim the horse without Buddy and I couldn't get in touch with him. I called Sarah and told her a story about a vet telling me the horse was sore and might have a broken bone.

That afternoon the horse won and I was in trouble. When Buddy called that night I told him the story, and he said he would call her and he would be back the next day.

"Don't worry, I'll take care of it," he said.

"Boy don't do that to me again. I can't take the pressure."

"I guess I should tell you I went to look at some land, and I know you are not crazy about the guys I went with."

"Who?"

"Just Dennis and some guys from Queens who I met. A bunch of Irish guys and we hang out in a pub one of the guys owns."

"So why wouldn't I like them, except for Dennis who is bad news?"

"Well, they drink and such."

"Look Bud don't make me out to be a saint, I have nothing against drinking, my family drinks and we had restaurants that sold lots of wine and beer. I drink every so often so that's not it. If it's something else then I draw the line. No drugs!"

"No, I guess they smoke some stuff and that's it."

"Buddy, I'm not your mother or keeper. Do what you want, but you have the world in your hands, and I know this is not what you want. Many of those people are users and losers they can only hurt you and that's all I'm going to say."

"Well you know I like to ski and they said if I would buy a ski lodge they would run trips from the pub to the lodge every week. They have loads of girls coming into the pub. Lots of airline people and it could be great. Would you like to be in?"

"Bud, I've got all to do to keep my head on around here. Thanks, but no thanks."

"Okay, let's see if we can get a good horse for Sarah. I spoke to her and she understands I don't claim from Poncho Martin. You have a hard time trying to improve on a guy like him."

Two days later we ran a winner in a $10,000 race and the horse was claimed, by Frank Martin. Sarah was furious, "That bastard took my horse and you said he was a friend."

"I never said he was a friend just that I never claimed his horses or he mine."

"Well that's changed now, claim anything he runs tomorrow."

"Look, let's be sensible. We can wait until he runs a good one."

"Buddy, you work for me and up to now I did everything you said. Now I'm telling you claim any horse he runs until I tell you to stop."

Thus began the war. We took his horse and he took ours every day. His owner was Sigmund Summer, a very wealthy builder and a guy who loved the races, he would come out almost every day. The war went on for about three weeks then Buddy claimed a horse called Lucky Richard for $20,000. Martin said Buddy was a fool and the horse was not worth the money. The meet ended at Belmont and Buddy sent the horse to race in a small stake at Liberty Bell racetrack. The horse won by five or six lengths and broke the track record.

The next day Lenny Goodman, the jockey agent came by the barn. "Buddy, Frank Martin and I were talking and he would like it if things went back to normal and stop all this claiming."

"Fine by me, but I didn't start it," Buddy said coldly.

"Well I think Frank was told your owner wanted to claim his horse and he got to her first."

Buddy and I stared at each other. "So that's what started all this? You tell Frank the next move is up to him. Right now I don't see any of his horses I'm interested in." Lenny left and the war was over.

Buddy was not coming to the barn every day. He would leave early and take one or two days off. This was not the Buddy I knew.

I did what had to be done at the barn and would be at the track in the afternoon with Sarah and sometimes with Bill. Buddy had the horses in good shape and we continued to win.

"I want to speak to Buddy about the winter, where is he going to send the horses?" Bill Levin asked.

"I think he is going to Maryland, the racing is not as hard as Florida, and I know he would like to rest some of the stock on the farm in Old Westbury." I answered without knowing what his plans were.

"Well you tell him I'm coming out to the barn Saturday and expect to see him there."

When Buddy called that evening I told him, and he said he would see me in the morning at the barn.

I was at home that evening when I received a phone call from one of the workers at the farm, there had been an accident and Joe Martin was hit by a car and taken to the hospital. I drove to the farm and found Joe's wife crying and in shock. Joe had let a van out of the farm area and was on the road trying to slow traffic when a car approached and the driver did not see him. He was hit at full speed and was killed on the spot.

It was a great loss, Joe was a fine man and loved the horses.

Buddy returned and I gave him the news. He was visibly shaken and had a deep affection for Joe.

"Frank, tell his wife that we will pay the expenses for the funeral and not to worry about staying on at the farm. Also I'm very sorry for her loss. You do it. I'm not good at that, then we better think about getting someone to take his place."

"Okay, but don't forget Bill is coming this Saturday."

"I'll be here and I just bought a ski lodge in Stowe, Vermont—the Norway Ski Lodge. You have to see it, it's swell."

"I think we should just keep that quiet for now Buddy, your owners might wonder if you are skiing when you should be at the barn everyday taking care of their horses."

"We have a great outfit, they don't have to worry."

"Buddy, people want you, not the second team. Bill is no fool. He even wants to get more horses, a good one he said."

"That's fine, I'll look for one and we will go to Maryland for the winter, and I don't think they will come down too often with the cold weather. You and Joe can handle everything and I'll call everyday.

"But Bud…"

"Wait, I'll be there and get us set up, but I'll just sneak away for a day or so."

I didn't like the way it sounded but just nodded and shook my head.

Chapter XXXII
Dead Man's Sale

We were making plans for the winter when one of the agents dropped off a sales book and spoke about the dispersal sale of the Harry Guggenheim's horses. Mr. Guggenheim was a wealthy horse owner who had many great horses and some of the finest blood stock in racing.

"Now that's the kind of sale I would like to go to," Buddy enthusiastically said. "No funny stuff in a dead man's sale. The bank handles all the money so horses go for fair prices, no kick backs, and no reason to run up the bids. We must get Bill and Sarah to go. You never know what we can get at a fair price."

"I think we should tell Sarah first, then Bill."

"You could be right, do it soon." with that he left the barn and I began to look through the sales book. It was obvious the bloodlines of the stock for sale were the best I had seen. I called Sarah and made a date to meet her for lunch at the track that afternoon. She was more interested in betting the races than talking about the sale.

"Look Sarah so far you have had great fun and have a nice stable, but this is the big time. You like to gamble, well this could be the biggest gamble you have ever made. This man had so many great horses and now you have a chance to buy into his knowledge and experience. There is no way we could ever get close to this blood."

"Sounds nice Frank, but I'm happy the way things are."

"Sarah did you ever think about the Kentucky Derby, and big races like that, well that's the kind of chance you could have."

"What dose Buddy say?"

"Sarah this is his idea, I'm just telling you so you can be ready when he asks."

"Okay, I'll think about it and speak to Bill."

"Great."

We left it at that, and the rest of the day I kept thinking how happy Buddy would be.

The next day in the barn I arrived very early with my big news.

"I think I sold her on the sale. She is going to talk to Bill, and she wants to speak to you, but it looks good."

"Did you check on the new feed?"

"I think it arrived yesterday." I softly replied.

"You know I changed the formula a little and I want everyone to watch their horses for any changes. Also, we may cut back a half measure on each horse as the new pellet is a little richer."

"Bud, aren't you excited about Sarah and the sale?"

"Why, I expected them to agree. I just wanted you to give them the message. My recommendation is enough for them. I don't expect them to question my judgment." He turned and walk out of the office.

I realized he wanted help. He asked me to call Sarah, but he did not want to acknowledge that I was of any help with shaping their decision. I accepted that he was the boss, but once again, I then saw another side of my Buddy.

Bill agreed and on November 17 we went to Belmont for the sale. Many of the big outfits were absent and lots of the "little guys" were there looking for a bargain. I went with Buddy as he looked over the horses. We had looked over the pedigrees and had come up with twelve horses that we liked. During the course of the sale we bought five yearlings. The most expensive was a beautiful colt of good size and body structure, he was a half brother to Never Bend, a great race horse. The problem was he had a very large knee that appeared to have been hurt.

When we looked at him Buddy examined his leg and I asked him if the knee was a deal breaker. "Frank I've had lots of claiming horses worse than he is, but he is young and you don't know if he will stand the training. This could go at any time, but we will never get a chance to get this blood. I have to take a chance." So he did, starting in the low twenties going up to the fifties and getting him for $52,000.

The under bidder was a very nice trainer named Lefty Nickerson. He came over to congratulate Buddy on the buy. "I sure liked him, but the knee stopped my owner. I wanted to go a little higher but he said stop. I think you got a good one, good luck Buddy."

I always liked Lefty, he was a real gentlemen and a very good horsemen and about this horse he was right on the money. Bill and Sarah were very happy and none of us knew at the time that every one of these horses would be a winner and the one with the knee was Bold Reason, who was a winner of seven races in a row after having run third in the Derby, and the Belmont, then won the Travers, the Hollywood Derby, the American Derby, the Lexington Handicap, and two allowance races before he was syndicated for about four million dollars, which at that time was the fourth highest syndicate price. The sorrow of it was Buddy didn't get to train him. But I'm getting ahead of the story.

After getting the horses, they were sent to a farm in Kentucky to be broken and trained for their racing careers. We relied on an old friend, Harold Snowden who was part owner of Stallion Station, a fine breeding farm in Lexington, Kentucky. Harold was a real horsemen, he lived and breathed horses. His sons, Hal Junior, Steve, and Bill were chips off the old block.

Many Kentucky breeders resented New Yorker's going into the breeding business, but Harold welcomed the competition. "Hell Frankie, how you all going to get bluegrass to grow up in New York? When those babies eat up on the bluegrass of Kentucky they get bigger and stronger than any others. Hell just look around." I did and what I saw was him at 6' 3", and Bubba at 6' 4" and Steve the same. Harold was right, they sure grew them big.

Harold liked Buddy and helped him many times. I grew to know him and admired him as a horseman and a man. He and his family were some of the finest people in the business.

During their lifetime Harold and his son, Bubba, bought and sold one of the greatest race horses in the game, John Henry, who earned over eleven million dollars racing. That is another story for another time but very interesting indeed.

Chapter XXXIII

Winter Racing Bowie, MD

Now the sales were over and we were on our way to winter racing in Bowie, Maryland. It was very cold in November as we set up in Maryland. Buddy was hard at work in the office and all the horses were getting used to the new barn.

"Buddy the vet is here, he would like to see you."

"Send him in."

The vet was a big man about 5' 10" and 250 pounds. He was dressed in a heavy winter jacket and had a funny little hat like a ski cap. His face was covered with a heavy dark beard. As we shook hands I thought he looked like Paul Bunyan.

"Nice to meet you, Buddy. I wanted to speak to you about the jug you ordered for the horses after the races. I've been using some new blood boosters and calcium things that I think would work for you."

Buddy just stared, this was Dr. Fox, he had a good reputation, Buddy had never used him but was told he was the best here.

"Nice of you to stop by, good bye."

"Well what do you think?" the confused vet asked.

"It was nice of you to stop by. I'll see you sometime... good bye."

The vet was speechless, silence filled the small office as Buddy sat behind the desk and this bear of a man just turned and left.

"What was that all about?" I asked.

"I will never use someone who questions my orders. If he does that now he may one day try something without telling me. I want people who understand they are to do what I say. If

I'm wrong it's my fault, when they have their own horses they can do what they like, here I'm responsible, so I make the call. Get another vet and be sure he follows orders."

The weather turned very cold and the training was hard on the horses and the men. We had a new rider, Tony Logursio. He had been injured and was returning to racing. I liked him very much. He and his agent would come by in the mornings with coffee and donuts and pitch in with the work, then he would ride some of the horses in their exercise period.

While the horses were on the track, Buddy would sit in the car with the heater on and watch the horses. One morning we arrived early and began to chop the ice off the water buckets in the horse's stalls. The wind was howling, the tractors had been on the track all night long plowing it in order to keep it from freezing.

Buddy called out, "Frank number five and twelve twice around."

That meant we were to send those two horses to the track and he would observe them from the car. Joe Porter had both horses ready to go. Tony was riding one and our barn rider, Frankie Costa, was on the other.

They completed the work and returned to the barn. Tony had his saliva frozen to his face from the cold. Frankie rode the horse into the barn and fell off on to the ground. He lay there in a fetal position groaning about being frozen. Buddy entered the barn at that moment and walked over to him and very calmly said, "You belong in Hollywood, not here. You're fired. Frank pay him off," and he walked to the office.

"Bud, you sure you want to fire him?"

He just looked up from the desk, then looked down again at the paper he was reading. He never answered.

I paid Frankie, and he was happy to go.

The next day Buddy told me he was leaving for his ski lodge, "We expect a big season. The guys from Queens have lots of girls coming up and they will have buses every weekend. I'd love for you to come, but I need you here."

"You know how I feel about ski trips, and I'm not sure I like all these new friends, beside being here with the horses and the guys is what I love."

"We will speak every day. You have the checkbook if you need anything, buy it."

He was gone. I missed him but loved being in on my own, so to speak. It was one of the coldest winters ever, but we survived and had lots of fun. Buddy would call and give orders, and when the weather was okay we would follow them but other times we would gallop in the barn, it was much warmer and better for the men and the horses. We still won our share of races. The meet was coming to an end, the weather was getting better and Bill and Sarah were coming to watch their horses. Buddy was coming back to help get the horses ready for the trip home.

We were in the Holiday Inn and Buddy was getting things in order when Bill called, "Frank please come to my room."

"Sure Bill, be right there."

Bill had just come out of the shower and was getting dressed.

"What do you know about our stalls in New York?" he asked.

"Buddy said he was waiting for the list to come out but he was sure there were no changes. Why?"

"I just received a call from that guy Gonzales in the racing secretary's office. He said we should get back to New York because we have no stalls. I was speechless."

"Can't be, why?" I gulped.

"Buddy will not get his stalls because he has to serve the thirty day suspension the track imposed over the Lefrak case."

"I don't believe it. That penalty was last year, and they never set a date, anyway they always let the horses in and then the trainer puts his assistant trainer on the papers till his suspension is over. I know Buddy never got the dates from the NYRA. When I asked him he said they would give him the information when we got back to New York."

"Well, for your information, the date starts on opening day and they won't let him back in. I want to know if you knew?"

"Look Bill, I didn't know any of this, and I'm sure Buddy did not know. Call him down and let's get this taken care of. I never heard of this kind of thing before."

"Call him," he said as he finished dressing.

"Buddy come to Bill's room, we need you."

"He will be right down." I sighed.

"Hi, what's up?" Buddy smilingly said.

Bill began to tell him the story. Buddy said it must be a mistake.

"I've been in the same barn for over twenty years, this suspension is bullshit. Everyone knows that, and I bring in more revenue to the state than any three trainers combined. I'll go back and take care of this."

"Buddy if you have trouble tell me, I will try to help, but if you lie it will only make it worse."

"Honest Bill, I don't know anything about this."

"Buddy, I put a lot of money into this game, and I depend on you. Are you sure you don't know anything about this?"

"Bill, I would not leave you hanging, trust me."

"Okay Buddy, I'm going back today and find out what's going on, and I want Frank to come with me."

"Sure, I'll be in New York as soon as I make arrangements to ship the horses."

I went back to the room and Buddy was very upset.

"They want to ruin me. I knew they would try after the strike but this is something I never thought they would do. They act like the good guys, but this is below the belt. Guys dope horses, pull horses, bribe people, and they get a slap on the wrist. I never received a notice about the date of the suspension. I could have served it any time. I never doped horses, or pulled horses, no penalties in twenty years and now this action."

"Buddy maybe it's a mistake? I'll go with Bill and try to get the true story."

"You do that Frank, but watch out these guys are lying and are out for my blood."

Bill left that night, and I left in the morning. We arranged to meet at noon at the track in the secretary's office. Bill spoke to Gonzales who said he made the call on his own, the association claimed they mailed Buddy a notice of the situation but he never responded.

"You know Bill, I'm not sure the paper was mailed," he confided.

Tommy Trotter came out and invited us into his office.

"Bill, we welcome you to racing in New York, but you have no stalls as of now."

"What do I do with the horses, and why did you take away the stalls?"

"We didn't take away the stalls, we just were unable to issue stalls to Jacobson because of his suspension. You can race at another track in another state, there is no bar on you or your horses. Or you might choose another trainer who has extra stall space."

"Will Buddy be coming back?"

"I can't say, but right now we have not decided if he will be given any stall space when his suspension is over."

"Look Tommy, I put a lot of money into the business and I like racing. I'm a New Yorker, and I want to race here. I don't know many trainers, but if Buddy is not coming back I will try to get someone."

Since I was close to John Campo, I suggested him.

"He's a fine trainer, but he has many horses now and I don't think he could handle your bunch, but a very good trainer and a fine gentlemen is Angel Penna. I know he has room in his barn, and he is well liked, and an excellent horseman. I would recommend him."

Bill asked me if I knew him.

"Only by reputation. He trains very good horses and does a good job."

"Tommy, I'll meet him and let you know."

We walked out and Bill asked what I thought of the situation.

"You know I love Buddy, and if he would go to another track I will go with him, but you need some place to put the horses now. Let me speak to him and see what he says."

"I'm not happy about him not telling us about this situation, if he knew I might have been able to help him. I don't like lying and if he did that I won't stand by him. You speak to him Frank, and let me know in the morning."

I said good bye and hurried to the apartment to meet Buddy. I told him what happened, and he was very quiet for a few minutes, pacing the floor in the apartment.

"I'll appeal. They can't do this to me. Call Win Klein and tell him to meet me in the morning some place in Queens."

"What shall I tell Bill?"

"You stay with him and let me know what he is doing."

I made the calls, Win said he would meet Buddy in the morning in a diner near the track. Bill told me to contact Penna and arrange a meeting.

Bill arrived at the Belmont backstretch at 9 a.m. for our meeting with Angel Penna. This was my first meeting with Mr. Penna and I was very impressed with his appearance. He had a strong handshake and a very handsome face. His hair was jet black and combed back in the European fashion. He wore a sport coat over a light blue shirt and a silk scarf around his neck. His tan slacks were well pressed and his shoe boots were polished. His dark eyes seemed to jump in his tanned face as he smiled and greeted us. He was from Argentina, he spoke with a slight accent and the meeting went well.

Bill took me aside and asked me what I thought. I told him the barn was in great shape and all the horses were well taken care of. This was a top operation. Bill asked me if I thought I could train the horses, "Thanks Bill, but at this stage of the game I couldn't do that to Buddy. Also I know they would not give me stalls and we need better than me right now."

We returned and spoke to Penna.

"Angel, I know your reputation, and I have a great respect for Frank Pagano. Would you have any objection to his being in the barn with the horses?"

"I know Frank was the assistant to Buddy. I will make him my assistant trainer if he would like."

"Thank you, Mr. Penna," I replied in shock. "I would like very much to work for you. I need to learn, and I know this would be a good place to do that, but I would like you to know if Buddy comes back and asks me, I will go with him."

"Good, so we will make the deal," he said and extended his hand.

This was one of the best years of my life, working for a wonderful man who was a genius with horses and a person of the highest principals. The stories of Mr. Penna would fill another book for those who would like to know about a life well lived.

I returned to Buddy and told him of the developments. "Good, I know Penna. He is a good guy, better than a lot of others. He will buy. He is not in the claiming game and when I win my case and get back I'm sure Bill will come back."

"I told them I would go with you when you were ready."

"Well, Win will try to get me back, but he says that it will take some time, and if I want to sue he will get me a lawyer who will be good at that."

"It's better you stay with the horses so I can know what's going on."

Buddy was not able to get back to the track before the suspension was over. We were in touch everyday and he kept some horses on the farm.

"I entered a horse to run and I'll be back at the track," he said.

The horse was scratched by the racing secretary.

Buddy called and was told the horse did not have a public workout at the track. Buddy said that was not a rule, the secretary told him a new rule had been passed that day and that horses training at a farm could not enter the track to work out and could not run if they did not have a workout at the track. The unofficial name of the rule was the Jacobson Rule.

I called Liberty Bell racetrack and spoke to the general manager, George Baker. He told me he would give Buddy thirty stalls to race there, and he could ship in to New York if he wanted to. Although I was working for Penna, I told Buddy I would go with him to Liberty Bell, he refused.

"I'm not going to any second-rate track. I'm a New Yorker and I belong here. I know I bucked the system but I've got rights and I'm going to win my court case. Why don't you quit and come with me?"

"Buddy what are you going to do if you don't train horses? We both know you will have enough trouble taking care of yourself. I've got a family and have to work, and I do love the track. Let's go to Liberty Bell. I know I can get Bill to give us the claiming horses. Mr. Penna doesn't want them. He trains good horses and wants to run in the big races, which is fine but Bill likes lots of action. What do you say?"

"No Frank, I want to try other stuff, the ski lodge, another model agency and I'm buying a building in the city and rent to models and stews, only women. It will be the hottest place in the city and guys will be fighting to get in. You can come and I'll make you a partner."

"Thanks Bud, I'll stay at the track, but we will be in touch."

So we went our separate ways, but stayed in touch.

Bill had success with Penna and he purchased a French horse called Semilent for $100,000. The horse won the Massachusetts Handicap and later hurt himself and was going to go to stud.

By this time I was working for Mr. Penna, who I admired a great deal and felt lucky to learn at his side, but also had more responsibility and pay with Bill.

"What do you think we should do about making this horse a stud?" he asked.

I was not sure. I told him to wait till I could get more information about the breeding business from a commercial basis. He agreed. It was at this time while going to the farm to see Buddy who was having weekend parties with lots of his new friends from the city and his new model agency, My Fair Lady that Buddy asked me to try and find a buyer for the farm.

"I'm doing so much and I borrowed some money from guys in Queens I just need to sell the farm."

"Bud, I'll try, but who are the people in Queens and how much do you owe?"

"Some guy named Brown, he owns a bar and he has helped me with the Ski lodge. He runs buses from his place to the Lodge and fills them with girls. Dennis introduced me and he has lots of guys around who have money. I don't think you would like them."

"Why not."

"I'm not sure but I think they are into some kind of drugs."

"Buddy, I told you before, I'm no saint, but you and I both don't like that stuff, you should never take any money from these people, they are the lowest next to guys who molest kids."

"That's why I didn't tell you, but I was desperate. The Ski lodge is great but it's seasonal and I need money to keep doing things."

"I don't know who to ask about the farm," I said.

"What about Bill? I heard his horse is a stake winner and with the New York program you could breed right here, also the land is very valuable."

"That might be an idea, he spent a lot of money for the horse and maybe he could get some back this way."

"Sure and I would help you get people to breed to the horse."

"I'll try."

"I know you can do it." The rest of the day we worked and I met some of the new girls from Buddy's agency. One special one was Mel Harris. She was eighteen years old, tall, slim with dark hair and a very attractive, but a different face. It was handsome with high cheek bones and a strong chin, she was charming and lively. Buddy had the group playing football and she was a very aggressive player. I remarked about her to Buddy.

"She is very smart and not shy I think she will do well in the business, I like her cause she's not my type and I won't have to worry about getting involved with her, just business and she will bring in other girls. Want a date?"

"Thanks, I think she is special but too young and tall for me and I've got lots of things to do."

I don't think Buddy or I would have thought how important she would become in the future to Buddy's relationship with other girls.

I spoke to Bill and suggested the purchase of the farm. He was very interested as he liked the location in Old Westbury only fifteen minutes from the Belmont race track. We had a meeting at his office and after discussion with his accountant and lawyer he decided to speak to Buddy about the purchase.

"Have him meet me at the farm on Saturday, about noon time and I'll get lunch." Buddy screamed into the phone.

"Frank this is great, You know I'll take care of you."

"Buddy I'm not doing this for that, I think it's good for him and I want you to pay those guys you owe and do well."

"I know Frank and I appreciate it you know anytime you want you can come with me."

"Thanks Bud, I won't forget."

We met and Buddy had a great lunch ready in his office at the farm.

"Buddy let's talk terms, how about a price for part check and lots of cash?"

"That sounds great, but can we talk alone?"

I was shocked Bill wanted me to stay and the guy I was pushing for wanted to talk alone.

"I'll check the stock," I said as I rose and headed for the door.

"Just a few minutes," Buddy said softly.

It was about ten minutes later when Buddy came down to the barn and spoke to me.

"It's all set, I'm having my lawyer get in touch with Bill's lawyer and draw up the papers. They have to do some investigation for debts and that stuff but Bill will give me some cash next week as a deposit, that will sure help, I'll see you then." He turned and drove off saying something about an appointment in the city.

"Well that was quick, he sure was in a hurry. Let's have a look around."

Bill smiled and he came into the barn.

It was about three weeks later we met again at the farm. Bill, Buddy and I.

"The deal was signed yesterday at the office, but today he gets the cash. Get that bag out of the trunk, will you Frank?" Bill said as he stepped out of his car.

I opened the trunk and found a brown paper bag that was quite heavy "This it Boss?" I asked.

"Yep, bring it up to the office and let's get a drink."

I put the bag down on the desk and Bill had a Tab I had a Coke.

"Think you are going to like running this place?" he asked.

"Sure, when I'm not at the Barn or the races."

"Don't worry you can get all the help you need."

"I just can't understand Buddy being so secretive about the deal."

Bill looked at me and said, "Sit down and let me tell you something, You will be with me for a long time, I have great trust in you and I know you know the business. Now I'll tell you what you have to learn, First you are a smart guy but you need to have a "Yiddisher Cup". That means a Jewish Head. You must control your emotions, when it comes to business, love or relationships. Everyone has some one in their life for whom they will be a sucker or a fool. That person can never do wrong in your eyes and you will make excuses for whatever they do to you or others. For you that's Buddy. Second when someone does something you don't like or is not fair you must not lose your temper but take action when it is in your favor and curb you Latin temper. The third thing is to read The Prince a very small book it is by Machiavelli. You told me Buddy went to take a course at Dale Carnegie and lives his life by it, you live yours by my principals, or at least try."

"Mr. Levin, Buddy Jacobson is here." one of the farm workers called.

Buddy said Hi and met with Bill they were together for about half an hour then Buddy came down. He was carrying the brown paper bag.

"Well he owns the farm, and I'm buying another building." He was standing next to me with his head down and not making eye contact.

"Frank, I'm giving you Billy, the pony on the farm, He is good for riding and I know your kids can ride him, also in the top of the barn is a small room with some stuff from the track, bandages and soap like that, you keep it. It's just a commission for helping me sell the farm. I'll call you and you can come into the city and have dinner."

He turned and went for the car.

"Buddy, You don't owe me anything, just pay the guys you owe and I'll see that Billy has a good home, at fifteen years old he has worked hard enough. See you."

And he was gone with a bag full of money about 200,000 and I guess we were even. He had helped me get started and Bill was right I never asked him for anything and was not upset when he didn't give me anything. Bill wanted the farm to become a showplace. "You have an open check book, make this place number one in the state," he told me.

I began to work with good help getting the farm in shape. I was at the farm one day and I received a visit from Dennis, Buddy's gofer.

"Frank I broke my leg skiing and I'm on crutches, I need a place to stay and I can do some work. I was hoping you could give me a job or a room till get this cast off.

"What about Buddy?" I asked.

"We had a big blow up, it was not my fault and he said he couldn't carry me right now so I left and got a ride out here."

I don't know why I did it but I let him stay and I called Buddy in the city. "Bud this guy was never one of my favorites but he was so sad I just told him he could stay for a few days I wanted to ask you what happened."

"Well we had some words and he is no longer with me, but I don't care if you have room and want to help him."

"OK well I'll let him stay for a while."

I told Dennis and he almost cried, he began to rant about how bad Buddy had treated him and how he just used people and after he had helped build the new apartments he never paid him and just turned him out.

He knew I had helped Buddy sell the farm and I had received the old pony as commission and how much Buddy received. I knew Buddy had paid $125,000 when he bought the farm so he did make a large profit.

Dennis stayed, and Rocky our night watchman, gave him a room and helped him get around. He rested a great deal and said he would not be able to work so he did not need a pay as he had some savings.

Things were going good on the farm and we brought Semilant out to stand at stud,. I hired a young man Artie

Armayer to help run the barn. He later became the farm manager when I became the General manager for Bill Levin's Gold Mill's Farms.

It was a Tuesday afternoon when I arrived at the farm. I had been at the track with Mr. Penna and we were looking over the arrival of the new two year olds Bill had purchased at the sale in Nov. Sarah and Bill had split and now all the horses ran under Bill's stable name Gold Mill's Farms.

Sarah had all the horses in her name and thought Bill would marry her but he was a married man who loved his wife and Sarah, but he would never think of leaving home.

"You think I'm going to wait around like some school girl?" she shouted at me.

"I know it's hard but people are beginning to talk at the track. They say you are dating a jockey."

"I have tons of men wanting to date me, so what?"

"I just thought you and Bill should talk it out."

They did and he was upset but said it was for the best. He gave her a large check, and she gave him all the horses, they parted as friends.

Sarah and I stayed in touch and Bill asked me to stay with him.

The Red phone on my desk was a direct line to Bill's office in the City When it rang it could only be one person.

"Hi Boss, what's up?"

"Nice to know you are there, I called earlier."

"We were going over the new horses at Belmont they look good."

"That's nice but you should know your pal called and wanted me to know you might need some help at the farm with the horses."

"What?, Who?"

"Buddy."

"What? I know you are kidding."

"No I'm not, he said the breeding program is wrong and your Vet is not giving the right shots to many of the mares and so on and on."

"I don't believe it."

"He knew lots about the farm and went on and on, sounded like he was drunk or high, I just laughed."

"I don't know what to say."

"Nothing to say, just wanted you to know about your hero. Remember what I told you about everybody having somebody. He did you a favor, now you know. By the way I'll be out Saturday with some friends, if you don't have any horses to run at the track try to be out early so we can show them around, have a nice day," and he hung up.

I sat behind the nice big desk I had just bought and slouched in the big black leather chair and glanced around the extra large office we had built and thought someone is trying to take this away from you. Then it hit me who would be giving information to Buddy, Dennis. I stopped for a minute, what about my 'Yiddisher Cup,' Fuck it. I'm Italian we don't always have the right cups. I rose quickly and called down to the barn

"Where's Dennis?" I shouted in a very angry tone.

"He's upstairs in the front room with Rocky having lunch." came the answer.

I don't remember just how many steps it took me to reach the front room which doubled as a lunch room and a lounge. Dennis still had his leg in a cast but was using only one crutch he was sitting at the table with Rocky talking. It appeared they had finished lunch when I stormed into the room.

"You fucking Judas," I screamed as I put one hand on his shoulder and the other on his throat. His chair tumbled back and he rose under my touch ending up against the wall.

"You bastard, you hate Buddy, you little prick I should stick that crutch down your throat."

"Easy Boss, you'll get a heart attack," was the quiet warning from Rocky.

"You want this boy out of here?"

I released my hold on the shacking Dennis who offered no resistance.

"I'm sorry Frank, you have been good to me I never meant to hurt you."

"You punk, the only one you hurt was yourself, get off this farm now, and don't come back. Rocky see he gets out, get his stuff and make sure he never comes back."

"I'll take care of it boss."

I went back to the office and tried to compose myself, Rule number one my first real test failed, hope I can do better next time.

It was about ten minutes later when Buddy called

"Frank I'm on my way out to see you wait for me."

I didn't answer I just hung up.

It was about forty minutes later when the noise of a car outside my window got my attention. I looked out and saw Buddy standing by the door. I left the office and went down to meet him. I kept repeating to myself, rule number one, he was standing with his head down not making eye contact and his left foot was poking at a small stone.

"What about it Bud?"

"I don't know what you are talking about, Dennis called and said he needed a ride, you told him to get out."

"That's right, you know why? Cause you and him have been trying to get me fired. Telling Levin I don't know how to run the farm."

He didn't answer, just kept kicking the stone than in a very slow soft voice just slightly raising his head he said, "Frank, would I do that? Do you think I would do that?"

"Buddy why would Levin lie?" I was starting to lose it.

He just shook his head. Dennis had put his bag in the car and Buddy turned and got into the car and drove off.

It was almost a year before we spoke, he acted as if he was offended I had accused him of saying these things to Levin. He left you with a feeling maybe I was wrong, even when I knew I was right.

I returned to the barn the next day and watched Bold Reason do his morning exercise under the watcher full eye of Angel Penna.

"You know Frank this horse could be a good one, but we must always watch for the knee. We will not go on a wet or sloppy track and we must do the leg up every day."

The next few months I spend observing Angel's techniques and his training ability. We became friends and I never missed a morning of work always looking forward to a new day of learning with him.

I always called Angel, Mr. Penna around the barn or any public setting. I felt it was the respect he deserved even though we were good friends. I was so happy when he told me about a very nice lady he had started to see named Elinor Kaine.

Elinor was a reporter and writer who was the first woman reporter to enter the Giant's locker room after a game. It was strictly taboo at the time for a female to be allowed access when the players were running around sometimes half clad or naked. She was a reporter and this was a story. She could care less if they had on clothes or tutus she wanted to go to press with the real story.

Elinor was from a Kentucky horse family and enjoyed all aspects of the racing and horse business. They were a great couple with so much in common and went on to become Mr. and Mrs. Angel Penna. They were a devoted couple and enjoyed many years together. It was wonderful that Angel had Elinor by his side when he moved to France to train for the Countess Batthyany. It was a magical and interesting move for them and one that Angel looked back on with some amusement, The French were a bit jealous and at the same time in awe of this foreign trainer that seemed to do no wrong. He won the Prix de l'Arc de Triomphe not once but twice along with many other big races.

Bold Reason was in his two year old year and doing well. Bill Levin was anxious to see the colt run. Angel refused to run the horse until he felt he was ready. Finally under pressure he let the horse run in December of his two year old year in Florida. The distance was too short and he did not win. He lost the next two races at which time after having brought his entire family and close friends to the track to see him run felt embarrassed and told Penna to just run him in a cheap $35,000 claiming race not caring if he lost him or not. I prevailed on him to please give the horse a chance and Penna, myself and everyone around the horse on a daily basis had confidence that he was indeed a great horse. Sure enough he finally broke his maiden in a seven furlong race.

We wintered in Florida and returned to New York in early March. We ran him in an allowance race in New York and he did not run well. The jockey was Jorge Velasquez and he came to the barn the day after he rode the horse and told us he felt the horse needed blinkers. This would keep his mind on his business and so the new piece of equipment was added. We immediately could see an improvement and we had high hopes for the horse and Angel was focused on getting him to the Kentucky Derby. Bold Reason was entered in the Derby which is always the first Saturday in May. Jean Cruguet was Angel's jockey and Levin agreed to use him in the race. As always there was a very large field for the Derby. It is safe to say that every owner, trainer and jockey wish to run in this most prestigious race in the United States.

Bill Levin was extremely excited and we invited thirty guests to join us on Derby Day at Churchill Downs. Our horse was an eighteen to one shot and not given much chance but we held high hopes.

Going into the first turn he was in 18th position in the race. For the rest of the race Jean Cruguet maneuvered him through the mass of horses and in a tremendous final stretch run finished a very impressive third where Canonero II won and broke the track record.

To say we were on cloud nine would be an understatement. I am not sure that we could have experienced much more joy if he had won. We felt vindicated and extremely proud of our horse and his unbelievable final stretch run. It was an amazing site to behold and I often go on YouTube to relive the event.

Churchill Downs has a very large private room where they hold a Champagne After Race Party for the owners, trainers and jockeys that were the top three horses that finish this the first leg of the Triple Crown. Also a number of dignitaries like the governor of the state, track officials and those well connected in breeding and racing may attend. It is a time to celebrate, make plans for future races and for possible syndications. My dearest friend, Harold Snowden, who was with us all through the week prior to the race was as happy as we were. He had prospects and hopes that Bold Reason might stand at his farm when his racing career was over.

Harold came to the party accompanied by another dear friend Liz Tippet who also had a horse running in the race that did not fare too well. "You know, I didn't give your horse much chance in the race but I have to say he ran a huge race." We were interrupted by the arrival of Jean Cruguet who was speaking French to another gentleman and both were in a great mood.

"Frank, I want you to meet my friend Pierre Bellocq." We shook hands and he congratulated us on our race. "I root so much for Jean, I know he will win many races on your wonderful horse."

He spoke with the most charming French accent and after a moment or so I said to him. "I know you, you are PEB!"

He laughed and said, "Yes, Yes" He was indeed the very famous French artist who did marvelous and coveted caricatures for the Daily Racing Form. A person had not really arrived in racing until PEB created a caricature of you and it appeared in this horseman's Bible. It was always a surprise and even though people would try and seek him out to draw or sketch them, it was a very difficult endeavor. PEB was his own man and he had the full backing of the paper and the track. To see your caricature in the paper good or bad was like receiving a great review for an opening Broadway play.

I invited PEB and Jean to join us at the hotel we were staying at. Levin was organizing a dinner party for all of his guest and friends in Kentucky. This was the real "beginning of a great friendship" to quote "Rick" from Casablanca. We remain in touch today and have swapped countries with my living in France and he and his lovely wife living in the USA. Pierre is still working as I write this book on yet another Mural to be this time at Belmont Race Track. His works also adorn the walls in Meadowlands, Churchill Downs and many other famous tracks not to mention any number of homes that have purchased his art.

This same evening I was introduced to a very handsome young man by the name of Joe McGinniss. He was casually dressed and accompanied by a lovely young girl carrying a large bag with camera equipment. I was told at the time that this young man was the author of the book "The Selling of the President" which had taken the country by storm. He was quiet and modest and spoke only of horses for the evening. He said that they were traveling the country in search of stories and enjoying the success his book was having. I met him from time to time at different racing events. Unlike Peb, I never got to know Joe as well as I would have liked but have followed his career and enjoyed his writing over the years. By the end of the evening it was obvious that this horse Bold Reason had propelled us into a serious position in the world of racing.

After the dinner and all of the celebrating I returned to my room and first thing I did was to call my Buddy. It was late in the evening but he picked up the phone immediately. Almost as if he was hoping to hear from me.

"Hi Buddy, I hope I am not calling too late."

"No, not at all Frank, you know you can call anytime.'

"Did you watch the race today?"

"Race, what race?"

"The Kentucky Derby, of course!"

"No, I was busy working on a new building."

"Bud, Bold Reason was third and ran one hell of a race."

"If only you had been with us it would have been perfect."

"That's nice, Frank, good for you "Come and see me when you get back to NY I want to show you the work I've done on the building."

With that he hung up. I could only imagine his feelings. Had I done the right thing by calling him? After all he had found and purchased the horse, he was at the center when we started this ride, how could I not let him know that he was thought of on such a special day.

Chapter XXXIV

See Buddy and Meet Melanie for the First Time

Things were going well for the stable and the farm. I was working at both and still in touch with Sarah Hall. She saw Buddy in the city and always invited me to join them for dinner, I was just too busy. It was on a Friday I received a call from Buddy, and although we hadn't spoken in months he acted is if it was last week since our last contact.

"Just thought you could have dinner tomorrow night in the city I need to speak to you."

"I'm not sure, is it important?"

"Very."

"OK what time?"

About eight at Elaine's"

"Fine see you then."

That was it. I wondered why I even said yes, but I did miss him and the crazy fun we had, and what could be so important?

I arrived on time and Buddy was already seated, he introduced me to three of the young girls at the table and that was the first time I met Melanie Cain.

She was about 5' 9" with a very nice figure, not as thin as the many other models, but she had a certain something in her smile. Her large brown eyes would sparkle and they always seamed to be open wide, like she was enjoying some thought or just trying not to miss something. Her complexion was peaches and cream. She was what every American boy was brainwashed to believe was a the ideal American girl, the girl next door with a touch of glamour. To say she was naive would be the understatement of the year. She was sweet and kind, and never seemed to understand her success or why she was admired. This was his new love and star of his agency.

"Mel's a great girl and a very good model. I wanted you to meet her."

"Buddy told me you guys were close and he wanted you to come work with him, it's nice to meet you."

"Nice to meet you Mel, Buddy gave me my start in the racing game and has always been a great friend."

"Frank, we are doing great and I did want to talk to you about our business and also how our building plans are coming. I would love it if you took an apartment in the building. If I have a number leases signed it's good security to get loans when necessary." Just then Sarah came in with her usual flair, still beautiful and bubbly. We hugged and were both surprised to see each other.

"I told Sarah I had a special guest tonight and that's you, Frank."

We all laughed and began to make small talk, Sarah was interested in the progress of the racing stable and Buddy said no trade talk tonight so we had a great dinner caught up with and got to know each other better.

As the evening came to an end Buddy called me to the side and told me our accountant Bernie Zipern would call me and had a business deal Buddy would like me to consider, I said I would meet Bernie when he called. I said my good byes and left.

Bernie called the following week and asked to see me at the farm. I told him to come for lunch the following day. Bernie was a friend and our accountant. He was about four years older than me, slight built and looked like a Jewish "Mister Peepers", a television character. He did Buddy's work for more than ten years and was accountant for about thirty other trainers and some track people. He loved horses and the racing game. His partner Robbie was the worker while Bernie would spend most of his time at the track getting new clients and keeping the old ones happy. Many times Bernie would end up with a piece of a horse when his client was not able to come up with the cash. He was happy to be an owner even if it was only five or ten percent, he was always looking for the pot of gold.

Buddy liked Bernie, but he loved to torment him. He would call him at home at any hour, day or night and then ask for a recipe for cheesecake or how he was feeling and Bernie would always say "Buddy, it's 3 am can I call you in the morning?"

Buddy thought it was funny, it upset me because I liked Bernie.

"Well Frank, did Buddy tell you about the deal?"

"No he said you would explain."

"It's his idea and he said you would take a share."

"You better tell me about it Bernie."

"You know I do some work in Puerto Rico."

"No, I never knew that."

"I do the accounting for a guy named Silver and one of his business's is The San Juan Diary, it's a magazine that is given out at the hotels and resorts in Puerto Rico. He wants to sell and retire, I think it could be a good business, and Buddy wants to buy it."

"Does it make money?"

"Right now it's in the red, they make money from the advertisements and they are owed lots of money."

"That's not good."

"They need a new management, and I know a guy who was working for the company but left about six months ago. He knows everybody and he can collect and get more business."

"Bernie, I don't know why I would want to be involved in a business so far away, and with so little control."

"Well I'll take a piece and I'll continue to do what I do now, go down every month and keep the accounts and check on this new manager, I think it will do great."

"Bernie, now tell me why Buddy wants this deal."

"I know you have helped me in the past Frank and you have been a good friend, Buddy thinks he can use the magazine to push some of the girls in his agency and also he wants articles about himself so he can put in a younger age like twenty-nine or thirty, but God don't tell him I told you."

"How much do you need?"

"Buddy will take two shares, I have two doctors that I do work for and they will take a share each I'll take one and if you take one I think I can sell two others. A share will go for five thousand. You know Frank you can go to Puerto Rico a few times and we will get great hotels on barter, no payment and the company will pay the plane fare."

"It's not my kind of deal, but if you need me I'm in. Buddy got me started and I'm doing very good right now so I'll do it, but you better take care of this, understand?"

"Yes, Sure, I understand thanks and please don't tell him what I told you."

I just smiled and shook my head and he left happy.

It was about another two months when I heard from Buddy. "Frank, need a favor."

"What can I do for you Buddy?"

"I'm at the Ski lodge and someone here has the clap."

"What?"

"We think this broad from Brazil Air brought it here."

"God, you better get a doctor."

"No need for that, Dennis has a friend working in a drug store and he can get me 100 hypodermic needles. I need you to ask the vet to get us 100 shots of Penicillin. I can give every one here a shot and it will be fine."

"Are you nuts, wait I know you are nuts. What I mean do you think I am nuts?"

"Look Frank it's not a big deal, I know the vet will do it for me, tell him I'll pay him cash. I can send it when the kid comes to get the stuff."

"Bud, I would like to help you, but I just don't want to fool with any kinda of drugs."

"This is medicine and not illegal in any way."

"It just doesn't sound right."

"Frank I need it please try."

"If I can do it I want you to promise never to ask anything like this again."

"Thanks, I knew I could count on you."

"You didn't promise."

"Oh sure, I promise."

I contacted a vet that was very friendly with Buddy. "Frank, I'll do it for you but never again. I know you are close to Buddy but I don't want him to know I got the stuff for him."

"OK Doc, this is it for me, never again."

He delivered a box to me and Buddy sent his "go for" down to pick it up. I never opened it but still felt guilty of something I just was not sure of what.

"Thanks Frank, I took care of everyone and things are fine now, see you in the city soon."

I was busy with Bold Reason traveling around with Bill and winning so many big races.

"Frank you must leave Penna, I want you to become my General Manager. You will oversee the Gold Mills Farms operations from racing to breeding and everything in-between."

Bernie came to the farm more often and tried to get me to go to Puerto Rico for a trip to see how the magazine was doing and have a vacation.

"Buddy saw this girl in the magazine and wants to meet her," he said.

"Told me to show you her picture."

"I just don't have time to go, but thanks."

He pulled out a copy of the magazine from his brief case and showed me the picture of a very attractive girl. She was very blond slim, with a beautiful clear complexion dressed in jeans with a rose colored top that left her midsection exposed. She was strumming a guitar and standing on a beach in her bare feet.

"Very pretty," I said as I handed the magazine to him.

The magazine was very professional, about six inches long and three or four inches wide. The paper was glossy and in bright colors and about sixty pages.

"Lots of ads, hope we are making money."

"Well we are getting out of debt, but no profit yet."

"Look Bernie, I know you go down every month and stay for a few days, and the business pays. I never saw a report of the income or expenses, are we going to get that?"

"Frank you can go down any time for a vacation, and no charge you are an officer of the corporation."

"I never knew that."

"Buddy told me to make you vice president."

"You never told me."

"I thought he told you."

"Bernie, you can remove me from the books, and if you ever use my name without asking me you will not be my friend, and I will be very upset. Understand?"

"Sorry Frank, I'll take care of it. Buddy wants to meet this girl and she is coming in next week from Puerto Rico. He told me to invite you to dinner in the city."

"Thanks but I don't know if I can make it."

"Frank, please come, Buddy is always nice to me when you are around and we can talk about the magazine."

"Call me next week I'll let you know."

The following week I went to the city to meet Buddy and Bernie at a midtown restaurant. Buddy wanted some place where he could meet the new girl alone and not have Melanie see him.

We exchanged greetings and he was happy to hear about the success of Bold Reason.

"Funny, I bought him with you and Levin and Sarah. Sarah named him and now both she and I have nothing to do with him. I'm happy you and Bill are together and get to have fun with a great horse."

"Bud, he was a great buy, and you are the guy who took the chance. It's funny how people rewrite history and stories get changed according to who's telling them."

Angle Penna did a great job with the horse. Levin gave up on the horse before he won and I begged him not to run him in a claimer only because I knew you believed in him. You know how much I respect you as a great horsemen, not always as a "business man." We both laughed.

"I'm sorry Sarah and Bill split but I still love Sarah and would help her anytime. Bill has been so good to me and my family. He has given me so much responsibility and everything I could ask for in a boss. But more than a boss he has become almost like a second father and friend. Being with you made it all possible, so no matter what I feel I can never say enough thanks!"

"Does that mean you will take an apartment?"

"You are a son of a bitch, yes, yes, have Bernie send me the lease."

"You always said I talk too much," and we laughed again.

Bernie arrived with the girl.

"Who's that?" Buddy said as they entered the restaurant.

They were at the entrance and we had a table in the rear but as they stood in the daylight the person with Bernie did not look like the girl in the magazine. She was thin as a rail, with a very poor complexion suffering from a severe case of acne, her hair was three shades of blonde and the texture of straw. She wore overalls of faded blue and sandals that had seen better days.

"My God, Frank tell Bernie to get her out of here. Don't let him come to the table. Give her some money and send her away, and tell him to leave, I'll call him."

I left the table and went to the entrance.

"Hi Bernie," I said as I realized the girl appeared to have a heavy drug problem.

"Buddy had to leave. He asked me to tell you he will call you, please see the young lady gets home."

Taking to the side I told him, "Bernie give her some cash and send her home, quick before he kills you."

Bernie gulped and took the girl by the arm and made a quick exit.

I returned to the table and we both began to laugh.

"That Bernie, he ran and won't stop till he gets home. He hates to make you angry."

"I know." Buddy smiled, "He may be the only guy in the world I can get to, wish there were more guys like him when I was at school."

"Why, did you have a tough time?"

"Let's just say a skinny Jew is an easy mark for some guys."

We left it at that and I saw another softer side of My Buddy.

"Frank you have to come into the city more often, like once a week. I want to tell you about the modeling business and you must take the apartment."

"I'll be in next week to sign the lease, and we will have lunch."

Chapter XXXV

The City

I arranged to meet Buddy on a Tuesday in the city at his new favorite place, Nicola's, the restaurant across from the model agency.

The owner was a long time employee at Elaine's and had left to start his own restaurant. It was on the same type of food and decor. The bar was in the front of the restaurant and the wooden tables were in the back. The walls were covered with pictures of current reviews of books and authors, many of whom were customers. After all, who doesn't like to go to a restaurant that features your book, or picture and a good review of your work. The food was Italian and continental and Buddy loved it. This was his hangout and dinner almost every night.

During lunch he told me of the business. "I advertise in small towns all over the country. We go to some and have a contest for young girls to become models. We do runway, they walk up and down and the winner gets to come to New York for three months rent free in one of my apartments and signs with us for a year. If they don't make it in the three month they can stay but have to pay rent and such or they go back home. Mothers beg us to take the girls, some are only fifteen or sixteen years old. They push harder than the girls."

"I see that would give you lots of new girls for the New York scene."

"Right, also the New York guys will do anything to get to be a judge at the contest or when we do a show in New York."

"Can you make any money?"

"That comes if you get a star, and my job is to make one just like a horse."

"I think I'll stick with the horses, my experience is that they are less trouble."

"Maybe, but if I told you the names of the guys who want to be my best friends just to get close to these girls you would flip. All the wall street guys, bankers, politicians, and even a couple of judges. Spend some time here and you will meet them all, would you like to be a judge at the next contest?"

"I know you are kidding."

"Why don't you come and work with me? I don't trust any of these guys I have around me."

"What about Dennis?"

"He is good to get the girls, he comes up with great ways to get the girls. He goes to the Port Authority terminal and watches for any of the young ones who look lost. He is young so they talk to him and he has a good line. He can change his story in a minute, and he loves to be important. But when the chips are down I know he would sell me out."

"So why keep him?"

"He has a brother and he is taking an apartment in the building, he has some money and he carries a gun."

"What the Hell is that about?"

"It's okay. He has a permit to carry, and since I never had a gun I feel he looks after the building."

"That is the sickest thing I ever heard. What kinda guys are you hanging with?"

"It's just the New York way, so I'll keep the brothers for now, just watch them more."

"This is nuts, I'll get Bill to take an apartment to help you out. I'll sign the lease and bring you the check. After I furnish it you may not see me too often, I like the girls but the guys are low life's and I can't forget what Dennis did on the farm."

I spoke to Bill who agreed to help Buddy by renting an apartment.

"It sounds like a good Idea, we can use a place in the city. You furnish it and when I need you, you can stay over. I can use it for some private meetings and you put in someone else's name."

So, Mr. Stein signed up for a ground floor apartment. I was on the farm when my secretary Lida Anderson called on the loudspeaker to tell me Mr. Jacobson was on the phone.

"Hi Bud, what's up?"

"I haven't seen you in a few weeks and you haven't furnished the apartment."

"Been busy maybe next week or so."

"If you could come in on Friday I have a decorator to help you and a good connection where you can get it done in one day."

"I'm not sure."

"Let me set it up it's important and I know Bill will like it when we finish."

"Well about 3 p.m., if we don't run into anything, is that okay?"

"See you then," click.

Our racing stable was having great success and I was busy traveling all over the country. I was now the general manager of a very large racing and breeding operation. Bill had purchased a large farm in Ocala, Florida. We had racing stables in New York, California, Boston, Florida and France. We also had a breeding operation in Argentina. The operation was Gold Mills Farms and the only way to keep it successful was to have lots of good people working with us, this I tried to do, and because of it I was able to get some free time for myself. Friday came and I kept my appointment in the city

"Frank this is Cindy she knows everything about decorating and will help you, you can pay her what you think she is worth. I told her you were my special friend and a fair guy."

Cindy was about 5' 2" with bright red hair, sparkling blue eyes and a peaches and cream completion. The fact that her face was so perfect could only be overshadowed by her size six full figure if such a thing is possible Her smile topped off her beauty. I was speechless.

"Hi Frank, Buddy told me you needed some help it will be a pleasure to work with you. I'll be happy to go over my work history with you and show you some of the jobs I've done."

I regained my composure and smiled.

"Cindy if Buddy says you are a pro I trust him, and besides, I think it will be fun to have your help."

"Good, then let's get started. If you have the key we can go into the apartment and I'll bring my book so we can pick some furniture."

The apartment was on the ground floor to the rear of the building. It had a large bay window which over looked an interior courtyard. The entrance was down three steps and was a large living room complete with a fireplace. The far end of the apartment had a small circular bar and a kitchen area. There was a circular staircase which led to the bedroom which was on the upper level. A well built bathroom was next to the bedroom and the view from this level could look out the bay window into the courtyard.

Bill liked the idea of the apartment. He said I could stay over if we were to have an early meeting or if we had a late one I could stay over and not need to drive out to Long Island. I also knew that although he would have a girlfriend he liked his privacy.

"Well Cindy we have lots of work to do to shape this place up."

"It's a snap, but I'll need your help. Can you spend some time with me?"

Could Babe Ruth hit home runs? That's the answer I wanted to give, but I wanted to be cool and not show my emotions, "I think I can arrange my schedule so we can get it done."

"Great, I'll draw up a plan and have it ready for you in about three days, I can call you and leave my number and we can meet when you are able."

"Sounds good to me." I was thinking this job may take longer than I thought.

She gave me some quick ideas about a couch some chairs and a juke box, I told her everything sounded fine. We ended the meeting and all the way out of the city I was thinking of how her short tight skirt just about covered the lower half of her beautiful body, three days seemed like a long time to wait. I said goodbye to Buddy but told him I would be back soon, he smiled, If he wanted me around he had the right bait.

I returned the following week and Cindy, true to her word had a plan for the apartment with a price list and some photos from a vendor.

"Wow, I thought you were just a pretty face this is very impressive," I said as I met her in the apartment.

She was wearing a very short skirt and a very light blue top which brought out her beauty even more. "Thanks, I wanted to be a model, but Buddy says I'm too short, so I have been doing this to keep body and soul together."

"Anyone as beautiful as you should have no trouble finding a sponsor in this big city," I laughed.

"Well sometimes the right sponsor is hard to take," and we both laughed.

I signed on to the plan and she began to make the purchase it took a few weeks but things were coming together.

The apartment was beautiful when she finished and I realized how this life was so easy to take, I began to spend much more time than I needed to in the city. I was very fond of this beautiful girl and could see lots of problems in this relationship. I believe we were getting too close but when I started to spend one or two nights in the apartment I was sure of it.

I settled our account with Cindy and Bill sent her a very nice check and ended a very pleasant interlude in my life.

Chapter XXXVI
Busy on All Fronts

Buddy called and asked why I had not been in for a while. I told him Bill had purchased a farm in Ocala, Florida and I had to oversee its operation. We left the fellow who we bought the farm from in charge of day to day operations and I would travel there once a month. "Come in one night for dinner. I have some stuff to talk to you about."

"Sure Bud, but not this week maybe next week would be better."

While I was fixing the apartment I met some of Buddy's new friends and spent some time with his girlfriend, Melanie Cain. When we were decorating the apartment I told Buddy I was going to pick up some pillows for the apartment. "Go to Macy's. There is a great store nearby and Melanie will go with you. She has to do some shopping."

"Are you sure?" I asked.

"Sure Frank. I like her to have company."

So we went off to shop. She was always pleasant and even in her everyday tank top and skirt she would get a great deal of attention because of her beauty. As we walked along she told me about her love for Buddy and how hard it was to understand him.

"You know Buddy always tells me you are his closest friend, but we don't see you much and you don't come to any of the dinner parties."

"Melanie, Buddy gave me my start in the business and if he was back at the track I would love to work for him, but I'm not happy with his new life, except for you. So I wish him well and hope you can make him happy."

"Well he takes care of me, makes sure I see my doctor and go to the gym to work out. I have a health problem. It's got to do with a sugar imbalance. He is always concerned. I like that but we don't go out a lot, just to dinner every night and see many of the same people."

"Melanie, when he works that's all he thinks about, but I can see he cares a great deal for you."

"I hope so, but he never talks marriage and I come from a family that believes in it."

"Just have patience. I think it will work out."

We arrived at the store and went to the bedding department.

"These are some nice pillows," she said and began to pick out some large bed pillows. At the same time she found a package of pillow covers and opened it.

"You have to check these. Sometimes they pack the wrong size."

She opened the pack and took out the cover and put the end of the pillow in her mouth while she opened the cover and tried to put the pillow in. Her arms were stretched out and she was wiggling around so her tank top slipped down revealing her very well formed breasts. I gulped and she continued to stuff the pillow into the cover not appearing to notice the mishap.

"Melanie, your top," I whispered.

She looked down and with one hand lifted her top and continued to fill the pillow case.

"This is good Frank. I think these will be good."

There were only a few people around so I don't know what the reaction was but she continued to make small talk and never mentioned the incident which gave me an insight as to how casual the human body was to the people in this business. I liked Melanie and when she would tell me of her experience with older men, who she felt were trying to be so kind to her, I could see she was in need of someone to take care of her and Buddy seemed right for her.

We returned to the building at 155 East 84th street, Buddy's building. His agency was on the ground floor and was a beehive of activity. I met a friend of Buddy's a fellow named

David Silbergelt. He was dressed in an army camouflaged uniform. He was a good looking fellow and was involved with the girl working at the desk.

"Who's the army guy?" I asked Buddy.

"He helps me here, something like you did at the barn...takes care of the cash and like that."

"Hope you know him well," I said.

"He goes with that girl you liked on the farm, Mel Harris."

"Wait...now you asked me if I wanted a date, I told you she was pretty, but too tall for me." We both laughed.

"Well Mel is close to Melanie and she asked her to speak to me about a job. I think he is going to marry Mel Harris."

"He is a green beret, I think, but I know he can get any kind of weapon from his base so he is popular with some of the guys around here."

"Nice people you deal with."

"I don't get into their business, but I can always borrow a few bucks if I need it."

I left the building after thanking Melanie and Buddy for the help and went back to the farm.

A few weeks passed and I was very active on the farm. Bill called and told me were to go to Ocala in two days. I was to visit our farm, Robin's Nest, and then meet with him at the Ocala Sales Company of which he was a share holder. George Steinbrenner, the owner of the Yankees is interested in buying my share of the Ocala Sales Company and I'm thinking of selling and getting more involved in the New York breeding business. What do you think?"

"Sounds great to me, and maybe we could sell the farm in Ocala so I could spend more time in New York."

"Why not? I would rather spend time here and be able to see the horses more. Let's work on it." It was good news.

As I finished the call Buddy called. "Hi Frank, can you come into the city this week?"

"I'm going to Ocala on Wednesday, maybe next week."

"What about tomorrow?"

"I'm not sure, let me check."

"Look I need to see you this week, come for dinner and you can leave early. I'll expect you at 6 p.m."

"Okay, but it has to be an early evening." It was always hard to say no to Buddy.

It was a few minutes to six as I looked for a parking spot near the restaurant. The city was very busy and warm. I entered and saw Buddy at a large table in the rear, he was not alone.

"Hi, Frank," he called, as I made my way to the table. Melanie rose quickly and gave me a kiss on the cheek.

"So happy you could come. Do you know the girls?"

"I don't think so."

"This is TC," and she pointed to a very beautiful, dark haired girl who was, I learned, Irish and Hawaiian with a figure that was great for a showgirl but much too much for a model. She smiled and said, "Hi." Next to her was a stunning tall, almost six foot, blond. She had the face of an angel. Her name was Alice and she had graced the cover of many top magazines. Her other claim to fame was her current date was Joe Namath, the football star. "And this is Taylor," she was equally tall and very slim, also very beautiful. She had dark hair and was of mixed race, negro and white, with the best features of each race. Her specialty was newsprint and after this night, any time I would see an ad in the *Times* or any paper nine times out of ten, she was in it. The other girl was a friend of TC's and also someone more suited to Hooters than anywhere else. She was attractive and if you could tear yourself away from her figure you would see a very nice face.

"Hi all," I said. What could you say in this company? Buddy had ordered some special dishes and we began to eat.

"Bud, what was so important?"

"We can talk later. The girls would like to hear about the horses."

"From me?" I asked.

"Girls, do you know this is one of, if not the best, horseman in the world," I said. "Yes Buddy, the guy who taught me about half of what he knows." I realized he wanted me to tell them who he was. He knew I would do it as I had for years with our owners. He could not do it himself but I could make a case for him. The girls were anxious to hear the stories and the evening went fast.

"Well we can do this again," I said. "I have to fly tomorrow off to Ocala to check the horses."

"Where do you fly into?" Buddy asked.

"Orlando, then I drive eighty-two miles to Ocala. I've done it about a million times or so it seems."

"That's where Disney World is, right?" Buddy said.

"Yes, I've been there lots of times. It breaks up the trip. I've gotten to know Mickey and Donald and all their friends."

"I've got a great idea. How about taking Melanie and some of the girls with you to Disney World? I've been promising Melanie I would take her but I can't get away, and I know she will be safe with you."

Melanie was all excited and speaking to some of the girls about the trip.

"I would like to but I have to go for work, and I can't stay as I have to get to a meeting in Ocala."

"Well, Babe would you like to go?" he asked Melanie.

"Buddy could I?" She was like a little kid, and Buddy was putting me on the spot.

"I think we can get Frank to take you. I know you will be safe with him."

"Frank, we won't be any trouble. I would like to see Disney World and I do need some time off. Can you do it?"

"Look, I'm on a National Airlines flight from JFK airport. If you want to come, I'll go with you. I know a union official who takes care of Disney World. He is a horse player and I think I can get you a room, but you will be on your own after that. Think about it and I'll see you there or I'll see you when I return." I rose and said goodnight. They were all smiles and a little under the influence. I didn't expect to see them in the morning. It was a bright sunny day and I was happy to get away for a few days and work but also relax. I remembered Buddy asked me to call, but I waited until I got to the terminal and called to say goodbye.

"Hi Frank, Melanie is on her way…got some friends with her. I do appreciate this. I wouldn't let anyone else take her. I know you will look out for her. She is such a little kid."

"Bud, I thought you were kidding. Sure I'll look out for her but you know I have to go to Ocala."

"Tell Bill. Maybe he will let you stay in Disney World, or take the girls with you to Ocala?"

"Can't do that, but I'll ask. How are they getting here?"

"I put them in a limo and they should be there by now...keep a look out for them. Call and let me know you get there safe and thanks."

"Thanks," not a word I was used to hearing from my pal. I went in front of the terminal and a large black limo approached. It stopped in front and the door opened and out stepped five of the most beautiful young girls in New York. They were all dressed in blue short shorts with bright orange t-shirts. Across the back of the shirt in bright script letters was the word "SURPRISE," the address 155 east 84th Street, New York was written below. This is what Buddy was going to tell me. He planned to open a restaurant in his building and call it Surprise. He had a lot of these t-shirts printed and was asking the girls to wear them around town.

This group was special. They were all the girls I had eaten dinner with the night before. People were stopping to take pictures and ask who they were. I decided to say that they were a women's basketball team and I was the coach. People accepted that. I felt like Gulliver among the giants. They were tall, and those legs just seemed to keep going higher and higher.

I went to the window and bought the tickets for the flight. Buddy forgot to send cash. I just put it on the company credit card. I called my office and had my secretary reach my union friend, Harry and make a reservation for some rooms on the grounds. I said I would call to check with her when I arrived in Florida.

It was a riot going to the gate to board the plane, one girl in the group would cause a stir, five would cause a riot. They were good sports and laughed and were pleasant to everyone. We had three sets of seats on the right side of the plane, one behind the other. Melanie and I sat together. The trip was three hours long and some slept, others just talked and talked. Melanie did most of the talking. She talked about her home, her family, and the job. She loved Buddy but he was so interested in the business and had little time for her. She wanted to take acting classes but he was not for it.

Her friend, Mel Harris, was younger but much smarter than she. "She knows things and she helps me," she said. I should get into other things and not depend on Buddy so much. Buddy does not think much of her boyfriend, David, and now he thinks David is stealing from the business. Mel says Buddy wants to do the business himself so that's why he wants David out. I just don't know."

"You know Buddy says he doesn't want to tire me out so he only has sex once in a while. I guess that's good cause he loves me and not only for sex. What do you think?"

"Well I'm no expert, but I think he loves you for everything.

We arrived in Florida and the people were all around us. "Are you a musical group? Are you making a movie or a Disney promotion?"

I just used the same line, "Basketball team." Lots of people asked if they could take a picture. The girls said sure, and they posed.

I rented a large car to fit six people and called my office.

"There is a special convention at Disney this week but Harry said he got you the last room in the Contemporary Hotel, it sleeps six. I thanked her and drove to the hotel. After checking in and asking if there were any more rooms available we went to the room. It was a very large room with two large beds and a smaller one on the far wall. It had a large balcony and the view was awesome, at least that's what the girls said. The girls made themselves at home. They began to unpack and make plans for the day. It was like a girls locker room. They changed clothes, some in the bathroom, others just where they were standing. It was as though I was not there. Alice changed into a white see-through dressing gown and sat in front of the mirror to make up her face.

"We left so early I can't believe what I look like," she sighed. The others began to follow suit. I began to feel it was time to leave.

"Don't go," Melanie said. "Stay and take us on the rides. You can spend the night. We have plenty of room."

"Thanks, that sounds nice but I have work to do."

"Come on...don't break up the party," they shouted as they playfully began to hug me.

"Look, I'll call my boss and see if I can get out of it." Which I knew was impossible.

"I'll go to the lobby and call. You relax and order some food."

I knew that would get them. I called the farm and spoke to Bill. He laughed and said, "Hop to it. I need you."

"I was thinking of having some lunch and then leaving."

"You know if it was any other time I'd be there with you but kiss the girls goodbye and grab lunch on the road."

What would I do with these young beautiful girls anyway, just show my age? He was right. I returned to the room to find lots of iced tea, cokes, and water with lots of ice. The food was shrimp cocktails and cheeseburgers. I grabbed a coke and a burger, kissed the girls, told them I would pay the room charges as I left and see them back in New York. They said they were sad and would stay for one night. I never saw all of them again. I only saw Melanie and once TC.

I met Bill Levin and George Steinbrenner and we had dinner. Bill told George about the trip I made and they both had a good laugh over how sad I must be. I laughed and went along with the joke. The next day Bill and George completed the deal and Steinbrenner purchased Bill's share in the Florida breeding company. Steinbrenner was very interested in breeding and the night before we had a long discussion about the potential of breeding a Kentucky Derby winner. Bill told him he would continue to do breeding in Florida but was interested in supporting the New York state breeding program. I met George on a number of other occasions and he was always interested in knowing how our breeding operation was going. I returned to New York and only spoke to Buddy once or twice the next year.

Bill had me traveling from pillar to post checking on all of the horses. There wasn't much time for the city life. On one occasion I had dinner with Buddy and Melanie and as it turned out Sarah Hall was in the same restaurant. Sarah looked great and was going with a very nice fellow, Joe Moose. He was a trainer who was an ex-football player. He was big and handsome and very much in love with Sarah. I heard later they married and moved to Florida where she started a catering business which was very successful. Later on she became ill with cancer and passed away. Joe was a devoted husband and cared for her until the end. Sarah was a great gal, a friend and a sport. During that meeting she asked me about what was going on in my life. I told her I met a girl from Mississippi who was young and beautiful and that I was very happy and wanted her to meet Judy. Sarah laughed and said, "Why Frankie, don't you know that if a girl from Mississippi puts her slippers under your bed, you'll never get her out of your heart or out of your head." She was very wise. I ended up marrying my little Southern belle.

Chapter XXXVII

Contact with Buddy After His Arrest

Life went on and things were good when the news of Buddy's arrest came on the air. I just told myself this couldn't be, not Buddy, not my Buddy. I spoke to the lawyer, Win Klein and he said, "Frank, I'm not the guy for this case. He just does not think he has a problem."

"He says he did not do it but he does not want to tell me things I need to know. He says he can't be convicted because he did not do it. That's not how it works. You and I are friends but he wants someone else, so let's hope he knows what he is doing."

And we left it at that. Buddy made bail and was back in his building. We spoke on the phone and he said, "No way will I ever get convicted. I didn't do it,"

"But Buddy, you have to prove it."

"No Frank, they have to prove I did it, and how can they do that if it's not true."

"I've got a good lawyer, and he is very confident. I'll be OK." "Come to the city on Friday and have dinner with me, and I'll tell you all about it. Thanks for calling. You would be surprised how many people won't take my calls. Well, I never had many friends."

I met Buddy in the city on Friday and we went to dinner.

"I wanted to have dinner alone so I could get your take on this thing. I rented an apartment to a friend of Dennis', well I met him with Dennis, he came from Queens and he owned an Irish bar. His name was Jack Tupper. He was a nice guy, always smiling. I knew he was into some things drugs, guns, and stuff like that but I liked him. He had a problem with his partner and there was a dispute over the sale of the bar, but he was to get his share and he wanted an apartment in the city. I rented to him, and I felt safe because I was having trouble with Dennis and his brother. They were stealing from me and the brother had a gun and always pulling it out saying he was small but the gun made him big. I told him to move. He did not pay the rent and wanted to stay rent free. Well we also had an Italian guy who was accused of blowing up a car in Long Island that belonged to a union official. He was going with that girl, TC and he was a nice guy but I know he did business with that David Silbegelt who stole more than $50,000 from me. Melanie was so crazy about Mel Harris she didn't believe me. She believed Mel who married the guy."

"Just wait up Bud. All these names and things...does it have to do with the murder."

"Sure, but you have to know all this first."

"Well, this guy Tupper started to talk to Melanie and wanted to go jogging with her. He asked me and I said sure, then I found out he had more than jogging on his mind. Well he told her my two sons, who were working with me, were not my brothers, like I told her and she asked Dennis and he gave me up in a minute. After all I did for him and his brother they were my worst enemies....well any one of the people Tupper was doing business with could have killed him, even the IRA."

"What did he have to do with the IRA?" I asked.

"Well his friend and a boss of the dope gang is Donald Brown. Do you know him?"

"Never heard of him."

"Well he used to buy guns from Silbegelt and sell them. He was connected to the IRA."

"Buddy how do you know all this stuff?"

"Everybody in the city knows this. Why Tupper's brother-in-law is an FBI agent, and after the murder he and three of his buddies came and cleaned out Tupper's apartment on their own. People said Jack was a stool pigeon for the FBI, he had no furniture and no phone. He was supposed to tape everything, people were afraid of him, he was a black belt and a strong guy. He had lots of fights in his bar and they say he never lost. He was nice to me and I trusted him. He would tell me lots of stuff that was secret and I never said a word to any one."

"Buddy all this is interesting but why did they arrest you, and why do they think you did this?"

"It was Sunday and I was working on my new building with the two Italian guys that have worked for me for a long time. I came back to 155 to check on the swimming pool, as we were installing a new light, you know the pool is on the roof but the bottom is in my apartment and guys like to come over and watch the girls swim. You can see right into the pool from the glass bottom. As I passed Joe Margarite's apartment I noticed the door was slightly open..."

"Wait a minute, who is this guy, Joe?"

"He was one of the guys with Brown. He did a lot of the drug stuff and served time in jail for selling drugs. He moved into apartment 7F, which is on my floor."

"So you, Tupper, and this guy all lived on the same floor?"

"Yeah, and also the Italian guy, Carlo Carrara."

"All on the same floor?"

"That's right. Well, I called out to Joe, but there was no answer. I thought he may have forgot to close the door so I went and opened it a little and called out again. I opened the door all the way and there was Jack, dead! I was in shock. I thought to call the police, but it would look bad for the apartment and I was in the middle of a big deal and the guys with the money might back out. Then I thought maybe someone was trying to blame me. They all knew Jack and I were at odds over Melanie. I closed the door and went back to the new building. I still didn't know what to do. You know me, I always want to solve problems so I decided to get rid of the body. We brought a wooden crate and the two boys helped me put the body inside. The boys loaded the crate and I told them to meet me at the new building. I asked them to dump the body. I felt they might not do it right, so I went with Sal who works for me to the parkway."

Buddy stopped talking for a moment. He gathered his thoughts and continued. "I drove up to the Bruckner Expressway where they had dumped the box. I left the parkway and was stopped by a cop who said they were looking for a car of the same description, so he called his station and they arrested me. They took me to the station and made me strip. I was standing there with no clothes and after a while a cop gave me a blanket to cover myself. They put me in a small holding cell right behind the desk and lots of people passed by looking at me like I was in the zoo. I sat on a small stool and tried to cover myself. I asked what I did and they just laughed. One guy asked me if I was sure I didn't know what I was being held for. I told him no. After a while I heard someone say a shooting. I told the cop I had never fired a gun in my life. I asked if that was it, and I said I could take one of those test to show I did not fire a gun. This big Irish cop named Sullivan told me to shut up. I know I did wrong but I never killed anybody."

"I'm glad you were released on bail, and $100,000 is not much for a murder case. I hope they find the real killer."

"Thanks Frank, this guy was involved with some bad people, lots of drugs and he had money problems with guys he owed and who owed him. He was a violent guy and the people who did this had to be very violent to take him on."

"Make sure you have a good lawyer."

"I think I have, but I'm not worried because I didn't do it. How can they ever take me to trial?"

"Buddy you are in the Bronx, the DA is Merola, and he has a bad reputation for wanting to win cases and he is very ambitious, wants to be mayor, or governor of the state. Don't take this lightly."

"Sure, I understand. I hope this gets over soon. I have a few big deals in the real estate business, and you know I would be happy for you to join me anytime."

"Thanks, Bud. I'm happy in my business and Levin is very good to me, but you know I would be happy to help you if I can at any time. Stay in touch."

I returned to the farm and thought about the story Buddy had told me. It was something he would do. I knew he was not a killer, not a violent person and he was so confident I felt better about the situation.

As time went on I began to hear about just who these people were that were involved in the life of Jack Tupper, the murder victim. Tupper was a young business man from Queens who was in the bar business and came to Manhattan to develop an Irish bar business but was later named in a huge federal drug case. He was young and handsome, in his early thirties, a black belt, a very strong and fit man. Jack was a six-footer of about 175 lbs who loved to workout, run, and keep fit. Buddy knew him from his bar in Queens and was happy to rent him an apartment. He liked Jack and felt safe with him around. So when Jack asked to take Melanie for a jog in the park Buddy was all for it. He felt it was good for her to have a friend and the she needed the exercise to stay in shape. Buddy was very protective of Melanie and felt she was in good hands with Jack. He never expected their relationship to change. He once told me, "I trusted him. He was my friend."

There was a group of men who came from Queens who were under investigation on suspicion of drug trafficking, and they were friends of Jack Tupper. Donald Brown was the "Boss" of the ring and was later convicted of drug trafficking. There were about sixteen others who suffered the same fate, but at this time they were all happy to see Buddy charged with the crime.

The papers were full of the story. "Love Slave or Murderer" was the headline. Many reporters said there was no case. Yes, he disposed of the body, but there was no proof he killed anyone. The political climate was strong for a conviction. Jack was from a fine Irish-American family, and his sister was a nurse married to a FBI agent. Buddy was a New York Jew who had battled the establishment and was a Brooklyn cowboy.

The Tupper family did not know Buddy but were convinced he killed their Jack. Why did they believe all the people who had so much to gain by having Buddy found guilty? These people wanted the case to go away. They did not want the spotlight to shine on their business and if it came out that it was a drug killing, many of them would be under suspicion.

There was an ongoing DEA investigation, many said Jack was an informer. He was very close to his brother-in-law, Tom Meyers, and had visited him in Puerto Rico just a short time before his death.

Buddy claimed Melanie had been with Jack on his trips and knew enough to help clear him but she was afraid to speak because of the fear of the action of the drug gang. The trial was delayed and postponed over and over. The papers wrote the DA must have a weak case as they had found no murder weapon and no DNA…just speculation.

Buddy and his team were gathering witnesses and Buddy was never in doubt he would be acquitted. "I didn't do it, so they can't convict me," was his battle cry. He worked hard and was making some big deals with the real-estate he had purchased. Jack was known to tape many conversations. If these could be found, it might prove who the killer was. The DA never revealed if the tapes were found.

I returned to work but kept in touch with Buddy. Many theories evolved and the police were unable to find this Joe Margarite who disappeared the day of the murder. Buddy questioned how hard they were trying. During this time Buddy met a new girl, Audrey Barrett. He asked me to come to the city to have dinner and I did.

We met in a small restaurant where he was not recognized.

"Frank, this is Audrey."

"Nice to meet you," I said. She was tall, slim woman with brown hair and large brown eyes set in a pleasant face. Her skin was clear and smooth and very white. She did not appear to use a great deal of makeup. She was very quiet and only spoke a few words.

It was obvious she was very impressed with Buddy and she hung on his every word. "Frank the case looks good. My lawyer says we have a very good defense and lots of people who are suspects, but I wanted to speak to you about the horse business. My son David is training and doing a good job. I told him if he needed anything he could call on you."

"Buddy your kids grew up with my kids. I consider them family. You know they can come to me anytime."

We ate and he spoke about his new buildings and the sale he was making with a million dollar profit. I left and wondered about the new girl. I found out later she was a model on 7th Avenue. She would work in the showrooms to model for the buyers and her slim figure would allow her to show off the garments in the best light. Girls who did not make it in the photo fashion business did this work which was hard and not very rewarding, so being with Buddy was being in a different and better situation. I never questioned her affection for him but I could see the many advantages the relationship would have for her.

I read more and more about the case. None of the racetrack people were coming to Buddy's defense, even the backstretch people forgot about his efforts in their behalf. Buddy was never involved in Jewish causes so it was natural no Jewish groups were interested in his case. He just continued to live as if he would never go to jail.

The trial was to be in January, but is was postponed again. The case was very weak and in March the DA decided to press Salvatore Prainito, the man arrested with Buddy, in order to have him testify against Buddy. He was accused of the rape of a young girl. The girl refused to press charges and claimed they were in love and wanted to get married. Her mother did not want the case to go to court and liked Sal and wanted them to be together.

The case went to court and Sal was found not guilty. Sal who was only a little over five feet tall and about 130 pounds was later charged with a larceny, for collecting unemployment checks but this case was dropped when the decision was made to charge him along with Buddy. Sal, who was born in Sicily, Italy and spoke very little English was only twenty-three years old but looked much younger because of his size and weight. He spoke very little and Buddy was to help him pay his legal fees. His lawyer claimed he heard the police refer to him as "that little dago bastard!" He told Buddy, "These guys are out to get you and don't seem to want to look for anyone else. I told them about the other people you mentioned but they just laugh. For some reason they want you, but they don't have any hard evidence.

Buddy told me of the conversation and was feeling good about the case.

Chapter XXXVIII
The Trial

It was not until the following year when the trial was to begin. Buddy and Sal had been indicted and on January 30 the trial began. It was the longest trial held in the Bronx and lasted eleven weeks. It cost over a million dollars and had over ninety witnesses. People testified for Buddy, stating he was not in the apartment when shots were heard, others stating they heard an argument in another apartment that day.

The case against Buddy was that he was obsessed with Jack Tupper for stealing his girl and killed him in rage. There was one witness who said she was riding by the dump when she asked her husband to stop the car so she could pick up two bicycles that someone had left by the road and at that point she saw the crate burning and some men, one of which was Buddy standing by the car. She called the fire department to report it and they came by to put out the fire and found the body. Her husband, who was in the car, said he did not see Buddy at that time and did not agree with all of her testimony. Her name was Estelle Carattini, and it was to come out after the trial that on the day of the arrest she was brought to the police station where Buddy was held and while he was in the holding cell she passed by and was able to see him. There was no line-up and it was a week after the arrest that she identified him. If this fact had been presented at the trial it could have been cause for a mistrial. Why was it that Buddy's lawyer did not bring it up?

Melanie testified she saw Buddy on the day of the crime and he appeared nervous and upset. She had no direct knowledge of his part in the crime but she was sure he did it. She was a woman who could not forgive Buddy for lying to her about his age and the fact that the boys were his sons and not his brothers. She knew now that all his friends knew of the deception and she felt the fool. Could those feelings have influenced her remarks? She did say she had seen Jack with large sums of money and she had counted it for him at times. She also had an arrangement to have her story written by Anthony Haden Guest.

Guest was called as a witness and testified Melanie had, before the trial, told him she was not sure Buddy did it. If she had said that at the trial it might have helped Buddy, but she never did. No weapon was found, no DNA, no evidence that Buddy was a killer, only the fact he was seen at the apartment building cleaning the rug and what the DA said was the crime scene. The transcript of the trial was hundreds of pages long and had many twists and turns. Many of the people who were later indicted in the drug case were happy to paint Buddy as a violent person which was not true.

As fate would have it, just a few days after Tupper's death, the newspapers in New York City went on strike. This would be the time that most of the investigating and collecting of evidence was taking place. By the time the newspapers started up again, Buddy had lost weeks of getting the truth out. Television was limited and did not cover the trial like they would today.

The first vote of the jury was six to six, a split. There was very heated discussions and after the first day they came back seven to five for conviction. They told the judge they were deadlocked and he sent them back for further deliberations. The jury was made up of three auxiliary policemen who were stationed in the precinct where Buddy was arrested. Can you imagine what the odds are, in a city of millions of people that three people from that precinct could all find themselves at the same time up for jury duty and arrive on the same jury. And why would Buddy's lawyer let them all serve? Why not object and choose other people?

His lawyer was Jack Evseroff, a very expensive criminal lawyer. After the case there were stories that while he was trying the case he was having his own problems with the DEA about drug related things. Were they true? Who knows? That's another story but that might explain some of his actions. These three auxiliary policemen were adamant for conviction. One threw a chair at a juror who wanted to vote for acquittal.

A retired subway worker, Michael Speller, who served on the jury later told a *New York Times* reporter, "They wore me down. Of the three auxiliary police on the jury, if it was now I would not have voted to convict. There was reasonable doubt."

Two women, who held out for a not-guilty verdict and changed to guilty after they said they tried to send a message to the judge but were told that could only be done by the foreman. Afterwards they gave Buddy's sister affidavits stating they believed Buddy was not guilty but were so afraid in the jury room they changed their vote.

So it was that Buddy was convicted but Sal, who Tupper's dad had commented, "My son would smash him like a fly," was found not guilty.

Buddy was remanded to the Brooklyn House of Detention, a new facility located on Atlantic Avenue, in Brooklyn, New York. This state-of-the-art building was considered escape proof and was to house prisoners waiting for sentencing or being made ready for transfer to other prisons.

Chapter XXXIX
The Escape

It was here on May 31, 1968, a warm sunny Saturday, that Buddy was to receive a visit from his new lawyer, Michael Schwartz. He arrived about 3:30 in the afternoon and was taken to a conference room reserved for lawyers and clients. It happened that the person visiting was not Mr. Schwartz, but a bartender friend of Buddy's named Tony De Rosa. He had done business with Buddy and was buying the ski lodge in Stowe, Vermont. But he was behind on the mortgage payment and Buddy agreed to forgive the debt of about $200,000 if he would come to the jail and switch places with him.

Buddy had grown a beard and shaved that day when his new lawyer arrived. Besides a razor he had a light summer suit and a shirt and tie in his briefcase. He waited until the guards changed shift and then left De Rosa in the room while he walked past three check points until he was at the last sign-out place. Buddy had practiced the signature over and over. He was left-handed and had very poor handwriting. We would joke that his hands were small like a woman's. He would claim they were like Wild Bill Hickok, the cowboy who was fast on the draw, but not good with a pen. Buddy told me he signed the book but he was lucky the guard at the check-out was busy telling a Spanish woman why she could not bring a basket of raw food in to her husband. She smiled at Buddy and asked him to drop the pass in the box on the desk. He began to panic. He had forgotten to take the pass. He shook the box and she did not check the signature just waved as he left and said, "Have a good weekend." He was out!

Later when he was captured, he told me this story.

"I can't tell you how I felt, nervous, happy, and scared. God, the sun felt good. I ran and then tried to slow down to look normal. I knew the car would be waiting around the corner. The street was quiet, not much going-on this part of town on Saturday evening. We were near the Brooklyn court buildings and since it was a weekend the courts were closed and there were very few people around. We drove to a side street and I went to the back of the car with my driver. We opened the trunk, and I bent down as if I was looking for something. He looked around and said, 'Go.' I moved into the trunk which had a blanket and a pillow, but it was very hot in there. I spoke to Audrey who was in the back seat and very nervous. I tried to reassure her and tell her everything would be fine. They asked me if I wanted a drink and I said, 'No, just drive and don't leave the car.'"

"We drove to Jamaica and I told them to drive to a side street so I could get out of the trunk, because the place I was going to was in a busy area. When we arrived they opened the trunk, I slipped out on a quiet street and into the back seat. I took off my shirt and tie and slipped on a light shirt and a baseball cap. We arrived at my friend's apartment and it was still light out. We went in and for the first time I felt relaxed. They had some food ready but I was not very hungry. I changed clothes and I had asked them to buy some wigs. I went into the bathroom and cut some of my hair so the wig would fit better. When it was dark, about 9:00 p.m., we left. My friend had rented a car and he was to follow us. I wanted to head towards California. I don't know why, maybe because I thought Dan Brown was out there, but I just wanted to get away. Audrey seemed happy, she never asked where we were going, which I liked."

Buddy paused for a second to gather his thoughts, then he continued, "I had about $5,000 and would make arrangements to get more. Before I left I had someone get me three phone numbers to different phones in the city. I would call the number at an exact time and then get three new numbers for the next week...never the same number always a different place. I should have made a code so if my system was discovered the party on the other end would be able to tell me not to talk for a long, but all great plans have problems. We arrived at the George Washington Bridge and we crossed over into New Jersey. There was no big search team, and I was very happy. We drove a few miles into New Jersey and stopped at a rest area I moved to the driver's seat and my driver and my friend took the rental car back to the city. Now we were alone, just Audrey and me. I began to drive and she moved close to me in the front seat. She held my arm while we drove and we did not speak. I knew she was not sure about coming with me but I had convinced her that it was the right thing to do. She said she loved me and this was a good way to prove it. We drove for about three hours and found a Howard Johnson Motel and took a room for the night. I was exhausted but had a hard time falling asleep. She cried a little but then fell off to sleep. In the morning we ate a little breakfast and began to travel. I drove for about three hours. I was happy to be leaving New York behind."

I just listened to Buddy tell his story. I know it felt good for him to tell me.

Buddy continued, "We left the parkway and in a small town I bought some camping equipment, a pair of boots for fishing and two fishing poles and tackle. Audrey found a store, I think it was a K-Mart and got some underwear, slacks, tops, and sneakers. She got me some khaki pants, three shirts and socks and a new baseball cap. We had lunch and she was feeling better, not as sad as the day before, she liked to shop. I told her we would travel towards the West and when we found a place we liked I might buy a farm or a ski lodge or some kind of business. As we traveled I would always look for a newspaper stand that might have a New York paper but it was hard to find in small towns, and I was never comfortable in the big cities. In Des Moines, Iowa we stopped in the local cemetery and I looked for tombstones that had deaths of young people or babies who would be about our age and probably never had social security cards. When we found them we took their names and dates of birth. I then went to the local library and looked up the obits for them and was able to get the names of their parents. It was then easy to go to the country clerk's office and get copies of birth certificates. Once we had the birth certificates we could apply for social security cards and also then get drivers licenses but only after taking the test..."

Buddy started laughing and said, "I took the name Lonnie Sherman Runbaugh...not too Jewish sounding. Maybe the track would like me better if I had trained under the name of Lonnie? Audrey became Rhonda Sue Guessford. Audrey, Rhonda not a big jump for her. It seemed to fit her pretty good. I also used the name Antony Zippoline. I kinda liked that name. It reminded me of being a New Yorker. After all, I was listed in the New York phone book for so long as Zzzyp. I always liked that move. Pretty cool, don't you think, Frank?"

I said, "Yes, Buddy. That is pretty cool."

"We made our way across the country, and I changed my appearance often. Sometimes I was an older guy, then a very preppy one, with topsiders for shoes but never work boots. I was clean shaven and bought some glasses. I liked to wear my baseball cap and I felt sure no one would recognize me. Audrey was moody, she missed the New York life. She liked to eat in very nice places, but I stayed in the diners and small restaurants. I moved often and never stayed in one place very long, but I tried to make her happy. When we arrived in California we had a few good days but I could see she was restless. I took her to some nicer restaurants, but money was slow coming so I guess I was a little tight with a buck. Anyway, I went to do some shopping and when I came back to the car she was gone, a note on the front seat. I panicked. Was she alright? I decided to make some calls to her brother and home and I found she was with her family. I guess this was too hard for her to do. It was great that she came with me in the first place but I thought she cared for me and would never leave. Does it seem to you that I have no luck with women?"

"That's some story, Bud. I guess I know who drove you."

"I know you do but I'm not going to say right now and I'll never tell who took me in. I'll tell you something, while I was in California and after she left, I wanted to speak to someone so I called a friend of ours that I thought I was very close to. He answered the phone and I said, 'Hi, it's me.' There was a long pause and the next thing I heard was the phone click. I never called him back but I understood that he might feel he had a lot to lose if he spoke to me. I wonder sometimes if he was in the same position and had called me, what would I have done.

The day after Buddy's escape the newspapers were full of the story withholds of pictures. Speculation about his whereabouts.

He was out of the country for sure was the consensus of opinion. I was interviewed and said I was happy he was free because I did not believe he did the crime. I also said, "Buddy will never leave the country. I spent too much time with him I know he would not be at ease anywhere else. It was not in his nature, just like killing was not in his nature." Time passed and there was less and less in the paper about him and soon there was nothing. I wondered where he was, if he was nearby or in the mountains, but there was no word.

Then, on July 9th, there were news bulletins, "Buddy Jacobson Captured in California!" What a shock. The great escape was over.

When the story was released it was not as exciting as it seemed. Like King Kong, the movie ape, it was not really the authorities who were responsible for his capture. There was no great police work. It was beauty killed the ape. Yes, the police had arrested him in a diner in Manhattan Beach as he was on the phone with New York, but what really happened?

When Audrey left him she went to her brother's house in California. Buddy went there but she was not there. He called New York and later found she had been arrested and was out on a bail of $350,000 for various crimes like helping in his escape, forgery for arranging the false papers for De Rosa during the escape, and lots more. She had her own lawyer and soon was not in jail but in a hotel under guard. She was cooperating with the DA. She knew who was helping Buddy and who was sending him money and how. She knew the telephone code and that David would be hearing from Buddy.

Now the DA moved against David. He was called into the office and told he was going to be charged with helping his father escape. He was to face at least seven years in jail and the DA assured him he would be placed in a cell with the worst sexual offenders. This was a promise. David left and did not volunteer any information.

Unbeknown to the DA, David was to receive a call from his father that very day. He told his father what had happened and Buddy made the most unselfish decision of his life. David was to call the DA and go along with the deal so long as he would not be charged.

Buddy said they were now in possession of the phone information and this was a good time to be sure David would not be charged. "We will never have this chance again," he told David. If Audrey talks you can be sent to jail and I would have no way to get any money. All our buildings might be seized and sooner or later I would be caught. It may hurt and people would have to think you did this but that's the only way it can work. With you outside maybe we can get proof I'm not guilty and we won't stop trying to do that, so call him and make the deal. David called the next day and after speaking to the DA he was assured neither he nor his brother would be charged if Buddy was captured. The DA even threw Audrey into the deal. When Buddy called the next day David did as he was told and spoke to him while the call was traced.

Buddy was calm when the police arrived at the Criterian Diner in Manhattan Beach and offered no resistance and "did not seem surprised," as per the arresting officers. I think he liked that it was more than a coincidence that he was in Manhattan Beach, California. Buddy was and always would be a New Yorker. Audrey was quoted as saying, "Buddy appeared to want to be caught."

Buddy told me later the hardest thing was to blame David but he did not want to appear happy about the arrest. In fact he was not, but he later said he was happy David did what he did. I'm sure now he would be glad to set the record straight.

Chapter XXXX

Buddy Serving His Twenty-five to Life

Buddy received an additional seven year sentence for the escape. He was sent to jail and would call me often…collect. While there only a short time, he was placed in solitary confinement for hiring two other convicts to dig a tunnel in his garden area. They were caught when the guard noticed a large amount of fresh dirt being dropped outside the garden. Shortly thereafter he was transferred to Attica prison, in upstate New York.

This had been the scene of a riot where the prisoners captured guards and destroyed much prison property. The riot was stopped after a number of prisoners were killed by the police. It's reputation now was for harsh treatment and strict discipline.

Buddy had a hard time for a while and then, by some stroke of luck, he was transferred to a less restricted area. He called me for the first time in many months and he was happy. "Frank, there is a refrigerator here and you can have a cold drink and I'm out of the cell during the day. Before, well you have a bathroom there on the farm go in and close the door. Now stay there for about fifteen minutes. Well just think of me in a similar place for twenty-three hours. That's how the other side is. This is heaven." We talked for a while and I realized how hard it must be for him but that was the only time he ever complained.

It was about three weeks later when we spoke again and this time it was not good news. He had been sent back to the other side, but why? "Well someone put something in the refrigerator and it was not legal. The skinheads had been after me, they don't like Jews. They made it look like I put the stuff in the fridge, but I didn't. I think the guards knew I didn't but someone had to go, so it was me."

"Can I do anything?" I asked.

"Not unless you're in here, but thanks."

Buddy's sister, Rita Costello, never gave up and she continued to work on the case. She hired private investigators and a new lawyer to try to have the case reopened. In the meantime, Buddy made good use of the prison library and now was getting a little more freedom. He began to help other prisoners with their appeals and with different legal motions. It got so you would have to have an appointment to see him.

One of his *clients* was a fellow called, "Little Ray." He was in for a violent crime and would meet with Buddy to write a legal appeal. Although he was short in statue, he had broad shoulders and a face that had been battered many times. He had a reputation of not caring what size his opponent was and in conflict he was the first to strike. It was obvious his formal education was limited, but he was streetwise. Little Ray was Italian and Buddy told him his grandmother was Italian so they had a bond. He also told him he had lots of Italian friends and one day he put Little Ray on the telephone so I could say hello to him. We spoke for a minute, and I thanked him for taking care of Buddy and told him I would buy him dinner at a fine Italian restaurant when he came home. Buddy said he was impressed and for as long as he was there he was Buddy's friend.

Time passed, David did well in the real estate department and also did whatever he could for his father. Rita never stopped trying to reach the truth and Buddy developed cancer. Rita lined up the surviving jurors and got affidavits as to their real feelings about Buddy's innocence. She got evidence that the pants presented at the trial were not Buddy's and that Buddy's pants had three red spots which were not blood as presented at the trial.

A black school teacher who said she saw the car on the side of the road almost two hours before the witness said she saw Buddy. This woman said Buddy was not there when she saw the car. Now she was principal of a school and she said when she came forward with the information originally the DA told her that she should not give evidence as there were "bad" people involved and it might be dangerous for her and her family. She was also told it would not be good for the state's case. With all the documents Rita had her lawyer ask for a hearing to reopen the case.

It is very difficult to reopen murder conviction cases but their lawyer, on a Friday morning, got permission to present his evidence on the following Monday. It was all to no avail. Buddy died that Friday night, May 16, 1989 at the age of fifty-eight at the Erie County Medical Center in Buffalo, New York.

Was it fate that he was granted a hearing date to reopen his case and possibly clear his name on the day he died? What a difficult hurdle that was to get over and only happened because of all of the work his loving sister and family did on his behalf to show his innocence. Did it make his passing easier or more difficult? I like to think it helped him and that the system he believed so hard in for so many years looked like it just might work after all.

That having been said, the courts never got to hear the evidence that was suppressed and or misrepresented. Nor did they get to hear from the jurors that were bullied into convicting him, or the people that stepped forward to say that they had knowledge of his being at another location at the time of the killing, or the shady people that he had allowed into his life that looked like they would have benefited more from the death of Jack Tupper than Buddy would have. Tragically there were two lives taken that day and both families suffered a great loss...two names that will forever be linked to "Murder on the Upper East Side."

All of this is yesterday's news as far as the courts are concerned, but not to his family and friends who even with the verdict of guilty believed in him and felt that justice had not been served. Was Buddy a warm fuzzy person that was loved by all that knew him? Of course not. But does this make him guilty of murder? Again, of course not. This short period in time, in a life of accomplishments, seems to have taken away or over-shadowed the person that he was. He was one of the greatest horse trainers New York has ever seen, breaking records that still hold today. Yes, many think him aloof, cold, and maybe uncaring. I saw a man that was shy and a man that had been hurt by life and faced a great deal of rejection…afraid to get too close. No matter how many races he won or how much money he earned, he would never be *accepted* by circles and clicks that ruled his chosen environment.

It was not my intention to focus on the murder, the trial, or the escape, but that is part of his life and had to be revisited and to tell some of the stories that he told me. His name cannot be cleared in a court of law and to me this was such a small part of who Howard Buddy Jacobson was. The clock ticks, the seasons change, and we sometimes put off dealing with what is important in life. That is why I opened the book the way I did. Because it was at the moment of his arrest that all of these memories came flooding in. Now, at the ripe old age of eighty-one, if I don't place these memories on paper, they will be lost forever. I want people to remember the person I knew. The man that was so much more than inmate number 80a3899.

Why am I writing this book? Why do I care if his story is told? I realized good or bad, love him, or hate him…he was and will always be, my Buddy.

Frank X. Pagano, Sr